Faulkner's Fashion

Faulkner's Fashion

Gender, Race, Class, and Clothing

Christopher Rieger

BLOOMSBURY ACADEMIC
NEW YORK • LONDON • OXFORD • NEW DELHI • SYDNEY

BLOOMSBURY ACADEMIC

Bloomsbury Publishing Inc, 1385 Broadway, New York, NY 10018, USA
Bloomsbury Publishing Plc, 50 Bedford Square, London, WC1B 3DP, UK
Bloomsbury Publishing Ireland, 29 Earlsfort Terrace, Dublin 2, D02 AY28, Ireland

BLOOMSBURY, BLOOMSBURY ACADEMIC and the Diana logo are trademarks of Bloomsbury Publishing Plc

First published in the United States of America 2024
This paperback edition published 2025

Copyright © Christopher Rieger, 2024

For legal purposes the Acknowledgments on p. vii constitute an extension of this copyright page.

Cover design: Eleanor Rose
Cover image: Two ladies in outfits by Bernard. Illustration by an unnamed artist for Art Gout Beaute, May 1924 © Mary Evans Picture Library

All rights reserved. No part of this publication may be: i) reproduced or transmitted in any form, electronic or mechanical, including photocopying, recording or by means of any information storage or retrieval system without prior permission in writing from the publishers; or ii) used or reproduced in any way for the training, development or operation of artificial intelligence (AI) technologies, including generative AI technologies. The rights holders expressly reserve this publication from the text and data mining exception as per Article 4(3) of the Digital Single Market Directive (EU) 2019/790.

Bloomsbury Publishing Inc does not have any control over, or responsibility for, any third-party websites referred to or in this book. All internet addresses given in this book were correct at the time of going to press. The author and publisher regret any inconvenience caused if addresses have changed or sites have ceased to exist, but can accept no responsibility for any such changes.

Library of Congress Cataloging-in-Publication Data
Names: Rieger, Christopher, author.
Title: Faulkner's fashion : gender, race, class, and clothing / Christopher Rieger.
Description: New York : Bloomsbury Academic, 2023. | Includes bibliographical references and index. |
Summary: "The first book-length study of clothing and dress across William Faulkner's novels and short stories"– Provided by publisher.
Identifiers: LCCN 2023019768 (print) | LCCN 2023019769 (ebook) | ISBN 9798765103944 (hardback) | ISBN 9798765103951 (paperback) | ISBN 9798765103968 (epub) | ISBN 9798765103975 (pdf) | ISBN 9798765103982 (ebook other)
Subjects: LCSH: Faulkner, William, 1897-1962–Criticism and interpretation. | Fashion in literature. | American fiction–20th century–History and criticism. | Short stories, American–20th century–History and criticism.
Classification: LCC PS3511.A86 Z954 2023 (print) | LCC PS3511.A86 (ebook) | DDC 813/.52–dc23/eng/20230629
LC record available at https://lccn.loc.gov/2023019768
LC ebook record available at https://lccn.loc.gov/2023019769

ISBN: HB: 979-8-7651-0394-4
PB: 979-8-7651-0395-1
ePDF: 979-8-7651-0397-5
eBook: 979-8-7651-0396-8

Typeset by Integra Software Services Pvt. Ltd.

For product safety related questions contact productsafety@bloomsbury.com.

To find out more about our authors and books visit www.bloomsbury.com and sign up for our newsletters.

Contents

Acknowledgments	vii
Introduction	1
Literary Clothing	2
Nonhumans and Things	3
Actor-Network-Theory	6
Clothes as Things	11
King Cotton	14
Fashion in Faulkner's Time	15
Faulkner's Fashion	18
Faulkner's Fictional Fashions	28
1 Clothing and Gender	33
Soldiers' Pay	34
Mosquitoes	40
The Sound and the Fury	44
Sanctuary	52
The Unvanquished	60
If I Forget Thee, Jerusalem	65
The Hamlet	70
The Town and *The Mansion*	73
2 Clothing and Race	77
The Sound and the Fury	80
"That Evening Sun"	83
Light in August	87
Absalom, Absalom!	92
Go Down, Moses	103
Intruder in the Dust	112

3	Clothing and Class	117
	Flags in the Dust	118
	The First World War Stories	123
	Pylon	131
	"Barn Burning"	135
	The Hamlet	136
	The Town and *The Mansion*	148
Works Cited		157
Index		164

Acknowledgments

I owe a huge debt of gratitude to Bob Hamblin, not only for his feedback on this project but for his mentorship and friendship for many years. I would not have been able to write this book nor have what success I did at the Center for Faulkner Studies without his help, support, and love. I hope I have built on the foundation that Bob and L. D. Brodsky began. The team in Special Collections and Archives at Southeast Missouri State University also have been great colleagues over the years, especially Tyson Koenig and Roxanne Dunn, and I thank them for all of their support. I appreciate Southeast Missouri State University as a whole for the years spent there and the privilege of guiding the Center for Faulkner Studies.

An earlier version of my discussion of the story "Victory" appeared in an article in *Studies in the American Short Story*, and I thank them for permission to reuse some of that material here. I appreciate the assistance of Amy Martin and her team at Bloomsbury, including their manuscript readers who provided much-needed and much-appreciated comments, criticisms, and suggestions that have certainly improved the book.

I see a lot of people in their book acknowledgments say that it took many people to make a book possible, but I frankly didn't get a lot of help from anyone on this (other than those already mentioned). I did the vast majority myself, so I thank myself for all the hard work.

Finally, and most importantly, I thank my wife and children for their love and support. By the time this book is published, I will have left the academic world for new challenges and adventures, and my family is both the reason for making that change and my main source of help in actually doing it.

Introduction

"There is much to support the view that it is clothes that wear us and not we them ... they mould our hearts, our brains, our tongues to their liking."
—Virginia Woolf, *Orlando* (1928)

"Thus in this one pregnant subject of CLOTHES, rightly understood, is included all that men have thought, dreamed, done, and been: the whole external Universe and what it holds is but Clothing; and the essence of all Science lies in the PHILOSOPHY OF CLOTHES."
—Thomas Carlyle, *Sartor Resartus* (1836)

There is no area of our lives or ourselves that clothing does not affect. The clothes we wear present a public version of ourselves to the world, but they are also our most intimate possessions, ones that touch our bodies daily. This combination of dressing to please oneself while also being mindful of the images of the self that clothing sends out to the wider world means that "dressing enacts one of the most complicated acts of daily existence" (Brydon and Niessen xi). For all of the people we know, live, and work with, we have seen their clothing much, much more than their bodies. Clothing, therefore, becomes a substitute for the body, but it is more than a substitute since we know that clothing projects more possible meanings than unclothed bodies. Clothing can be read as a text with all the attendant complications of the "author" of the text and the "reader" of the text reaching different interpretations about meaning, not to mention the potential destabilization of texts themselves in the wake of deconstruction and the theory boom. In the following chapters, I argue for the importance of clothing in William Faulkner's fiction and examine how that importance manifests in both the symbolic meanings of clothing but also in the significance of garments as material objects.

Literary Clothing

The novel, with its focus on middle-class striving and the ordinary details of everyday life, is particularly fertile ground for clothing as fictional detail and symbol. A character's dress can immediately provide characterization, and the potential symbolic, metaphorical, and metonymic effects of clothing allow writers to use garments in complex, multilayered ways. Literary dress and fashion studies have not been prevalent in Southern Studies nor Faulkner Studies, though critics in other areas have examined this topic more frequently. "Dress makes the body what is," according to Simon Gatrell, who in his 2011 study *Thomas Hardy Writing Dress* argues that "the issue of the relationship of dress to identity is perhaps the one Hardy addresses with most persistence throughout his writing" (5). Other single-author studies of literary dress include books on Margaret Atwood, Emily Dickinson, Franz Kafka, and Herman Melville,[1] while Clair Hughes's *Dressed in Fiction* ranges from Daniel Defoe and Samuel Richardson to Henry James and Edith Wharton, and the essays in *Fashion in Fiction* analyze a variety of texts from North America, Europe, and Asia. In an article on clothing in the work of Faulkner and Erskine Caldwell, Sylvia Jenkins Cook expresses surprise at the relative dearth of fashion and clothing approaches in the field of Southern Studies "because literary dress has proved elsewhere amenable to cultural inquiries into societies like the South that have been highly stratified in terms of wealth, gender, race, and class" (3). Babak Elahi's *The Fabric of American Literary Realism* offers incisive and original analysis of clothing and social mobility in late nineteenth to early twentieth-century American fiction, covering works by Twain, Chesnutt, James, Dreiser, Cahan, Yezierska, and Cather. Elahi's book focuses on class issues, but clothing also is implicated in all types of social and cultural discourses. As Jessica Munns and Penny Richards put it in their introduction to *The Clothes That Wear Us: Essays on Dressing and Transgressing in Eighteenth-Century Culture*, clothes "are never merely useful nor merely ornamental; rather, they are part of societies' signifying systems and, therefore, are part of the way in which relationships, identities, and sexualities are imagined and contested, formed

---

[1] See Cynthia Kuhn's *Self-Fashioning in Margaret Atwood's Fiction* (Peter Lang, 2005); Daneen Wardrop's *Emily Dickinson and the Labor of Clothing* (University of New Hampshire Press, 2009); Mark M. Anderson's *Kafka's Clothes: Ornament and Aestheticism in the Habsburg Fin de Siècle* (Clarendon, 1995); Stephen Matterson's *Melville: Fashioning Modernity* (Bloomsbury, 2014); Clair Hughes' *Dressed in Fiction* (Berg, 2005); and McNeil, et al., *Fashion in Fiction* (Berg, 2009).

and enacted" (27). Clothing is both the most personal possession we own, since it literally touches our bodies every day, and also our most public in the ways it presents a version of ourselves to the world. Munns and Richards link this aspect of clothing as part of our sense of self to the larger economic and cultural structures of modernity with which Elahi's book is concerned:

> As always with issues of representation, dress can be seen as concealing or revealing, as a disguising overlay or as the manifestation of the unification of inward essence and outward appearance. Finally, the paradox we live with was born: fashion as a product of capitalist industrialization coinciding with individualism appeared to support a self-fashioning through dress that was only possible given a system of mass-consumerism.
>
> (27)

Faulkner's brand of modernism follows closely the period Elahi examines and is surely influenced by the literary realists who, in Elahi's words, "attempted to negotiate between collective and individual agency, and to represent both the material and the metaphoric significance of America's new consumer-driven culture" (38).

Indeed, the connections between clothing and identity construction in literature have been studied in texts much earlier than the realist novel on which Elahi focuses. Stephen Greenblatt's classic study *Renaissance Self-Fashioning* (1980) is not focused on clothing as much as the idea that "the self" becomes something to be created (as opposed to inherited or merely inhabited) in sixteenth-century England in ways that are quite different from what came before. I take inspiration from Greenblatt's notion of self-fashioning individual identity and will discuss his work later in the introduction (as well as Matterson's study of Melville) in conjunction with Faulkner's penchant for using clothing as a way to explore the construction of identity. While the metaphoric and symbolic meanings of clothing as expressions of the self are perhaps more readily noticed by readers and critics, if not always easily interpreted, it is the less obvious but also important aspect of clothing as physical object that I want to emphasize equally in this book.

Nonhumans and Things

As far back as 1986, anthropologist Arjun Appadurai coined the phrase "the social life of things" in a cross-disciplinary essay collection by that name that brought together historians and anthropologists calling for more attention to things themselves: "we have to follow the things themselves, for their meanings are inscribed in their forms, their uses, their trajectories. It is only through the analysis of these trajectories that we can interpret the human transactions and calculations that enliven things" (5). These wide-ranging essays trace the lives of a variety of things, showing how they accumulate and discard meanings and values as they move in and out of the roles of commodities. Movements in the humanities and social sciences in the twenty-first century have further sought to decenter humans in favor of concern for the nonhuman, including animals, technology, climate, commodities, landscapes, and geophysical systems. The "nonhuman turn" is the broad moniker given to these developments in a 2015 book of essays by that name that grew out of a conference hosted by the Center for 21st Century Studies at the University of Wisconsin-Milwaukee:

> Given that almost every problem of note that we face in the twenty-first century entails engagement with nonhumans—from climate change, drought, and famine; to biotechnology, intellectual property, and privacy; to genocide, terrorism, and war—there seems no time like the present to turn our future attention, resources, and energy toward the nonhuman broadly understood.
>
> (Grusin vii)

This nonhuman turn finds binaries like human/nonhuman and subject/object to be problematic in the ways they remove agency and even meaning from the nonhuman world in favor of social constructivism. The various approaches clustered together under the rubric of the nonhuman turn share with or borrow from the related philosophical movements of object-oriented ontology (OOO) and speculative realism. Scholars of the nonhuman turn are mindful of objections that their approaches might objectify humans or work against liberatory scholarship that rejects the figuring of humans, particularly those in minority groups, as subhuman things or objects or commodities. Scholars of the nonhuman turn see their work as very much compatible with politically liberatory scholarship, arguing that understanding how nonhuman agents affect human and social realms is a necessary step toward progressive change in society. As Timothy Morton puts it in his essay in *The Nonhuman Turn*, "the lineage that brought us slavery and racism is also the lineage that brought us the anthropocentric boundary between human and nonhuman" (167). Similarly, Rebekah Sheldon's contribution to the collection notes that after some early antagonism between feminism and OOO, common ground has been found, particularly in the emerging field of feminist new materialism, which "has moved away from the critique of neutrality and toward the recognition of the wholly nondiscursive agency of other-than-human forces" (195). Jane Bennett, in her essay in the same volume, suggests the nonhuman turn is a response to two twenty-first-century trends: "a growing awareness of the accelerating concentration of wealth within neoliberal economies, as expressed by the Occupy movement and by the renewed vitality of Marx-inspired political analyses" (223). The project of rethinking the distinction between people and things can be part of antiracist, antimisogynistic, and anti-neoliberal discourses and practices.

Bill Brown, one of the leading scholars of thing theory, discusses in a 2001 article, and later in his book *A Sense of Things*, the mutual influence of subjects and objects, or "how inanimate objects constitute human subjects, how they move them, how they threaten them, how they facilitate or threaten their relation to other subjects" ("Thing Theory" 7). Brown focuses on things in texts, often literary texts, to show how material objects began to take on a greater importance in American culture during the second half of the nineteenth century, asserting that new forms of mass production and distribution during and after the Civil War fueled demand and the growing sense of being possessed by things. Brown calls the 1890s "the era now recognized as witnessing the origin of American material culture studies" (108). In *A Sense of Things*, Brown shows how writers like Sarah Orne Jewett—writing in the same era on which Elahi's literary clothing study concentrates—make things and possessions central to their fiction at the same time that museum curators place new importance on objects as story-telling texts (108). Popular magazines devoted to using objects in home decoration began to proliferate, including *The Ladies Home Journal* in 1883, *Good Housekeeping* in 1885, and *The House Beautiful* in 1887. Hubert Spencer's influential *The Principles of Sociology* (published in 1897, the year of Faulkner's birth) also places emphasis on material objects, claiming that each person's "nature inheres not only in all parts of his body, but in his dress and the things he has used" (116), and Brown links Henry James's fictional representation of objects with that of his good friend, the painter John Singer Sargent, as two artists portraying a Gilded Age United States defined by its possessions (136). For Brown, this emphasis on material objects makes direct connections from the 1890s to regionalism and to modernism:

> Could it be that William Carlos Williams's great modernist dictum ["no ideas but in things"]—however clearly it expresses a post-romantic effort to erase (rather than to overcome) the subject/object division—is a relic of the museal and local-colorist imperatives of the 1890s? ... the most domestic of American

modernsims may have pursued a materialism adamantly expressed by the curatorial anthropologists of a preceding generation: the faith that thoughts could be found in, and expressed by, things.

(124–5)

Faulkner's emphasis on material goods in his fiction, then, may grow out of a new focus on objects inculcated during his early years which became a mainstay for many modernist artists, a sort of "materialist localism" (124), a phrase Brown uses to express how the local and regional intersect with a new attention to things in modernism. Faulkner's fictions are often set around the turn of the century as he explores the rise of consumer culture in a rural Southern setting. Jay Watson has examined Faulkner with a move away from "modernism as aesthetic innovation to a broader cultural assessment of modernism in concert with modernity" (*Modernity* 7). The prevalence, even "referential excess" (76), of things and objects—especially clothing—in Faulkner's fiction, then, builds on that of his realist predecessors and also reflects the "agrarian roots of modernism" that Watson argues are just as important as the more readily acknowledged urban origins.

Actor-Network-Theory

Bruno Latuour is the theorist most associated with Actor-Network Theory (ANT), and his book *Reassembling the Social: An Introduction to Actor-Network-Theory* makes the case for reimagining sociology. In particular, ANT wants to push back against the tendency to say individuals are often under the sway of "society" or "culture" or that these nebulous constructs influence their actions and instead to reexamine or look more closely at what specific things and objects are acting on us:

> As soon as you believe social aggregates can hold their own being propped up by "social forces," then objects vanish from view and the magical and tautological force of society is enough to hold *every thing* with, literally, *no thing*. It's hard to imagine a more striking foreground/background reversal, a more radical paradigm shift. This is of course the reason why ANT first attracted attention.

(70)

Latour makes clear that ANT is more complicated than claiming that objects have causal agency; it is not a "return to technical determinism" (70 n. 81).

For the purposes of this book, however, ANT's emphasis on objects is the most relevant aspect of the theory. While I do not want to caricature or oversimplify ANT, I also do not have the space to discuss all aspects of it, and so I will focus on ANT's reconceptualizing of the role that objects play in the social realm:

> The main reason why objects had no chance to play any role before was not only due to the definition of the social used by sociologists, but also to the very definition of actors and agencies most often chosen. If action is limited a priori to what "intentional," "meaningful" humans do, it is hard to see how a hammer, a basket, a door closer, a cat, a rug, a mug, a list, or a tag could act ... By contrast, if we stick to our decision to start from the controversies about actors and agencies, then any thing that does modify a state of affairs by making a difference is an actor.
>
> (71)

This does not mean that objects determine the action nor that they are now seen as the cause instead of the effect nor that objects do things instead of humans, but rather that "there might exist many metaphysical shades between full causality and sheer inexistence" and that nonhuman actors can participate in social phenomena (72). Latour does away with the division between the material and social worlds in order to more accurately account for the roles of objects that have been cordoned off and neglected by the social sciences that have clung to such divisions (though not, it should be emphasized, in order to claim some sort of symmetry between humans and nonhumans). It is not difficult to see, for instance, that animal or plant substances ingested into the human body induce certain effects on humans. While other interactions with nonhuman entities may not be so obvious nor direct, it is surely not a giant leap to suggest that indirect encounters with material objects result in things acting on humans in subtle ways.[2]

Thus my focus on clothing in this project is meant to bring something from the background to the foreground, to show that clothing in literature, and in Faulkner's work in particular, is not "mere" description, not only backdrop for

---

[2] For example, if a woman's perseverance in an unhappy marriage is said to be caused by "the power of the patriarchy" then nothing has really been explained, analyzed, or dissected. Rather a substitution has occurred whereby the term patriarchy is meant to explain human actions. This substitution of an invisible force makes invisible actual things that are actors in this process: clothing could be one of these, along with other people (e.g., priest, father, mother, teacher) and innumerable other objects (e.g., books, advertisements, jewelry, government documents). Bringing the obscured objects into the foreground can be done by the artist and by the critic.

the more important work of human characters, but actually integrally connected with human activity in myriad ways. While in theory many other types of objects could also prove amenable to study following ANT's ideas, I argue that clothing is not only more prevalent than almost any other sort of object, but also that clothing is more significant than other objects.[3]

Jane Bennett's work of political theory and feminist new materialism, *Vibrant Matter: A Political Ecology of Things*, was inspired partly by Latour's critiques and reforms of sociology, and she borrows some of his ideas and terminology to argue for a vitality of things that can act as "quasi agents" to influence both humans and nonhumans: "My aspiration is to articulate a vibrant materiality that runs alongside and inside humans to see how analyses of political events might change if we gave the force of things more due" (viii). Bennett argues that one key to doing such analysis, that is, treating nonhuman things seriously as actors, requires one to appear naïve or foolish at times since one must resist entrenched assumptions and common sense that have privileged the human to the exclusion of all else. She argues that resisting the urge to demystification is important since demystification always wants to reveal the hidden human power that is "really" behind the appearance of nonhuman agency: "What demystification uncovers is always something human … Demystification tends to screen from view the vitality of matter and to reduce political agency to human agency. Those are the tendencies I resist … If we think we already know what is out there, we will almost surely miss much of it" (xv). I want to follow Bennett's lead here to resist anthropocentric impulses and to remain open to a variety of possible ways that clothing interacts with humans, even at the risk of sounding naïve or foolish.[4]

Bennett suggests that the type of "cultivated, patient, sensory attentiveness to nonhuman forces operating outside and inside the human body" needed for this kind of project is something she has learned from, among others, Thoreau, Kafka, Whitman, ecofeminist philosophers, Wendell Berry, Barry Lopez, and Barbara Kingsolver (xiv). In other words, literature is one of the places where nonhuman actors and their influence in the "real" world can be made most visible; writers

---

[3] One imperfect measure of the prevalence of clothing is the keyword database in Digital Yoknapatawpha. There are over 500 separate keyword entries of clothing in the database, while the common objects "guns" and "cars" have only about 50 entries each. This is a rough and imperfect measure because keywording in Digital Yoknapatawpha is an ongoing project, as well as the fact that what gets keyworded is a somewhat subjective process. Still, the sheer number of clothing references gives some idea of how ubiquitous clothing is across Faulkner's body of work.

[4] Latour also argues that it is necessary and important to risk appearing "absurd" (5), "childish" (73), and to be rejecting "common sense" (4, 12) in order to take seriously these sorts of ideas.

are people who may be most attuned to the influence of the nonhuman on the human. In her justifications for advocating for the vitality of things, Bennett also explains that the conception of matter as innately dead and passive contributes to humans' destruction of the planet: "The figure of an intrinsically inanimate matter may be one of the impediments to the emergence of more ecological and more materially sustainable modes of production and consumption" (ix). In this sense, this book is an extension of my earlier work *Clear-Cutting Eden: Ecology and the Pastoral in Southern Literature*, in which I argued that during the Great Depression, Faulkner and other writers of the US South began to present humans as part of an interdependent network with the natural world and that this reconceptualization of nature as active agent was directly related to more progressive treatments of race, class, and gender.

Extending the ideas from that project into this one seems logical if perhaps not obvious. Sometimes the link between fashion and the natural world is direct and obvious:

> In the period roughly between 1860 and 1921 the fashion for plumage in women's hats led to a hideous carnage, first of British birds such as gulls and kittiwakes (sometimes their wings were pulled off the living birds which were then left to die in slow agony in the sea), later of the exotic species in the British Empire and the third world.
>
> (Wilson 221)

In Faulkner's world, the links are more indirect and primarily through King Cotton. If cotton is transformed into cloth and clothing, is it no longer part of nature? Surely human and mechanical interventions have altered a plant into something else, something that exists on a continuum of human-nature or cultural-natural and not necessarily a thing that ceases to be natural and exists only as unnatural object. At the least, the agency that I argued the natural world has in my earlier book does not completely disappear when cotton is altered into a new state of being.[5] Moreover, the environmental destruction of the South in the late nineteenth and early twentieth centuries that I argued inspired writers to envision new literary interactions with nature is part of the clothing industry in Faulkner's time and now. Soil erosion and depletion from cotton farming, as well as pollution from textile mills, were problems in the 1930s and 40s, and while

---

[5] Bennett, following others, ends her book by suggesting "a discursive shift from environmentalism to vital materialism" (111), which might enhance public actions toward more sustainable practices (see Chapter 8).

they still are in some ways, we now understand that diversification away from cotton also has disastrous environmental effects. A 2021 study by Stand.earth, a supply chain research firm, showed that many of the world's most famous fashion brands are likely contributing to deforestation of the Amazon rainforest through the complex supply network of Brazilian leather (Pitcher). Moreover, microfibers from synthetic fabric make up 90 percent of the microplastic pollution in the Atlantic Ocean with machine washing of clothes being the primary conduit for these pollutants to reach the oceans and be ingested by fish and plankton (Matei). Another study found that in 2019 "an estimated 4,000 metric tons—or 13.3 quadrillion fibers—were released into California's natural environment." The study's authors provide context for that huge number of nearly invisible fibers by noting that it is 130,000 times larger than the number of stars in the Milky Way galaxy (Gammon).

The "vital materialism" that Bennett argues for can also be traced to Faulkner's era. Philosophers like Henri Bergson and Hans Driesch are major figures calling themselves "critical" or "modern" vitalists, contributing to what Bennett calls "an outbreak of vitalism" just before the First World War (63). While Henri Bergson's ideas about time and duration have received much attention in Faulkner studies for their influence on the author's narrative techniques, Bergson's philosophy of vitalism is a precursor to the work of Bennett, Brown, Latour, and others. Bergson's *L'évolution créatice* (1907; published as *Creative Evolution* in 1910) opposes the materialists of the day who understood nature and matter to be purely mechanistic, arguing instead for an *élan vital*, a vital force in matter, but not separate from it (not a soul, for instance, that could exist apart from matter): "Nature was not, for Bergson and Driesch, a machine, and matter was not in principle calculable: something always escaped quantification, prediction, and control" (63). Bennett situates their scientific vitality in a wider popular debate about how change occurs, spurred by recent scientific discoveries: "The ensuing debate was simultaneously moral and scientific: the vitalist-mechanist controversy combined discourses of freedom and life with studies of morphology and matter" (82). This brings the notion of nonhuman actants into the realm of the political in several ways. Discourses of freedom and liberty inform political debates that lead to world-changing events, such as world wars and economic depressions. Nonhuman actants resemble political bodies in that both are composed of assemblages (to use a term of Deleuze and Guattari), that is, loose groupings of heterogeneous elements so that agency is dispersed rather than localized in a single, autonomous individual, "a congregational understanding of agency … an actant never really acts alone" (Bennett 20–1). Furthermore, this connection between a political body and a material thing need not be thought of as simply figurative, since assemblages might include both human and nonhuman actants: "Assemblages are ad hoc groupings of diverse elements, of vibrant materials of all sorts" (23). This is not to suggest that all participants in assemblages exert equal agency. The power of actants depends on many factors, but recognizing that material objects and nonhuman actants play *some* role in human affairs can broaden our understanding without implying that things are equal to humans. Though I do not pursue this line of thinking this far, the concept of panpsychism, the idea that all matter has some form of consciousness which grows stronger as physical objects become more complex, has recently been posited in some scientific and philosophical circles.[6]

Timothy Morton has gone beyond the idea of assemblages, using OOO to posit the category of *hyperobjects*, "things that are massively distributed in time and space relative to humans" (1). Morton's introductory examples in *Hyperobjects: Philosophy and Ecology After the End of the World* include black holes, the Everglades, "the Lago Agrio oil field in Ecuador," the biosphere, the solar system, "all nuclear materials on Earth; or just the plutonium, or the uranium," or "the very long-lasting product of direct human manufacture, such as Styrofoam or plastic bags" (1). While I do not have reasons to delve deeply into hyperobjects in this book, I mention them because they afford obvious instances of objects that exert influence on human affairs, which act independently of human consciousness, desire, or behavior, and thus provide a foundation for understanding how more mundane objects and commonplace things might also be actants on a smaller scale. We might think of hyperobjects in Faulkner's canon as examples of nonhuman actants: the way the stock market (a hyperobject) influences Jason Compson IV's actions in *The Sound and the Fury*, the impact of the great Mississippi River flood in *The Wild Palms*, or the institution of tenant farming in "Barn Burning."

Clothes as Things

While a study of things, objects, or commodities in Faulkner could conceivably choose from any number of objects (or all of them), I contend that clothing is the single most important material thing running through his corpus. Focusing

---

[6] See David Skrbina's *Panpsychism in the West*, the first comprehensive study of this subject.

on one type of object allows for a more coherent, more in-depth study than examining all things, though certainly there are numerous important objects that might be similarly explored. One needs only to think briefly to start compiling a list of things, tools, and objects that are not only important symbolically, but play the role of agent or actant by influencing human behavior: Quentin's watch, Caddy's wedding invitation, and the red tie in *The Sound and the Fury*; the ledgers and the metal detector in *Go Down, Moses*; the scythe and the Sutpen house itself in *Absalom, Absalom!*; the toothpaste in *Light in August*; airplanes in *Pylon*; to name but a few. Following the ideas of OOO, actor-network-theory, and the other philosophical developments that treat things seriously in and of themselves, I want to understand items of clothing in literature as complicated objects that interact with their human wearers and viewers. But clothing is also more than a thing.

In her landmark study of clothing in visual art, *Seeing Through Clothes*, Anne Hollander asserts that clothing can and should be analyzed as more of a craft like pottery, tapestry, or furniture. "Clothing might be thought to claim the more serious kind of attention given to architecture," Hollander says, in the way it expresses "something extruded onto the surface of a complex cultural organism and expressing its prevailing taste and attitudes," but this is still insufficient for analyzing dress:

> [T]he primary function [of a garment] … in the main tradition of Western dress, is to contribute to the making of a self-conscious individual image, an image linked to all other imaginative and idealized visualizations of the human body. Any such garment has more connection with the history of pictures than with any household objects or vehicles of its own moment—it is more like a Rubens than a chair. Western clothing derives its visual authenticity, its claim to importance, its meaning and its appeal to the imagination, through its link with figurative art, which continually both interprets and creates the way it looks.
>
> (xiv)

It is this aspect of clothing that elevates it above other similar objects and material goods, she argues convincingly, while also noting that the decorative aspect of garments has led to dismissals of interest in clothes themselves as shallow or facile:

> Unlike sex and art, dress usually fails to qualify as serious *in itself*. Clothes themselves are believed to be merely shifting ephemera on the surface of life, and so it is very easy to consider them trivial and to concentrate instead on the

seriousness of what they mean ... to treat clothes as if they were metaphors and illustrations. To be objectively serious about clothing has usually come to mean explaining what they express about something else.

(xv)

Besides echoing Bennett's point about the need to pay attention to often overlooked things, Hollander's commentary helps to explain why clothing is such a rich field for academic study: garments operate on multiple levels simultaneously, as both concrete objects reflective of social and economic conditions of their time and place, as well as abstract artistic statements about metaphysical concerns. Clothing, according to Hollander, is an artform itself: "If anything, clothes are rather like conventional expressions in a literary form, of which the canonical examples have been assimilated by the reading public" with individual garments functioning more like "public readings of literary works in different genres of which the rules are generally understood" (xv). While Hollander is talking about visual representation of clothing in art, I hope to follow her lead while applying her ideas to representations of clothing in literature.

Roland Barthes, in *The Fashion System*, devotes an entire book not to fashion *per se*, or what he calls "real Fashion," but rather to writing about fashion, what he refers to as "written Fashion" or "written clothing," even suggesting that Fashion cannot exist without being written about: "without discourse there is no total Fashion, no essential Fashion" (x-xi). Ultimately, Barthes suggests that studying writing about fashion is a synecdoche for studying literature; both are examinations of how to "convert the real into language" through description (12). *The Fashion System* is routinely disparaged as one of Barthes's least successful efforts (even by Barthes himself), full of virtually impenetrable semiotic analysis. However, Malcolm Barnard, a scholar of visual culture and author of *Fashion as Communication*, argues that the book's final section redeems it: "It would perhaps be more accurate to say, however, that while the first part of *The Fashion System* is correctly described as 'two hundred pages of head-splitting analysis,' the last seventy pages have been lauded as both witty and accessible" (96).

Barthes, however, analyzes not clothing as a thing, but the language and discourses of the fashion industry in a particular place and time. Whereas Barthes's book pursues a semiotic analysis of French fashion journalism and a linguistic analysis of how fashion communicates, I am more interested in charting a different course inspired by his overarching argument that writing about fashion and clothes provides a rich and multifaceted subject for exploration. Barthes seeks to pin down precise meanings, rules, and formulae for the language of clothing whereas literary analysis requires reading clothing as ambiguous with contextual and overlapping meanings subject to change and multiple interpretations. Some broad associations are certainly possible, the sort of conventional literary expressions to which Hollander refers: angularity suggests masculine and curvilinear feminine; darker colors insinuate more serious and somber meanings than lighter ones; or corsets and petticoats indicate restriction while looser clothing signals freedom. Particularly in the hands of a modernist writer like Faulkner, the meanings of clothing are context-dependent and interact with other objects, symbols, and themes in each work. I seek to combine analyses of clothing as object, commodity, exterior expression of interiority, authorial method of characterization, material manifestation of culture, and a component of gender, racial, and class identities. Clothing does not merely reflect social and political change but is always situated within culture and can even act as a site or tool of transformation. Barthes also touches on the importance of clothing in the construction of the self, writing that because it touches the body, clothing functions "simultaneously as its substitute and its mask" (236). Miss Quentin and Deacon in *The Sound and the Fury*, for instance, both utilize garments and fashion to fashion masks or personae but also to help create new identities for themselves while reacting to and even manipulating cultural assumptions about race, gender, and sexuality in the process. Or as Elahi puts it in *The Fabric of American Literary Realism*, "Clothing marks the space where individual self-production meets broad social construction" (4).

King Cotton

There are few better examples of a thing that exerts influence over peoples' lives than cotton. The cotton industry, especially during the King Cotton era, is also an example of Morton's hyperobjects, with the tentacles of agriculture, global trading markets, and textile manufacturing reaching far, wide, and deep across US society, economics, and culture, and indeed across the entire globe. Gene Dattel, in *Cotton and Race in the Making of America*, acknowledges the prominence and agency of nonhuman things in the history of cotton: "Although we may not wish to acknowledge it, the cotton boom was a perfect example of how machines and technology control human destiny" (30). The wealth and power of the United States and Europe were largely produced by cotton, and Dattel quotes Marx's dictum that "Without slavery you have no cotton; without cotton you have no modern industry" (x).⁷ Cotton remains economically vital for decades, "America's most important foreign export from 1803 to 1937" (293), as clothing industries worldwide expand their reliance on cotton. Sven Beckert's *Empire of Cotton: A Global History* argues that the story of cotton as a commodity "is also the story of the making and remaking of global capitalism and with it of the modern world" (xi). Beckert emphasizes how cotton is one of the main drivers of the socioeconomic hierarchies and inequalities that Faulkner explores in his postage stamp of native soil, "the vast divides that still structure today's world, the divide between those countries that industrialized and those that did not, between colonizers and colonized, between the global North and the global South" (xiv).

Cotton as a thing displaces millions of people and causes untold suffering. Slavery and the replacement systems of tenant farming and sharecropping kept millions in enforced states of subjugation, ignorance, poverty, and sickness, with repercussions felt well into the twenty-first century. Native Americans were displaced in order to provide more acreage for farming (Beckert 113), while the clearing of millions of acres of land and monocrop farming caused significant and long-lasting environmental damage.⁸ The raw cotton shipped out to manufacturing centers only to return as finished clothing sold back to those who labored to grow the plant are like, as Faulkner says in *Go Down, Moses*, "two threads frail as truth and impalpable as equators yet cable-strong to bind for life them who made the cotton to the land their sweat fell on" (245). This is not to minimize the human actors who willingly created and upheld the institutions of slavery, sharecropping, and tenant farming, of course, but rather to create space for an ancillary discussion of how cotton as a thing in itself becomes almost totemic in its power and influence.

Fashion in Faulkner's Time

In her history of nineteenth-century women's dress reform, *Pantaloons and Power*, Gayle V. Fischer shows how dress reform was closely allied to the feminist and suffrage movements, providing a symbolic corollary to the political protests

---

⁷ The Marx quote comes from *The Poverty of Philosophy*, in which he goes on to say, "Cause slavery to disappear and you will have wiped America off the map of nations" (111–12).
⁸ See *Clear-Cutting Eden*, especially pages 8–11, 29–30, and 145–6. See also Don H. Doyle, *Faulkner's County: The Historical Roots of Yoknapatawpha* and Albert E. Cowdrey, *This Land, This South: An Environmental History*.

and challenging of conventional power relations: "For women to take control of their appearance, to distance themselves from a primarily ornamental identity, primarily dependent on men and devoted to pleasing men, was intrinsically transgressive" (4). Nearly three years after the famous Seneca Falls Convention of 1848 that is often credited with launching the women's suffrage movement, "Elizabeth Smith Miller, Elizabeth Cady Stanton, and Amelia Jenks Bloomer strode through Seneca Falls, New York, in short skirts with "Turkish trousers"—and pantaloons and women's struggle for power came together for the first time in U.S. history" (79). The wearing of men's pantaloons in public was immediately controversial, leading to extensive national newspaper coverage of women's dress reform (by reporters who soon christened the women's trousers "bloomers"). Political associations of clothing continued in Faulkner's time, particularly the decade he begins writing, the 1920s.

The mass manufacture of goods, popularized by Henry Ford, was applied to most industries in the 1920s, including the clothing industry, and electric sewing machines were a boon for factories and homemakers alike. New technologies not only helped expand the fashion industry, but also inspired fashion choices, as when, for instance, leather jackets and cloche hats became popular for flying and driving (Herald 8) and scarves stiff like propellers were tied into "airplane bows" as part of the larger "machine aesthetic" (18). War-time clothing also inspired new everyday garments, while politics and clothing were linked throughout the decade, often in unsavory ways. Benito Mussolini's black shirts marched into Rome as part of the "top hat revolution," Hitler's brownshirts copied the Italians' use of uniformly colored civilian clothing, while the Ku Klux Klan used white robes as symbols of their terror campaign, and the new president of Turkey, Mustafa Kemal Ataturk, forbade wearing the traditional fez for men and discouraged the use of the veil for women as part of a secularization and Westernization campaign.

Women's dresses became looser and more streamlined, allowing for a freedom of movement in line with political freedoms that women in the United States and Europe were attaining. Parisian fashion often included African influences, while American designers found inspiration in the art of the Harlem Renaissance and jazz clubs of New York (21–5). The flappers accelerated the trend toward shorter hemlines, and new materials for stockings helped popularize the somewhat scandalous trend for flesh-colored stockings beneath shorter and shorter dresses. Men's fashion also became less formal and more colorful with college students preferring blazers and flannel trousers to three-piece suits (29). Movie stars, both male and female, began to replace the aristocracy as fashion icons and trendsetters, and the major French fashion houses began to use Hollywood to gain exposure for their wares (37).

Although the 1930s are commonly associated with deprivation, poverty, and economic collapse, the fashion industry continued to thrive and innovate throughout the decade, experimenting with cheaper and more versatile fabrics, cutting prices and producing more ready-to-wear garments for mass markets. "Despite failing economies, many women saw it as their duty to be fashionable" (Constantino 28). The shift to films with sound gave Hollywood even more influence in popular culture, and some of the world's top designers came to work for the top film studios, including Coco Chanel hired to work part-time for MGM (33).[9] Both men's and women's fashions shifted to more broad-shouldered looks than had been popular in the 20s (22–3), while hats continued to be *de rigueur* for men. The sleek lines of airplanes found their way into women's fashion, especially in the Art Deco style (36), even as the 1920s flapper styles were replaced by more shapely garments and trousers became more acceptable for women's wear (16). Innovations in synthetic fabrics, bias cutting, halter-necks, and backless gowns popularized more revealing and form-fitting styles for more liberated women (44).

Military uniforms influenced both men's and women's fashions in the 1940s, while war-time rationing, restrictions, and embargoes sparked innovations in clothing manufacturing and design (Baker 11–14, 28–9).[10] After the war, French designer Christian Dior popularized "the New Look," featuring curvaceous lines and "the sheer extravagance of yards and yards of fabric" (24), while American fashion houses challenged the supremacy of the French stalwarts that were heavily criticized for continuing to operate normally under Nazi occupation (36, 57).

While it may be tempting to think of Oxford, Mississippi, as a backwater town, far removed from the centers of fashion and these trends, this characterization is stereotypical and misguided. Jay Watson argues that Faulkner depicts the modernity of rural spaces through "numerous suggestive examples of

---

[9] Chanel worked only briefly on a handful of films in 1931, just months before Faulkner began work at MGM in May 1932.

[10] The two-piece swimsuit that came to be known as the bikini was invented at this time in direct response to the US government's order to reduce the amount of fabric used in women's swimwear in order to curtail textile waste (Baker 19).

modernizing elements and energies that move from rural to urban space rather than, as a more conventional notion of the social geography of Yoknapatawpha County would have it, the other way around" (*Modernity* 43–4), going on to cite historians who characterize rural Mississippi as quite modern and technological in many ways (71). As Faulkner grew up, his hometown newspaper, the *Oxford Eagle*, featured the latest clothing and fashion on its pages regularly. A teenage Faulkner would have seen in 1914, for instance, front pages dedicated almost entirely to news of the Great War, while inside The Leader, a clothing store on the Square, placed daily ads featuring pictures of the latest styles in what were routinely the largest advertisements in every issue.

Similarly, *The Mississippian* student newspaper at the University of Mississippi in 1919–20, when Faulkner enrolled as a student, was full of ads for clothing stores in Oxford, Meridian, Jackson, and Memphis. A typical eight-page issue often contained ten different ads for clothing stores, as well as more for tailors, cleaners, and jewelers. The clothing stores' advertisements appealed to the college crowd's desire for the latest fashions, with lines like "New Hats Received Most Every Day" and "The Snappy Stuff. That's what the young fellows want; that's what we have for them" (Jiggits Collection, University of Mississippi). *The Scream*, the university's humor magazine, had an ad for Neilson's (a clothing store on the Square still in business) in its March 1925 issue with the tag line "The Well-Dressed College Man is the Keenest Style Authority Under the Sun" which then went on to detail their new, up-to-date styles: "Wider shoulders, narrower hips, shorter coats, the smart English slacks" (Faulkner Periodicals Collection, University of Mississippi). The May 1925 issue had columns titled "What The Well Dressed Man Will Wear" and "What The Well Dressed Woman Will Not Wear This Year," while page eleven included a drawing by Faulkner of stylishly dressed people boarding a train for "a show" (Faulkner Periodicals Collection, Box 1). In short, the seemingly provincial Oxford was part of global multimedia networks that disseminated not only news, but the latest trends and styles even to the small towns and hamlets far from the urban fashion centers.

Faulkner's Fashion

Throughout his life, Faulkner was preoccupied with self-presentation, public image, and crafted personae. Numerous biographers have discussed and analyzed these tendencies, and James G. Watson, in *William Faulkner: Self-Presentation and Performance*, identifies these as motifs running throughout Faulkner's life and fiction: "Self-presentation and performance are manifested in Faulkner's life in his regularly putting himself forward in the guises and disguises of a moment—gentleman dandy, soldier, and farmer are familiar ones—as well as in his art, where these and other personae are separate but interlocking elements of fictional representation" (5). Thomas McHaney similarly comments on the "impersonations, imitations, fabrications, fictional personas, role-playing, and legends about himself that Faulkner employed in both life and art" (163). Clothing was a major element of Faulkner's public guises, and Watson examines Faulkner's fashion in carefully staged photographs in Chapter 2 of his book. Oxford photographer J. R. Cofield, who made over 100 pictures of the author, recalls Faulkner's fondness for clothing, costumes, and cameras, and notes that he had a penchant for changing outfits multiple times in a day, enjoyed mixing styles to the horror of others, and owned a wardrobe "that would equal, if not surpass, that of the former Prince of Wales" (Webb and Green 111). The earliest photograph that Watson analyzes in terms of self-performance is his book's cover image, Faulkner posing in his backyard just before leaving for New Haven in 1918 in the "uniform costume of a Young Dandy in a Mississippi college town of the period: dark, tailored suit, coat fashionably drawn back from a tattersall vest, high round-collared shirt and broad striped tie" (19). Joseph Blotner explains that the young Faulkner would spend most of his money on fancy clothes, often from Phil A. Halle Department Store in Memphis. He was the first boy of his age in Oxford to own a "Styleplus" dress suit, bought for $25 at Halle's (the equivalent of about $700 in 2023), and he often had his mother alter his clothes, "especially to make the legs tighter" (Vol. 1, 180). Faulkner enjoyed standing out in Oxford, both for his style and his seeming lack of material prospects, the combination of which led to his nickname of Count No 'Count and even inspired his detractors to parody him in *The Mississippian* in 1920, writing "wouldn't this be a fine University if all of us were to wear sailor collars, monkey hats, and brilliant pantaloons; if we would 'mose' along the street by the aid of a walking prop … Wouldn't that be just too grand?" (Vol. 1, 269). The cane, which one friend referred to as a "swagger stick" (Webb and Green 103), was an important accoutrement for the image Faulkner was trying to effect. Thorstein Veblen specifically cites the "walking-stick" as one of the examples of an item of clothing "suggesting the wearer cannot when so attired bear a hand in any employment that is directly and immediately of any human use … It not only shows that the wearer is able to consume a relatively large value, but it argues at the same time that he consumes without producing" (170).

In her discussion of the origins of the dandy in *Adorned in Dreams*, Elizabeth Wilson notes that cut and fit were more important than flashy clothes in a description of the dandy that sounds like it is depicting the young Faulkner specifically—or at least the image that he wanted others to see:

> The role of the dandy implied an intense preoccupation with self and self presentation; image was everything, and the dandy a man who often had no family, no calling, apparently no sexual life, no visible means of financial support. He was the very archetype of the new urban man who came from nowhere and for whom appearance was reality.
>
> (181)

The dandies "invented Cool," says Wilson as they tried hard to look like they were not trying in "a kind of performance of aristocracy" (182). Faulkner's cultivating of this dandy image worked quite well, as he acquired a reputation in Oxford as a bum "who should be driven out of town" (Cofield 108) and a young man whose lack of prospects and financial support made him unfit in the eyes of the Oldhams to marry their daughter Estelle. Wilson's reference to the apparent lack of a sexual life for the dandy does not mean that dandies were not sexual. In fact, the preference for tight-fitting clothes was meant to be erotic, and, though it was not originally, dandyism by the end of the nineteenth century became more openly associated with homosexuality, especially through public dandies like Oscar Wilde. In *Gay Faulkner*, Phillip Gordon summarizes Faulkner's affinity for Wilde as an outcast (48–50) and also suggests that Faulkner may not have been bothered by Oxford denizens conflating his dandyism with homosexuality and perhaps even encouraged it through a rather public courtship with Ben Wasson (29–34). That is, Faulkner's predilection for sartorial dandyism dovetails with what Gordon calls "Faulkner's actively and intentionally acting out a homosexual identity" (29), regardless of whether any sexual activity between the two men occurred. While Faulkner's style of dress may be read as a reflection of the outsider persona he embodied in Oxford, the clothing itself might also be an agent or cause of his outcast status, perhaps even further pushing him to explore identities and behaviors outside the accepted norms of his place and time. Certainly his clothing may be just a reflection of his mental state and choices, but a causal role for clothing should not be precluded simply because clothing is nonhuman. Surely Faulkner's dress had effects not only on those viewing him with suspicion and disdain but also upon his own mental state, self-conception, and identity.

Shortly after the above referenced dandy photograph, Faulkner exchanged one costume for another, this time the dashing military uniform of a young pilot. Trying on this new identity of soldier recalls Judith Sensibar's analysis of Faulkner's obsession in his early poetry with "the quintessential masker himself, Pierrot," the stock character of commedia dell-arte (*Origins* xvii). Sensibar's study of Faulkner's poetry demonstrates the centrality of Pierrot, his shadow, and his masking in not only the writer's apprenticeship poetry, but also in his later Yoknapatawpha fiction and, indeed, in his life:

> His [Pierrot's] impostures, his narcissism, his protean, androgynous character attracted the young poet who often appeared to imagine himself as an actor in his own dramas—dramas that were, in their essence, dream visions. Faulkner was drawn to the mask of Pierrot as he was drawn to the uniform of a World War I Canadian Royal Air Force officer.
>
> (xviii)

Changing dress means changing persona, and Faulkner was clearly taken with the war hero pilot role that he would inhabit intermittently for years, and this persona included a new name (adding the u to the family name), a new birthdate and birthplace (May 25, 1898, in Finchley, Middlesex, England), and new religion (Church of England), in addition to the costume of a rank he never achieved (Blotner, Vol. 1, 210–11). Blotner even suggests that Faulkner's predilection for fashion was part of the appeal of joining the war effort: "And for one with a taste for smart, trim clothes, what could be more attractive than the slim boots, shining leather harness, peaked cap, and light blue of the RAF?" (210).

Faulkner was dissatisfied with the reality of his cadet uniform, an "ill-fitting costume" that was "unsuited to his self-image" (Watson, *Self-Presentation* 18, 24), and he complained about it in letters home with an accompanying sketch. A month later, a sketch in another letter to his parents was of an officer's uniform, and Faulkner promised this would be his new uniform, "my sure enough one," within a matter of weeks (*Thinking of Home* 89). Of course, the war ended before Faulkner was even close to achieving officer status (and even before a single solo training flight), so he bought himself a complete officer's uniform before returning to Oxford: "As usual, where clothes were involved, he had ordered the best—a garrison cap made by William Scully, Ltd., Montreal, the smart, blue-gray belted tunic, trousers, and a trench coat complete with the flaps and equipment rings that made it combat-worthy as well as smart" (Blotner, Vol. 1, 229–30). Getting off the train in Oxford wearing this outfit, ornamented with a cane and a limp (later adding a fictional metal plate in his head), Faulkner lapped up the attention from bystanders and other returning veterans who saluted him because he wore an "overseas cap" that indicated he had been to Europe in the war. He would have noted the difference in how he was perceived and treated due entirely to what he wore; indeed, his reason for purchasing the officer's uniform was in order to exploit the power of the clothing's nuances to act on strangers and enhance his reputation in Oxford. Faulkner reveled in this persona and costume that he wore "at home, around town, and also to dances in neighboring towns" all while his brother Jack was missing in action (232). His brother John recounts basking in his brother's reflected glory as he tagged along at seventeen, noting that "our own returned soldiers saluted Bill in his Sam Browne belt and monkey cap ... They turned up their noses at our own officers who had not been over and refused to acknowledge them in any way" (*My Brother Bill* 139). The brothers are downright conspiratorial in this uniform masquerade, with John commenting that Bill "did all right in his British officer's uniform" at local dances before casually mentioning, "He lent it to me several times. I liked it too" (139).

As Donald Kartiganer has noted, this role playing continues throughout Faulkner's life, including such personae as

> the English Dandy, the bohemian poet, the town bum, the Southern aristocrat, the ex-bootlegger and gun-runner, the romantic suitor, the cynical father of illegitimate children, and eventually the hard-working farmer who happened to do some writing on the side. But his greatest role, the one he played the longest and most insistently, and which represents his deepest personal involvement in the clash of Old South and modernist forces, is that of the World War I aviator.
>
> (627–8)

In a 1943 letter to Estelle, Faulkner clings to the story of a First World War plane crash to explain his current leg and back pain (Rollyson, Vol. 2, 243–4), and in a letter that same year to his nephew and godson Jimmy, who was preparing to head to war, Faulkner revisits the same lie about his "crack-up in '18" and solemnly asserting, "I would have liked for you to have had my dog-tag, R.A.F., but I lost it in Europe, in Germany" (*Selected Letters* 170). Later in that same letter, Faulkner bemoans his inability to join in the war effort with a sartorial lament that he cannot don the uniform again: "I must stay in civilian clothes" (171). In 1946, when working with Malcolm Cowley on *The Portable Faulkner*, Faulkner writes three separate times to get Cowley to change or remove the R.A.F. First World War references in the introduction (215, 219), though still refuses to admit outright that he made up his war stories entirely. Perhaps his description of Chick Mallison's overly elaborate ROTC uniform in the 1949 story "Knight's Gambit" reveals the author's true feelings of being an imposter: "the khaki serge true enough such as real officers wore but without even the honest stripes of N.C.O.'s but instead, the light-blue tabs and facings of R.O.T.C. like the lapel badges of fraternity pledges, and the innocent pastless metal lozenges such as you might see on the shoulders of a swank hotel doorman or the leader of a circus band" (205–6). Joel Williamson notes the importance of Faulkner's enlisting in Canada, rather than closer to home, in the creation of the "cosmopolitan" persona he was creating, "not simply another American 'doughboy' in a rough cut, ready-to-wear, ill-fitting uniform" (185). Thus, his soldier costume and persona can be linked with the post-war Bohemian poet persona that included his 1925 sojourns to New Orleans and Europe.

Sensibar compares Faulkner to "pathological imposters" in terms of his numerous instances of acting, borrowing, and plagiarizing without remorse (*Origins* 43), and she asserts that father-son conflicts may be the root of his behavior: "When Faulkner the poet pretended to be his great-grandfather or his own wounded brother, he was acting out those conflicts" (44). Watson also notes the prevalence of father-son conflicts in Faulkner's early novels (*Self-Presentation* 128); however, in his later fiction, he learns to control and depict such conflicts in his characters' lives rather than act them out himself. We can see the beginnings of this change in his first two novels, *Soldiers' Pay* (1926) and *Mosquitoes* (1927), "while not imitative like his poetry, draw their main characters and settings from the counterfeit worlds of the would-be soldier and would-be artist" but with a new ironic distancing which allows him to comment on the imposters and poseurs whom he resembles (54). Even when he is able to gain some ironic distancing from his material and perhaps to see himself as the character/impostor play-acting in real life, Faulkner never quits role playing. In a chapter called "Life Masks" in *William Faulkner, Life Glimpses*, L. D. Brodsky compares the famous Faulkner fox-hunting portrait with the R.A.F. uniform photos and the First World War aviator persona that Kartiganer says was his longest, most personal role:

> These portraits forty years apart represent costumed incarnations of the same man attempting to project an image at once ideal and real. As a "wounded," "decorated" flier and as a fully garbed aristocrat accustomed to riding to the

hounds with the most elite Virginians, Faulkner could accept himself as a success: a man's man who had succeeded in pursuits requiring courage and skill; a man of action, arrested in perpetuity by the camera's all-discerning eye.

(Brodsky 32)

Brodsky links this need for masculine posing with Faulkner's numerous affairs, quoting from Estelle's letters that he "feels some sort of compulsion to be attached to some young woman at all times" (29) so that he can still see himself as desirable and masculine. Faulkner's desire to project an image through words, behavior, and clothing is a lifelong preoccupation, one that he translates to his fiction since he understands, on some level, the need for people to project images of themselves through clothing and also how, as a novelist, he can telegraph aspects of character through sartorial choices.

Faulkner was not the only one in his family known for style and fine clothing. Estelle was always thought more fashionable than most in Oxford, and her marriage to the worldly and wealthy Cornell Franklin supplied her with high-end and exotic fashion items. Blotner's notes indicate that Estelle was the first to buy clothes at Arthur Halle's store in Memphis, with Faulkner following her lead. Estelle was not only a consumer of fashion, but also a creator. Blotner relates that she remade her wedding gown into an evening gown (Blotner Papers, Box 2480), and she always dressed Jill in "exquisite handmade clothes" (Rollyson Vol. 2, 192), even organizing fashion shows to exhibit the gowns she made (Sensibar, *Love* 5). Jill herself grew to have "exquisite taste in clothes ... cultivated by her mother" (Rollyson, Vol. 2, 278). A family friend recounted to Blotner that Estelle's son and daughter, Malcolm and Victoria, "were better dressed than other children," and described both Faulkner and Estelle as "glamorous," with Estelle seeming to the locals "like a visiting movie star, beautiful, with beautiful clothes, gowns out of VOGUE" (Blotner Papers, Box 2480). Sensibar refers to their marriage as a "private theater" and argues that husband and wife both delighted in role-playing: "the two had acted together since childhood and shared equally in an attendant love for costume" (*Love* 9). In an interview with Sensibar, Jill Faulkner says her parents were always "playing a role," and that both would change clothes to suit the particular part they were playing at the moment (12). Even Ned Barnett, the Faulkner's butler/yard man/handyman, "loved to dress up" and was known as "an elegant gentleman" (Blotner Papers, Box 2480) who even "wore a tie when he milked or chopped kindling ... [and] would appear in frock coats inherited from the Young Colonel" (Blotner, One Volume 261).

Brodsky's interview with Albert "Buzz" Bezzerides, a scriptwriter with Faulkner at Warner Brothers who befriended the author, letting him live in his house for months at a time in 1944 and 1945, sheds additional light on the idea of Faulkner's role playing. Bezzerides not only knew Faulkner well during his time in Hollywood in the mid-1940s, but he also talked with many friends and relatives of the author as Bezzerides worked on the 1979 PBS film *A Life on Paper*. The knowledge Bezzerides gained of the author's personal life directly and indirectly leads him to conclude that in the 1950s, Faulkner "seemed to have become a victim of his own legend and was living a part that seemed totally false: the esteemed writer, the Nobel winner ... He was living a role that seemed fraudulent to me. It seemed sad to me ... I feel strongly he must have been aware of the fraudulency of what he was doing" (77). Bezzerides speculates that at the root of Faulkner's issues was his desperation to avoid the burdens and responsibilities of the oldest son role, taking care of all the problems from extended family members. The role playing, posing, and costuming all seem like attempts to avoid being who he felt fated to be but did not want to be (74–5). Emily Stone (the wife of Faulkner's early mentor and friend Phil) agreed with Bezzerides's assessment and felt that Faulkner donned protective armor so that no one could see his true self (Webb and Green 98–100).

Many friends and acquaintances commented on Faulkner's sartorial style later in his life, well after his dandy and war hero phases. The tweed jackets Faulkner favored were seen by some as an affectation, but William Evans Stone V thought differently: "I am rather of the opinion that it was Bill's method of identifying himself with the aristocracy—and he was to the manner born—and also with the hill farmers of North Mississippi, for whom he had great compassion" (Webb and Green 78). J. W. "Bill" Harmon, who owned a clothing store at which Faulkner shopped, said the author "didn't wear what we would call conventional clothing" and adds that "he wore blazers and things that were two or three years ahead of the style generally worn in this part of the country" (91). Despite this trendiness, Harmon echoes Stone's depiction of Faulkner as moving between high fashion and shabbiness: "He wore that old trench coat from World War I until it almost fell to pieces" (92).

According to Dorothy Commins, the wife of Faulkner's long-time editor and friend Saxe Commins, when the Faulkners phoned the Commins to tell them that Faulkner had been awarded the Nobel Prize, the conversation immediately turned to Faulkner's concern that he did not have the proper clothing to wear to the ceremony and that he wanted to rent, rather than buy "a full dress suit and a silk hat" (Commins 195). The next day, Faulkner called Saxe in his office and provided his measurements over the phone, which Commins then took to Fifth Avenue Formal Wear. Donald Klopfer related the story to Dorothy that Faulkner had liked the suit so much, he wanted to keep it:

> The clothes fit Bill reasonably well. However, when Bill returned from his momentous journey, he told Saxe and me that he had noticed that the king had two satin stripes on his trousers, while he (Bill) had only one. At Saxe's suggestion Bennett [Cerf] and I presented Bill with the clothes he had worn at the presentation ceremony, but not before Saxe had had the extra satin stripe added to Bill's trousers.
>
> (Commins 196)

This anecdote demonstrates how attentive to detail Faulkner was when it came to fashion, as well as the importance he placed on his appearance. His preparations for a 1954 trip to Brazil for the US State Department reveal a similar attention to detail and awareness of fashion as he writes to the Commins to request a suit that he left at their house and to ask that Random House buy him a new pair of shoes for the trip: "I want English shoes, Church is the maker, evening shoes. There is a shop on the west side of Madison, somewhere between Fiftieth St. and Tripler's, I have seen Church shoes in the window" (210). Faulkner would probably be both flattered and horrified to know he was named by *Esquire* magazine as one of the "75 Best Dressed Men of All Time" (February 17, 2010).

Just because Faulkner was attentive to fashion and dress does not mean he always dressed well. Dorothy Commins also mentions a visit Faulkner made to their home in February of 1956: "That trench coat! I had seen it on Bill so many times. It was threadbare at the wrists. The inside rim of the collar was stained a brownish tan that no cleaning could remove. Not so his hat! That was a dapper little affair, alpine-shaped with a perky little brush peeping out of the band that encircled the crown" (223). It seems Faulkner's perpetual worries about money often conflicted with his proclivity for fine clothes. Commins remembers that on his many visits to their house Faulkner sometimes wore "a full-length kimono that must have been handsome in its day. It was made of silk, a very dark purple. The hem was padded with cotton wadding to weight it down. Now the edge of the hem was so frayed that I could see bits of the wadding struggling to come through" (224). Cofield surmised that he never "threw away a single garment that he ever owned" (Webb and Green 111), and he remembers Faulkner in "the early thirties" refusing to dress up when the Associated Press requested photographs:

> His attire consisted of the old tweed hoss coat, with a red bandanna stuffed in the pocket; and his pants—that luckily did not show in the picture (I also cut out the bandanna)—were white seersucker, washable, with red paint splattered all over them. He was unshaven and his hair was unruly, very much so. But do you think I would have had him any other way?
>
> (109)

Faulkner always said how much he liked these particular pictures of him, likely because he was playing against type by refusing to conform to typical author portraits.

Similarly, when Faulkner visited Delta State College in May of 1952 to speak to the Delta Council, an organization of planters, farmers, and businessmen, he was an internationally renowned figure who was being asked to speak about race relations, psychology, religion, and international affairs. Blotner recounts that Faulkner used his clothing to play the role of the common man for the speech. When Bob and Alice Farley arrived at Rowan Oak to drive Faulkner to Cleveland, they found him dressed in wrinkled cotton seersucker trousers, a shirt with "a badly frayed collar," an old, belted jacket that was now much too small for him, and a felt hat that Farley said looked like it was from 1915:

> "You ready to go to Cleveland," [Farley] asked.
> "Oh, is this the day?" Faulkner replied, his eyes glinting.
> "It sure is."
> "Can I go like this?"
> "You can if you want to."
> "Let's go."
> As they pulled out of the driveway to start their eight-mile drive, Farley mused over his friend's appearance. He thought that he had obviously made up his mind to play the Lafayette County farmer.
>
> (Blotner, One Volume 1415)

As Robert Hamblin says of this incident:

> [I]t is extremely hard to believe that anyone, even an absent-minded author, would forget the date scheduled for him to make a significant speech on an issue of grave concern at the invitation of an important organization and before a large audience that would include the governor of the state and other important

dignitaries. More likely, Faulkner deliberately chose his attire to identify with the hard-working, self-reliant Americans who were the subject of his remarks.

(165)[11]

Faulkner's speech that day centered on the theme of the individual versus the government, and he was particularly vitriolic in his indictment of the federal welfare system, showing that he understood keenly how to dress and act the part for a given audience, while also using his dress to protect and insulate himself, putting a barrier between his inner self and the public. As these numerous examples indicate, Faulkner understood and manipulated the connections between clothing and identity (real and perceived) throughout his life. This life-long fascination with fashion and its effects appears in his fiction in myriad, complex, and overlapping ways.

Faulkner's Fictional Fashions

A brief example from *As I Lay Dying* illustrates the multifaceted confluences of dress and identity in one of Faulkner's novels. Clothing is rarely mentioned in *As I Lay Dying*, perhaps not surprising given the Bundrens's position outside the modern economic world of mass-produced, store-bought goods. On the few occasions clothing is mentioned, it is related to the novel's larger questionings of identity. To prepare for Addie's funeral at the house, Anse changes into his best Sunday clothes, "wearing his Sunday pants and a white shirt with the neckband buttoned," and the new outfit seems to transform him into a new man:

> It is drawn smooth over his hump, making it look bigger than ever, like a white shirt will, and his face is different too. He looks folks in the eye now, dignified, his face tragic and composed, shaking us by the hand as we walk up onto the porch and scrape our shoes, a little stiff in our Sunday clothes, our Sunday clothes rustling, not looking full at him as he meets us.

(86)

Donning these new clothes, Anse is able to inhabit the role of grieving husband, altering not only his physical appearance, but also the ways he acts, his demeanor,

---

[11] Hamblin adds that "Faulkner's attire, by the way, would prove especially fortuitous for Bern Keating, the photographer from Greenville, who was destined to shoot on this day some of the most impressive photographs of Faulkner ever made" (165).

and the way others perceive and interact with him. Vernon Tull's narration makes clear that the other men gathered for the funeral also behave differently, their stiff clothes producing a stiff demeanor, "not looking at one another" as they strain to make idle small talk (86–7). Anse's new persona is a milder instance of the crises of identity that threaten to overwhelm the Bundren children after their mother's death, particularly Darl, Dewey Dell, and Vardaman.

Dewey Dell also wants to believe in the power of clothing to affect both the wearer and her audience. Just before reaching Jefferson, she changes into her best set of clothes, "her Sunday dress, her beads, her shoes and stockings" (229), hoping to blend in with what she assumes are more sophisticated town people and to transform herself by dressing the part of the confident consumer who knows what she wants, covering up or disguising her interior country girl. As Faulkner puts it in *Sanctuary*, "Empty wagons passed him and he passed still more women on foot, black and white, unmistakable by the unease of their garments as well as by their method of walking, believing that town dwellers would take them for town dwellers too, not even fooling one another" (111).[12] Unfortunately for Dewey Dell, there are forces more powerful at work than the subtle influence of dress. Moseley exerts patriarchal power and privilege to intimidate and infantilize Dewey Dell, chiding her moralistically (though his willingness to sell poisonous cosmetics suggests a highly selective ethical concern for life and women). Rather than helping her blend in, her clothing marks her immediately as "a country girl" (242) and, combined with her country demeanor, draws more attention to her body. Paradoxically, Dewey Dell must stand out in order to be seen and heard as a woman, but also blend in as a woman who is as respectable as the other women in town. MacGowan and his crony fixate on her appearance, and her combination of naivete and attractiveness leads MacGowan to see her as easy prey. Rather than the clothing helping to disguise herself as something else, her body—what is underneath her clothes—is exposed both figuratively and literally as her pregnancy is laid bare and she is sexually assaulted in the pharmacy basement. It is a particularly egregious example of clothing's inherent dual function of defining the limits of the self while also connecting the self to others and the world. Mosely sees her as a respectable woman who should simply submit to the respectable institution of marriage, suggesting she align her inner desires with her outer proper appearance. MacGowan sees a "pretty hot

---

[12] Lena Grove similarly tries to be mistaken for a town dweller at the beginning of *Light in August* (3–4).

mamma" (242) trying to disguise her inner desires with an outfit of respectability. The male gaze incorporates clothing into its own version of who a woman is, and Dewey Dell is powerless to resist the violations of the patriarchal system.

Because items of clothing are signifiers, they, like words, may be interpreted differently. In fact, Addie's description of a word as "just a shape to fill a lack" (172) applies to clothing as well. Dani Cavallaro and Alexandra Warwick even refer to clothing as the ultimate example of Lacan's *objet a*:

> In psychoanalytic terms then, we are offered an explanation for that "arbitrariness of fashion" as a system that goes beyond a simple Marxist or feminist analysis of fashion as a mere function of capitalism or patriarchy. It suggests ways in which capitalism or patriarchy can actually co-opt the psyche in their operations, and why the seductions of fashion are so difficult to resist. The purchaser and wearer of clothing is not simply a brainwashed adherent of a transparently exploitative system, but a participant in a complex process of self-determination. Items of clothing are objects of desire that hold the promise of completion, the last piece necessary to close the gap; but because they are inherently condemned to failure, the subject's desire turns to another piece, a new object to fulfill that desire.
>
> (35)

Other things in the novel behave similarly to clothing in this respect, such as the train coveted by Vardaman, Jewel's horse, the graphophone that Cash desires, and Anse's false teeth. All give the illusion of fulfillment, but even if they are attained, they will not fill the lack.

We also see these objects fulfilling the roles of actants throughout the novel, compelling specific thoughts and behaviors in characters. Perhaps the thing that influences people the most throughout the narrative is the coffin. In many ways, the coffin as an object is the most important "character" of the book. It is a liminal object, not a person, but containing one, or at least the body of one, yet, as the novel reminds us again and again, Addie continues to be a dominant force even in death. Her ability to influence her family members' thoughts and actions is not limited to their memories of her; the coffin containing the body precipitates the journey to Jefferson, dictates the action in the river crossing scene, and compels Jewel to burn himself to extricate it from the barn. It is the shape of Addie's wedding dress that dictates the shape and (im)balance of the coffin, and it is the coffin that dictates much of the action in the novel.

These themes of identity and identity creation that we see in Faulkner's fiction and in his own life are a major aspect of how I explore and analyze clothing in Faulkner's work, and this approach is more common in other analyses of literary fashion. Greenblatt's notion of self-fashioning individual identity in *Renaissance Self-Fashioning* is an influence, although he ultimately does not focus on clothing's connection to identity construction to the degree I do. Greenblatt's argument that the time period he examines is a unique moment of change sounds an awful lot like Faulkner's era as well: "there is in the early modern period a change in the intellectual, social, psychological, and aesthetic structures that govern the generation of identities" (1). During the sixteenth century, Greenblatt argues, individuals gain more say over their "passage from abstract potential to concrete historical embodiment" (1) as the influence of cultural institutions begins to wane. This same negotiation between the individual and larger cultural forces in the fashioning of identity is prevalent in Faulkner's time, as Michael Zeitlin has argued in a discussion of Faulkner and the Frankfurt School: "In Faulkner's view, the broadest problem of his time was that the distinction between the individual and the general society was collapsing altogether, the individual losing his or her power to resist the invasive agencies and coercive seductions of the latter" ("Faulkner, Marcuse" 55). The tension between individual autonomy and coercive cultural forces often plays out in the minds and on the bodies of Faulkner's characters, capturing a time when individual identity is becoming less a product of birth and predetermined class rank—a fixed identity projected outward—and more of an individually fashioned thing that has a private, interior component as important as the public one.

This attention to identity creation is also the focus of one of the more recent single-author studies of literary clothing, Stephen Matterson's *Melville: Fashioning in Modernity* (2014). Similar to Greenblatt, Matterson asserts that the modern person of Melville's time had to invent himself rather than inherit a preordained place: "Melville's sense of the relation between self-invention and clothing engages me most in this book, how dress comes to be part of the narrative of the self" (3). However, he explicitly limits his analysis of Melville's use of clothing to the symbolic meanings as they relate to identity, excluding the material culture of clothing. Where my approach differs from Matterson's (and Greenblatt's) is in my addition of analysis based on ANT and OOO to the more symbolic meanings that relate to identity formation.

The following chapters are organized by their primary modes and subjects of analysis: gender, race, and class. Of course, there is often overlap in how clothing relates to these areas, but dividing the chapters in this way allows for the foregrounding of these contentious categories of political and individual identity and to emphasize the importance of clothing in constructing selves that negotiate these realms. The chapters together aim to demonstrate how clothing and fashion reflect Faulkner's life, his cultural environment, and his characters, while also revealing how items of clothing can affect human thought and behavior as quasi agents or actants. The first chapter, Clothing and Gender, examines how clothing is implicated in and impacts gender power dynamics in Faulkner's world. Faulkner examines how both masculine and feminine clothing influence identity construction, including military uniforms and flapper fashions in his early work. Androgynous clothing that destabilizes traditional gender categories interests Faulkner in the 1930s, while later novels shift to an examination of Eula Varner's sexuality. In all his works, Faulkner is attuned to both the power of garments as objects and the role of dress in creating a sense of self and an individual identity in a male-dominated society that sees clothing as something that should contain female sexuality and becomes alarmed when it does not.

Containment emerges as an important theme in the second chapter, Clothing and Race, as well. In this case, it is racial boundaries that must be maintained but which Faulkner reveals to be a futile endeavor. Faulkner's limited perspective as a white male leads to more emphasis on outer appearance and on role-playing in relation to race and clothing. Reinvention of the self through clothing does emerge as a possibility for Black characters, if not a main focus for Faulkner, especially in the novels of the 1940s, whereas his more pessimistic visions of the 1930s often leave broken identities and clothing reduced to rags and scraps. Using objects to redefine the self as a fully formed modern subject is a struggle for many of Faulkner's Black and mixed-race characters.

Using clothing as an object to remake the self is perhaps the dominant theme of the final Clothing and Class chapter, though again success at doing so is severely limited. Fashion is a marker of modernity as well as class, and many characters struggle to cast off the shackles of the past. The lure of clothing and things as commodities is related to the class striving that drives multiple characters. Flem Snopes is the most successful in terms of improving his class standing, although his stagnation in the latter half of the Snopes trilogy is indicative of Faulkner's lack of focus on identity creation with regards to class, as image becomes more important. As with gender and race, clothing plays varied roles and fulfills disparate functions in relation to class, notably as both an extension of the body and a shield for the self. These functions, along with the struggle for identity creation through clothing and the power of clothes as actants, are threads that connect the following chapters and weave a larger picture of Faulkner's fixation on fashion in fiction.

1

Clothing and Gender

Studies of clothing and fashion (both literary and otherwise) have often been dismissed as superficial or trivial, and this is surely in part due to fashion being historically and stereotypically thought of as a woman's field. Ironically, this same gender bias has probably curtailed the number of literary clothing studies. Matterson argues, for instance, that Melville's use of clothing has been ignored because men's clothes are more prominent in his fiction than women's (34–5). The connections between clothing and gender in Faulkner's fiction often center on oppositional relationships, exhibiting what Malcolm Barnard claims in *Fashion as Communication* is clothing's ability to subvert traditional power structures: "fashion and clothing may indeed question and oppose the continued existence of class and gender identities in society, and show how they may be used to dispute and disrupt the positions of power and status that go with those class and gender identities" (127). Faulkner's critical examinations of gender depict the same struggle between individual identity and cultural norms that Cynthia Kuhn finds in her analysis of clothing in Margaret Atwood's work: "The clothed body often becomes a battleground as Atwood's female protagonists respond to divisive cultural scripts through self-fashioning" (5). In addition to its connections to identity formation, the power of clothing as an actant is displayed repeatedly, as specific garments often influence characters' thoughts and actions. Faulkner also plays with the symbolic meanings of clothing, particularly the military uniform as it relates to masculinity, while women's associations with sin and sexuality are interrogated through an array of different garments. For female characters, the key terms that emerge are excess and containment. Women's bodies and therefore clothing are often sites of overflowing sexuality and femininity that men find threatening and therefore must be constrained, covered, and bound.

Soldiers' Pay

Faulkner's first novel, *Soldiers' Pay* (1926), while often neglected in critical studies, is important for this project for how it treats the theme of containment of women's bodies and for how it utilizes the author's fascination with military uniforms in the tale of a badly wounded and scarred First World War veteran returning home to Georgia. Clothing also becomes significant as an external representation of characters' interior lives. Donald Mahon's train ride home that opens the novel clearly has connections with Faulkner's own return from Canada by train to Oxford, as discussed in the Introduction. Cadet Julian Lowe, like Faulkner himself, is depressed because "they had stopped the war on him," though the civilians on the train are deferential to the military garb if not the men: "When I see a uniform, I respect it like it was my mother" (14). The power of this military attire is evident when Lowe first meets Mahon; he notices and respects the injured man's uniform right away: "He saw a belt and wings, he rose and met a young face with a dreadful scar across his brow" (21). This initial description of Mahon links his scar and his clothing: both are exterior markers that communicate something of his character and experiences to others. Lowe, surely channeling Faulkner's own sentiments, feels his own brow and longs for what Mahon has:

> To have been him! he moaned. Just to be him. Let him take this sound body of mine! Let him take it. To have got wings on my breast, to have wings; and to have got his scar, too, I would take death to-morrow. Upon a chair Mahon's tunic evinced above the left breast pocket wings breaking from an initialed circle beneath a crown, tipping downward in an arrested embroidered sweep; a symbolized desire.
>
> (41)

The details of the uniform shared by Faulkner and noted by Lowe are indicative of the desire that concludes Lowe's reverie: desire for combat, experience, and glory, translated in the novel (and arguably in Faulkner's life) into a desire for sex and women. Faulkner explores Lost Generation themes of alienation, psychological trauma, and sexuality in the novel, and clothing plays a significant role.

Lowe compares his own hat with Mahon's as a synecdoche for masculinity, the white band signifying lack of combat and lack of manhood, "the cadet's conspicuous mark of shame" (136) as Michael Zeitlin describes it in *Faulkner,*

Aviation, and Modern War: "his hat severed by a white band, upon the table the other man's cap with its cloth crown sloping backward from a bronze initialed crest" (*Soldiers' Pay* 41). The scar-like description of Lowe's hat band signifies the opposite of Mahon's scar, a war wound that is incontestable proof of battlefield action and conveys as much about the man as his uniform. Lowe seethes that he "would have got wings in two weeks more" (46), but the war ended too soon, and he overtly links his lack of military clothing and embellishment to his perceived lack of virility, asking Margaret Powers, who is accompanying Mahon home, "you don't like him better than me because he has wings and a scar, do you?" (48). Uniforms become another prop for a performative masculinity. Lowe tags along briefly and then quickly exits the novel, only writing letters to Margaret expressing his sincere if naïve emotions for her, while she, along with ex-soldier Joe Gilligan, escort Mahon home for nebulous reasons. Gilligan seems to take pity on a fellow soldier who clearly cannot care for himself, while Powers has a sense of guilt and obligation since her own husband was killed in the war before he received a letter from her declaring their hasty pre-war marriage a sham. Mahon can barely speak and has trouble comprehending what is happening around him, so why are Gilligan and Powers so taken with him that they immediately change their lives to take a stranger to a small town in Georgia? It is the uniform and the scar that act on to them and compel their deeds—the objects, not the person—and they surely must feel much of what Lowe expresses. To emphasize a point made in the Introduction, I am not arguing that clothing-as-object is the only actor or cause here, only that it is important to recognize that things, not only people, influence human behavior: "any thing that does modify a state of affairs by making a difference is an actor" (Latour 71).

While Mahon does virtually nothing over the course of the novel, he is nonetheless the controlling center of the story around which the other characters swirl. Zeitlin likens him to Pierrot, a character who "darkly reflects the dimly articulated preoccupations, fears, and desires" of the characters around him ("Passion" 355): flying ace, returned war hero, resurrected son, youthful lover, returned fiancé, and, for Powers, a replacement of her dead husband. Mahon's blindness, muteness, and lack of memory make him a perfect blank slate onto which these roles may be projected, but so do his uniform and scar. The military uniform, by design, is the same as many, many other uniforms (aside, of course, from details designating honors, rank, etc.). That is, the uniform makes Mahon more generic, and many critics have noted the Mahon/man pun that makes Donald into something of an everyman figure. His scar, too, becomes the collective wound of the war or even the broad ailment of the human condition. Faulkner's narrator even pays homage to the uniform itself as active subject and seducer of young women at the beginning of the war:

> O Uniform, O Vanity ... Up to that time, uniforms could all walk: they were not only fashionable and romantic, but they were also quite keen on spending what money they had and they were also going too far away and too immediately to tell on you. Of course it was silly that some uniforms had to salute others, but it was nice, too. Especially, if the uniform you had caught happened to be a salutee. And heaven only knows how much damage among feminine hearts a set of pilot's wings was capable of.
>
> (184)

This personification of uniforms echoes Lowe's earlier infatuation with the uniform, its insignia, and meaning, though here we also see the object become subject, the uniform given its due as an actant albeit in figurative language.[1] Faulkner is clearly drawing from his own experiences returning home in uniform detailed in the Introduction, including the responses and actions that a uniform can compel in those observing it rather than wearing it. It is worth emphasizing that Faulkner is using uniforms for more than just metonymy, synecdoche, or symbolism. The clothing does not stand in for or represent the man. As Faulkner well knew, the deeds of the wearer may not, in reality, match what the uniform conveys, but the outfit itself is what compels actions and attitudes from others.

Januarius Jones, representing the crass, uncomprehending civilian population, boorishly pursues Margaret, Cecily, and Emmy over the course of the novel, barely bothering to look at Donald and discounting him as a romantic rival. This demonstrates how Donald has been feminized by his injury with the uniform perhaps his last vestige of masculinity. His physical attractiveness, speech, and capacity for sexual activity have all been devastated by his wound, but he also fits Patricia Yaeger's description of how Faulkner's women can only enter the historical world by being "scarred, marred, or mangled by their environments" and consequently enduring a social death of "ostracism, psychic exile, and sexual segregation" (198–9). Thus, Donald's feminization from his war wound battles the masculinizing power of his uniform, and his betrothal to Cecily is

---

[1] Faulkner captures Lowe's feeling in a line from *Absalom, Absalom!*: "the most moving masssight of all human mass experience ... the sight of young men, the light quick bones, the bright gallant deluded blood and flesh dressed in a martial glitter of brass and plumes, marching away to battle" (97).

in limbo throughout the novel. The overweight Jones is the antithesis of the dapper war hero in uniform; instead, his appearance in his uniform of tweed is referred to disparagingly multiple times: "baggy in gray tweed" (52); "slovenly in his careless unpressed tweeds" (243); "a fat and shapeless mass palely tweeded" (283). Jones's pants actually determine much of his action in the story, behaving as quasi-agents, to use Bennett's term. Upon first meeting Donald's father, the rector of an Episcopalian church, Jones ruins his pants with a pail of dirty water on the way into the house, forcing him to borrow a pair from the elder Mahon. This, in turn, leads to embarrassing first encounters with Emmy, who sees him pants-less, and Cecily Saunders who laughs at him in the ill-fitting clothes of the rector. These slights anger Jones and color his relationships with both women for the remainder of narrative (with his pants mentioned no fewer than five times), most of which he spends lecherously pursuing both of them, as well as Margaret Powers. The ignominy of wearing another man's trousers throws him off and leaves him desperate to reassert himself through callous conquest of women. Clothing inspires both admiration and derision in *Soldiers' Pay*, altering peoples' behavior accordingly.

Donald Mahon, before he wore the uniform, refused to conform to the day's fashion in his youth (wearing "neither coat nor cravat" in a photograph [64]). He rejects custom for practicality, and he is identified with nature in the flashbacks to his pre-war days. "Could you put a faun into formal clothes?" Jones rhetorically asks his prim and proper father (65). Emmy recalls her youthful dalliance with Donald wistfully and notes how he would roam the countryside for days at a time: "He wouldn't never have a hat or a coat, and his face was like—it was like he ought to live in the woods. You know: not like he ought to went to school or had to dress up" (121). The primal scene on which Emmy fixates is when she loses her virginity to Donald after swimming naked together. The lack of clothing signifies a true baring of the soul to one another, at least as far as Emmy is concerned, and she cannot handle the fact that he now does not recognize her at all. Their nudity in nature suggests opposition to or casting off of social conventions to expose the true self, although her feelings of guilt and shame also link the scene to an Edenic idealization of innocent childhood. Returning home from her tryst with Donald, her father threatens to beat her, and she runs away, appropriately to work for a dressmaker (124–5). In the present, she tries to recapture her youthful feeling by lying down in the damp grass, but now her wet clothes only remind her that it's almost washing day (297).

Gender and class issues intersect and overlap in the character of Emmy, who laments wearing "coarse dresses and shoes while other girls wore silk and thin leather" (270), and her garments now reflect her station in life as the servant for the rector. Margaret tries to befriend Emmy by offering her a fancy new dress "that doesn't suit me for some reason," but Emmy responds, "I don't go anywhere, and I got clothes good enough to wash and sweep and cook in" (118). While Emmy imagined before the war that her prospects in life might be trending upward through possible marriage to Donald, she now seems resigned to wear the clothes of her station, the "badge of servitude," as Veblen describes the liveries of domestic servants (79). This recalls the role of dress noted by Sandra M. Gilbert as having fixed symbolic meanings tied to one's social roles: "[U]ntil the middle or late nineteenth century most people wore what were essentially uniforms: garments denoting the one form or single shape to which each individual's life was confined by birth, by circumstance, by custom, by decree" (196). Thus, Margaret's offer of fancy clothing as "dress-up things" (118) has no relevance for Emmy's current life, relegated to the status of the silk dresses that only "other girls" wear. Appropriately, she settles at the novel's end for Januarius Jones, "a fat and shapeless mass palely tweeded" (283). Emmy ultimately cannot envision herself as a modern woman and cannot self-fashion an identity that rejects the patriarchal conditioning she accepts. Her maid's clothes are a uniform that denotes her rank and status as much as Donald's.

Of course, Donald's life prospects were not circumscribed nor ruined by his one-night stand with Emmy, only hers. He goes on to get engaged to Cecily before the war and even marries Margaret when Cecily cannot bear to go through with the wedding after it. Margaret voices a complaint familiar to many of Faulkner's women characters: "Men are the ones who worry about our good names, because they gave them to us. But we have other things to bother about, ourselves. What you mean by a good name is like a dress that's too flimsy to wear comfortably" (100–1). So women must sometimes take off the dress, literally and figuratively (like Addie Bundren "dressed in sin" [174]), as a rebuke to the patriarchal dictates that women maintain "a good name" for the honor of men. The "New Woman" of the 1920s can be seen in Margaret Powers, but traditional patriarchal attitudes about women's sexuality dominate the small-town setting of the novel.

In Faulkner's second novel, *Mosquitoes*, nakedness and shedding of clothes becomes linked to a progressive discarding of antiquated values and a willingness to explore the true inner self unencumbered by social norms. *Soldiers' Pay*, by contrast, depicts a society still dominated by old white men who cannot or will not relinquish their calcified attitudes. When Cecily's father enters her bedroom, he accosts her with "Do nice girls sit around half naked like this?" (126). She replies, "Maybe I'm not a nice girl" and puts on "a flimsy diaphanous robe" (126), a precursor to Miss Quentin's kimono, as well as presaging Caddy's response to why she let a boy kiss her: "*I didn't let him I made him … What do you think of that?*" (133). The dress that Cecily wears to the dance near the end of *Soldiers' Pay* is twice referred to with the same phrase, the "glass-like fragility of her dress" (200, 202), and another woman warns her that the dress is see-through: "See right through you. Stay out of the light" (201). Cecily by now has a reputation in town as a fast woman of loose morals who has been seeing another man while her fiancé was away at war, and this breach of decorum taints her in the minds of the townspeople. What's underneath her dress, both literally and figuratively, is shameful and should be hidden away. The pre-war innocence of nakedness in Emmy and Donald's skinny-dipping episode is replaced by a post-war repression, a preference not to confront the naked truth. "How ugly men are, naked," Margaret thinks (178). The willingness to shed social restrictions and confront the exposed truth is celebrated by the artists and faux artists of *Mosquitoes*, but here the painful truth is better covered up and ignored. Unconsciously at least, Cecily desires the attention the dress brings. That is, she has been lying to herself, her parents, and the town about intending to continue seeing Donald to make him feel better and even going through with the marriage. She wants to be done with this charade, to have her façade seen through, as it were, and to run off with George Farr. Choosing this dress to wear to a public event invites further scorn; the dress causes the reactions that will further drive her to forsake Donald and elope with George, in turn cementing her pariah status. The dress is scandalous, not her, and this incident illustrates another of clothing's dual features: it both conceals the body but also draws attention to that which it conceals. Cecily here is also a forerunner of Faulkner's later women characters in that her sexuality is barely contained by her clothing, and the reaction of those around her is to demand she be covered and hemmed in.

Donald Mahon's scar is perhaps like clothing in the sense that the visible exterior reflects in a muted, palatable way the scarred interior of not just himself, but all of the shell-shocked First World War veterans. A "breach of bodily boundaries" is a recurring theme and fear in Western society and art, whether it be through contamination, bodily invasion, or bodily collapse (Cavallaro and Warwick 5). Cavallaro and Warwick's fashion study connects this theme to

Julia Kristeva's notion of abjection, "the expulsion and rejection of everything that threatens the subject's existence as an autonomous and differential entity" (xvi). However, the abject is never truly suppressed: "In particular, it resurfaces whenever we are confronted with marginal or threshold phenomena that elude unproblematic classification and remind us that the body is only precariously bounded" (xvi). Mahon's scar, which causes other characters to feel sick, to cry out, and to faint when they see it, is just such a bodily breach, a reminder of contamination, invasion, collapse, and death. Clothing is therefore similar to the scar because it also blurs the line between self and other, it "reinforces the fluidity of its frame by raising the somewhat uncomfortable question: *where does the body end and where does dress begin?*" (xvii). While dress is meant to divide clearly the self and others, it also is the margin that "links the biological entity to the social ensemble and the private to the public" (xvii). Cecily's see-through dress makes everyone uncomfortable precisely because it destabilizes what is body and what is not; what is private and what is public; and what is intimate and what is shared. Mahon's scar also seems to bring the interior to the surface disturbingly and suggests that others, perhaps everyone, has the same ugly wound inside.

Mosquitoes

Mosquitoes continues Faulkner's use of clothing symbolically and his revelations of how clothing can be an actant or quasi-agent in human affairs, building on the ways that uniforms affect people in *Soldiers' Pay*. Julius Wiseman, usually referred to as "the Semitic man," voices an object-oriented philosophy toward the end of *Mosquitoes* after witnessing his fellow passengers flirt, court, and attempt to seduce one another throughout the trip, as Faulkner anticipates Latour and the fashion critics I rely on in this study: "Who was the fool who said that our clothing, our custom in dress, does not affect the shape of our bodies and our behavior?" (252). Indeed, the shape of bodies, as accentuated and revealed by clothing, induces the lust that drives much of the action of the novel, and Faulkner perhaps voices baldly in this apprentice novel what is more nuanced, implied, and buried in his more accomplished later work. As the party gathers on the boat, the *Nausikaa*, for the first time, Faulkner's initial attempts at characterization rely on clothing. Mrs. Maurier dons a yachting cap to get in the mood and "her guests in their colored clothing gathered, dressed for deep water in batik and flowing ties and open collars, informal and colorful with the exception of Mark Frost, the ghostly young man ... He wore ironed serge and a high starched collar" (53-4). Other references to clothing abound in the first "Ten O'clock" section: "a florid stranger in heavy tweeds" (54), "a soft blonde girl in a slightly soiled green dress" (54), an insolent youth in a "slanted stiff straw hat" (54), and "narrow coat" (55). Pete's refusal to part with his straw hat becomes something of a running joke throughout the novel (though not much more than that), while the other characters are continually disrobing. The hostess, Mrs. Maurier is "horrified" that her niece does not wear stockings or shoes on the boat (59), and her bare legs are emblematic of the characters' casting off of social restrictions on the water. The multiple swimming scenes require characters to change into swimsuits or underwear, signaling a loosening of inhibitions as the guests break the ship's rules for the first swim (80).

This first swim has Mrs. Maurier's niece, also named Patricia, change into "her brother's underwear—a knitted sleeveless jersey and short narrow trunks" as a swimming outfit (82), and she subsequently, perhaps consequently, bests two of the men in some playful wrestling in the water, literally stepping on Dawson Fairchild and Major Ayers and forcing them underwater until they give up. It is as if her man's clothes have given her the confidence to subdue and dominate men in ways that she does not on dry land. As she climbs out of the small rowboat, one of the men swings her by the hands back onto the ship's deck and she has a "sensation of flying" momentarily and exhilaratingly: "for an instant she stopped in midflight ... high above the deck while water dripping from her turned to gold as it fell ... and in her face the passionate ecstasy of a child" (83). This feeling of freedom, being loosed from daily burdens and conventional restrictions, is what most of the characters chase throughout the novel, and the older ones envy the innocence and boldness of the young. There are repeated references to disrobing and nakedness, and this motif highlights the novel's themes of hiding the true self yet longing to cast off the roles and constraints imposed on individuals by social and cultural mores, "a kind of letting down of the bars of pretense, you know; a kind of submerging of civilized structures before the grand implacability of nature and the physical body," as Dawson Fairchild puts it (245).

The characters long to feel a freedom symbolized by the shedding of clothes, but when they achieve it, it is not always a positive experience, especially seen in Patricia running away with David only to be driven back by the mosquitoes and the swamp. Patricia's decision to cajole David into running off with her is precipitated by her swimming naked in the mist at dawn, an exercise in losing herself, stripping herself down as it were until she feels "this limitless vagueness whose center was herself" (171). Jenny, too, has a similar crisis of identity "feeling again her world become unstable and shifting beneath her" as she "gazed into the dark water" (235), prompting her to run inside, undress, and stare at herself in the mirror: "She didn't know what it was she wanted, except that it was something" (236). Patricia knows that she wants to be different, a rebel, but her running away quickly seems foolish and naïve as she daydreams childishly about never living in a house: "We'll just go around like this, camping" (178). She succeeds in acting rather than simply talking, in contrast to most of the characters ("the utter and heartbreaking stupidity of words" [194]), but ironically the reality of running away is far less pleasurable than the abstract idea of it. As the mosquitoes start biting her in the swamp, Patricia suddenly puts on the stockings whose absence had earlier horrified her aunt (179), then adds David's shirt on top of her bathing suit, and her own dress over that (187–8) in a desperate attempt to layer protective clothing against the biting of the real world. Words and ideas prove futile in the face of actions and things.

All of the repeated doffing and donning of clothing in *Mosquitoes* works with the novel's theme of uncovering truth that is shrouded by layers of concealment, whether that is words masking deeds, artistic pretensions obscuring vapidness, posing covering up one's true self, or conventional conformity hiding unconventional sexuality. Minrose Gwin and Phillip Gordon have particularly analyzed male homosexuality and homoeroticism in the novel, while many critics have commented on the more overt instance of female homosexual desire. As the characters shed their clothing, their true and hidden desires are exposed. In her article "Did Ernest Like Gordon?: Faulkner's *Mosquitoes* and the Bite of Gender Trouble," Gwin argues that Talliaferro is attracted to Gordon, noting Talliaferro's inept displays of heteronormativity and his attraction to Gordon's half-dressed body in the novel's opening scene. Talliaferro, a wholesale buyer of women's clothes, watches Gordon's "hard body in stained trousers and undershirt" (7) while dressed more repressively in "his own pressed flannel … [and] his stiff straw hat … [that] flaunted its wanton gay band above the slim yellow gleam of his straight malacca stick" (9). Gwin also details four scenes in Faulkner's typescript deleted (apparently by the publisher) from the published final version, each of which further develop homosexual or queer themes and characters, most prominently a more extended version of the lesbian encounter between Patricia Roby and Jenny Steinbauer watched voyeuristically by the lesbian poet Eva Wiseman (134–5). Gordon further argues that Julius Wiseman and Fairchild are a couple (81), and the numerous attempts at heterosexual coupling throughout the novel also underscore that away from dry land and unencumbered by the clothing and inhibitions that usually constrain them, the men and women let loose the repressed and stifled thoughts, words, desires, and actions that have been kept covered up. The failures of almost all of these attempts, though, perhaps suggest that some clothing, some covering of these base desires, is appropriate and important, something Fairchild grasps at the novel's end: "When the statue is completely nude, it has only a coldly formal significance, you know. But when some foreign matter like a leaf or a fold of drapery … draws the imagination to where the organs of reproduction are concealed, it lends the statue a warmer, a more … speculative significance" (339–40). Or as Mrs. Wiseman says as she convinces Jenny to wear a more conservative, less revealing dress, "A little flesh is worse than a little dynamite" (213).

In addition to these symbolic meanings of clothing, there are a few instances of garments exerting a certain agency as things. Often these are minor moments where glimpses of underwear or skin as clothing shifts give rise to lustful feelings in the watchers. When Jenny changes into Patricia's clothes, she and Mrs. Wiseman both are caught off-guard by the difference it makes. "It's far more exciting than a bathing suit," Mrs. Wiseman tells her, insisting that she should not go around the men in this tight-fitting dress and convincing her to change into something more conservative to maintain decorum (213). This presages Faulkner's later concerns with excess and containment of feminine sexuality in his major works. During her brief sojourn off the boat with David, Patricia's "muddy stockings and her stained dress" suggest a moral dirtiness along the lines of Caddy's muddy drawers, especially since a leering man watches her pour water on herself "sopping her dress" in an image of a failed attempt at purification (22). At the conclusion of the trip on the *Nausikaa*, the first lines of the Epilogue focus oddly on Jenny's dress: "Lake water had done strange things to Jenny's little green dress. It was rough-dried and draggled, and it had kind of sagged here and drawn up there. The skirt in the back, for instance, because now between the gracious miniature ballooning of its hem and the tops of her dingy stockings, you saw pink flesh" (311). After all that has happened, the dress is what gets the initial and primary attention, as well as the way it reveals what's underneath because of the changes it and its wearer have been through. The dress is a symbol but more than that. As an object, it too has been transformed and played its part in its wearer's transformation. The power of items of clothing to influence people in *Mosquitoes* is confined to their ability to titillate and stimulate, important aspects, to be sure, that are expanded upon in later novels.

The Sound and the Fury

Clothing in *The Sound and the Fury* functions almost entirely on the symbolic level; that is, clothes are not so important as items of fashion or even as things, as much as for what they represent to characters and readers. Benjy's clothing gets caught on a nail in the fence, triggering his first-time shift (4), and while this could be said to show the clothing as an actant, the real significance is that he gets stuck in a liminal position between two states, not *how* he manages to get snagged on the fence. Benjy rarely notices clothing in his narration, with the notable exception being items of Caddy's clothing that he fetishizes as replacements for her. The slipper that he uses to soothe and comfort himself (70, 72, 316–17) has no real importance as an item of clothing, but only because it represents his missing sister. It is important as an object, but primarily for what it represents, rather than for its own qualities as a thing. Yet it is also true that these two aspects of the item are impossible to separate. The smell of trees may carry rich symbolic meanings, but it is also literally embedded in the fibers of her clothes. Likewise, when Caddy at fourteen wears a new hat and dress, Benjy shies away from her because these garments represent a new Caddy, a sexually maturing young woman who will leave her brothers. Jason accurately diagnoses why Benjy pulls away, almost rechristening his sister to match her newly fashioned identity: "'He dont like that prissy dress.' Jason said. 'You think you're grown up, dont you. You think you're better than anybody else, dont you. Prissy'" (41). Benjy pulls Caddy's dress multiple times (47, 69, 124, 149) as if removing her "grown up" clothes will undo her sexual maturity and keep Caddy with him in a state of arrested development.

Of course, the more famous symbol of Caddy's muddy drawers, the focus of her brothers' gazes as she climbs the pear tree to spy on Damuddy's funeral, also carries symbolic meanings of sexuality with the added element of sex as dirty or wrong. This interpretation of the muddy drawers as emblematic of sexuality has been a critical truism for years, and certainly it is valid, though in a sense it privileges the male view of (white) female sexuality as inherently sinful. Recent critics have expanded on the garment's meaning, Stephen Kern, for instance, seeing it as a symbol of trauma that gains force over time for the Compson brothers (121). Susanna Hempstead argues that this muddy underwear signifies to Quentin, Jason, and Benjy "more than sensuality" and represents Caddy's willfulness "and in them they can see the reflection of their own decay" (35). These ideas are a helpful push toward the themes of excess and containment that become increasingly prominent in Faulkner's feminine clothing. I echo Hempstead's thinking that linking the garment only to sensuality or sexuality leads to "a reductive understanding of these female characters" (35) and would emphasize how they represent death as well. Not only is Caddy boldly viewing Damuddy's funeral from her elevated vantage point in the tree, but, as I have detailed elsewhere, Faulkner suggestively links sex and death throughout *The Sound and the Fury*.[2] The dark stain on the white cloth is the blot of death that imprints our existence. In one sense, Quentin and Jason may intuit the clothing as failing to contain their sister's sexuality, the stain seeping out from within. But this permeability of clothing also works the other way, failing to stop the taint of death from reaching our bodies. "It done soaked clean through onto you," Dilsey tells Caddy (72). Thus, the muddy drawers reveal the folly of all defenses we might raise against death: Benjy's ignorance, Quentin's faith in inherited codes, Jason's rage and denial, and even Faulkner's art.

The power of the muddy drawers and their lingering trauma results in Jason's fixation on his sister's sexuality—and on that of her daughter as a proxy for the missing sister. Jason is nearly obsessed with Quentin's clothing, repeatedly describing her kimono almost coming off, leaving her "dam near naked" (184), and practically fantasizing about sexually assaulting his niece because of her revealing dress:

> [S]o I stood there and watched her go on past, with her face painted up like dam clown's and her hair all gummed and twisted and a dress that if a woman had come out doors even on Gayoso or Beale street when I was a young fellow with no more than that to cover her legs and behind, she'd have been thrown in jail. I'll be damned if they dont dress like they were trying to make every man they passed on the street want to reach out and clap his hand on it.
>
> (232)

---

[2] See "'The Front Door and the Back Door of the World': Flowers, Sex, and Death in Faulkner and García Márquez," pages 108–24 in *Faulkner and García Márquez*.

A woman in public is an object on display, so her clothing receives lingering attention and lurid interpretations to which men are simply not subjected. Quentin had earlier threatened to tear off this same dress in the car with Jason, attaching her symbolic value to it as a commodity: if Jason's money has paid for her clothing, she will refuse to wear it (187–8). Interestingly, Caddy sends money specifically for a new "easter dress" (190) for Quentin, an item that might symbolize Caddy's rebirth in her daughter, a cleansing of both of their sexual "sins" through a wardrobe change, but Jason never uses the money for its intended purpose, leaving his niece to wear the revealing dress he is both attracted to and repulsed by. In fact, the forty dollars he steals from Caddy's money order replaces the same amount he had given Lorraine for a dress (194), further linking Quentin to his sexual desires through clothing. Whether Quentin's dress is actually as revealing as Jason claims or her kimono is really as flimsy and prone to opening as he says cannot be known. What is important is how he discusses them, for his descriptions of her dress reveal not her character, but his. It should also be noted that Quentin is a strong, rebellious, independent female character who wears feminine clothing, as opposed to Drusilla Hawk and Charlotte Rittenmeyer who, as we will see, both express female empowerment through men's clothing. Perhaps Quentin's willfulness explains Jason's linking of sexuality and race. He does not accuse Quentin of dressing like a Black woman; rather, he sees her clothing as one manifestation of her true inner self and her imagined sexual behavior as another, accusing her of behaving "like a nigger wench" (189). Jason's need to contain the threat of women and African Americans from exceeding their "proper" place finds expression in his constant attempts to cover his niece's body.

Jason's own clothing is never described, so we only see how he obsesses over garments that he associates with sexuality, how Quentin's clothing, for instance, becomes a portent for her sexual intentions. The man with the red tie is especially infuriating to him because the fashion statement is so bold and signals to Jason a type of masculinity beyond his ken. Three times he asks himself, "what the hell kind of a man would wear a red tie" (232, 234), and his outrage at his niece's sexuality becomes bound up with the race and class resentment that seethes throughout his section of the novel. The fact that this man is part of a traveling show angers Jason as much as his presumed sexual relationship with Quentin, fitting the larger pattern of Jason's rage at his reduced class standing compared to earlier generations of Compsons and Bascombs. Jason worries that chasing the pair around town without his hat makes him look "like I was crazy too" (233), showing his concern for social propriety and tradition that he masks through insults. The tie enrages him not only because of what it might symbolize, but also because Jason considers himself the guardian of traditional morality and communal standards, sartorial as well as sexual. The red tie and gasoline smell combine to make him ill and indicate his unsuitability for the modern world and its changing values. As John T. Matthews says, "he's as anchored to the past as either of his brothers, he just doesn't realize it" (97–8). Matthews's analysis details how economic resentment motivates Jason and how he "constructs a full-fledged narrative to account for his life," one that rests on blaming others for all of his problems: "Jason's story functions as a suit of armor against his daily woes" (103). Jason reveals a glimpse of his soft underbelly beneath his armor at times, such as when he stands with Caddy after his father's funeral: "We stood there, looking at the grave, and then I got to thinking about when we were little and one thing and another and I got to feeling funny again, kind of mad or something" (203). Clothing often acts as a shield or armor, "a protective barrier meant to insulate private fantasies" (Warwick and Cavallaro 47), but Jason's protective barrier slips at times, just as his clothes fail to protect him when he attempts to track Quentin and the man in the red tie through the countryside on foot and gets "beggar lice and twigs and stuff all over me, inside my clothes and shoes and all" (241). In Jason's section alone, clothes are quasi-agents that affect human behavior in three different ways: the flimsy kimono triggers sexual arousal and causes Jason to leer at, ridicule, and attack his niece; Quentin's dress, because of its status as commodity and its provenance, causes its wearer to attempt to rip off her clothing in public, leading to another physical confrontation; and the red tie symbolically implicates Jason's masculinity and reminds him of his reduced class and status, exacerbated by his stolen three thousand dollars "with his invisible life ravelled out about him like a wornout sock" (313).

In Quentin's section of the novel, clothing acts in yet another way, more as the shield, armor, or disguise function mentioned in relation to Jason, as well as Faulkner's own frequent costuming and role playing. On June 2, 1910, the day he has chosen to commit suicide, Quentin wears a brand-new suit, and Shreve mocks him for "all that primping" (82). Shreve even presciently suggests Quentin is dressed up for a funeral, referencing a Hindu custom of a wife throwing herself on her husband's funeral pyre: "Say, what're you doing today, anyhow? All dressed up and mooning around like the prologue to a suttee" (101). His clothing choice seems inauthentic to Shreve, and others also pick up on this. His suit causes the watch repairman to query, "What're you celebrating today? ... That boat race aint until next week, is it?" (84). The boys he encounters who are fishing also feel compelled to ask about his dress: "They looked at my clothes. 'You looking for work?'" (119). Quentin's costume betrays his feeling of not really belonging, as a small-town Southerner at Harvard, as older brother who does not exhibit traditional masculinity, and as an adherent of an outdated chivalric code in a modern world.[3] This dressing to project an external version of the self and conceal the true self is a continuation of the posing we see in various flashbacks, whether telling Caddy he has had sex "lots of times with lots of girls" (151) or threatening Dalton Ames like a sheriff in the Old West: "I heard myself saying Ill give you until sundown to leave town" (159).

Quentin knows, of course, that his various poses merely cover up (badly) the despair and nihilism inside, and this may help explain why he recognizes similar costuming in Gerald Bland—and why Bland angers him so. Bland also claims to have had sex "lots of times with lots of girls," but his misogyny is closer to Jason's bile than Quentin's desperation. Bland seems to overdress fashionably like Quentin when he practices rowing on the river: "Either he or his mother had read somewhere that Oxford students pulled in flannels and stiff hats, so early one March they bought Gerald a one pair shell and in his flannels and stiff hat he went on the river ... His mother came down in a hired auto, in a fur suit like an arctic explorer's" (90–1). The seemingly virile and masculine Bland glides across the water in his fancy clothes while Quentin can only sink beneath it in his blood-stained, gasoline-soaked suit.

Quentin's descriptions of the fashionable Gerald combine mockery and jealousy, his scorn betraying attraction:

> [S]itting in his attitudes of princely boredom, with his curly yellow hair and his violet eyes and his eyelashes and his New York clothes, while his mamma was telling us about Gerald's horses and Gerald's niggers and Gerald's women. Husbands and fathers in Kentucky must have been awful glad when she carried Gerald off to Cambridge.
>
> (91)

Quentin's attentiveness to Gerald's hair, eyes, and even eyelashes suggests a sexual attraction despite his revulsion at Bland's morals and character. The merging of Gerald Bland and Dalton Ames in Quentin's mind is not only because both

---

[3] This connects Quentin to Melville's characters, who Matterson argues are often dressed in the "wrong" clothing. For Quentin, though, this is not a sign of social mobility, but rather being out of step with or behind the times.

treat women like "they're all bitches" (160), but also because of their fashionable appearances: "Dalton Ames. Dalton Ames. Dalton Shirts. I thought all the time they were khaki, army issue khaki, until I saw they were of heavy Chinese silk or finest flannel because they made his face so brown his eyes so blue. Dalton Ames. It just missed gentility" (92). The same fixation on the eyes of both men suggests more than just sartorial envy, and Quentin's attraction to Dalton Ames has been a staple of critical and classroom discussions for many years. Quentin cannot get over those shirts, and they help make "Dalton Shirts" appear as a heroic figure against whom the effete Quentin can never measure up: "he looked like he was made out of bronze his khaki shirt" (158). Quentin's envious awe at Ames's martial appearance recalls the effects of the uniforms in *Soldiers' Pay*, with Quentin in the role of Lowe feeling an inferior masculinity reflected in another's clothing. After the fight with Bland, a sad echo of his failure with Ames, Quentin's sole preoccupation is cleaning his clothes before committing suicide. Though Shreve says, "Oh forget your damn clothes" (165), the clothing has become imbued with the memories of failure, and Quentin cannot just forget them, the Compson blood on his clothes bringing to mind his sister's hymenal blood that vexes him so. He puts some of his bloody clothes in a bag and changes into new ones but attempts to clean the blood from his vest with gasoline before putting it back on (172, 178). The strong smell of gasoline links Quentin's failures to Jason's later ones, both stemming from the brothers' inability to accept their sister's sexuality.

While Caddy's muddy drawers in the tree are echoed by Quentin wiping mud on to his sister's clothes years later ("the mud flatting her bodice through her dress it smelled horrible" [137]), there is another less noticeable connecting thread in Quentin's section. As he walks around Boston with the little Italian girl looking for her home, Quentin, for no apparent reason, fixates on one house in particular: "In the center of an untrimmed plot enclosed by a fence of gaping and broken pickets stood an ancient lopsided surrey and a weathered house from an upper window of which hung a garment of vivid pink. 'Does that look like your house?' I said" (131). Why does he notice only this house, and why does he assume that it could be hers? After the alleged kidnapping has been adjudicated by the Squire, Quentin again notices this house while riding away in Mrs. Bland's car: "We ... passed the house where the pink garment hung in the window" (146). The garment perhaps reminds Quentin of the "orchard pink and white" (122) that he visits with the fishing boys a bit earlier that day, but it more significantly recalls blood, not only the virginal blood of

Caddy that he is prepared to die for, but also his blood that Caddy draws when she scratches him in retaliation for his smearing mud on her: "my hand came red away streaking off pink in the rain" (138). They decide "we better try to wash it off in the branch," but the blood and "stink" (138) will not come off easily, as Quentin learns with his suit vest. But perhaps he does not want the stain removed in any case, needs it as a constant reminder. Thus, he erects a sort of shrine in his dorm room with the unopened invitation to Caddy's wedding at its funereal center: "It lay on the table a candle burning at each corner upon the envelope tied in a soiled pink garter two artificial flowers" (94). The stained pink garter brings us back to Caddy's soiled drawers and the pink garment in the window, as well as forward to the other Quentin, his namesake, who apparently reprises her mother's behavior while also breaking free from the cursed Compson family, leaving behind only one thing, a haunting reminder of those traumatic muddy drawers, when she climbs out of her window and down the same tree her mother once scaled: "On the floor lay a soiled undergarment of cheap silk a little too pink" (282).

Focusing on clothing may not always produce startling new interpretations to upset the critical consensus, but it can, I hope, offer new angles on major themes, as well as draw attention to texts not as often discussed as the major novels. The connection of "Red Leaves" to Faulkner's major works is perhaps not obvious, but an eye on clothing may suggest commonalities with *The Sound and the Fury*, both written around the same time. "Red Leaves" was Faulkner's second published short story, appearing in the October 25, 1930, issue of *The Saturday Evening Post*, and written sometime between 1927 and 1929 (Towner and Carothers 164). In this story of Native American slave owners, Moketubbe seems to have some sort of unspecified physical and mental debilities, suggested through the narrative's preoccupations with his "broad, flat, Mongolian face," his "unfathomable lethargy" (320), and a body "diseased with flesh" (321, 327). The curious adjective "dropsical" is used to refer to both Moketubbe (321, 335) and Benjy (274). Although his mental issues do not seem as profound as Benjy's, Moketubbe is similarly obsessed with footwear, in this case patent-leather slippers with red heels that his father, Issetibbeha, brings home from Paris. These slippers are initially associated by Issetibbeha with the power to rule the tribe: "When you are the Man, the shoes will be yours. But until then, they are my shoes" (316–17). The son continually tries to fit the slippers onto his feet from age three to sixteen, at which point he steals them. Fearing the theft is a sign of impending patricide, Issetibbeha gives the shoes to his son hoping to appease him, though he intuits that it is not "the same if I give the slippers to you" (321), implying the necessity of a Freudian father-son power struggle.

Moketubbe becomes entranced by the slippers at age three, the only objects that rouse him from his state of "complete and unfathomable lethargy" (320), a fact that recalls the description of Benjy as having been "three years old thirty years" (17). This passage about Moketubbe's fascination with the slippers at age three is followed immediately by a description of his mother and her clothing: "Moketubbe's mother was a comely girl whom Issetibbeha had seen one day working in her shift in a melon patch" (320). This juxtaposition, as well as the similarities with Benjy, suggests that the slippers are perhaps a replacement for Moketubbe's mother. Issetibbeha is attracted to this unnamed woman at least partly because "he may have remembered his own mother" (321), and this doubling and conflating of mother and mate (replacement mother) echoes the mother/Caddy linkage in Benjy's psyche, similarly channeled into shoes.

The slippers in "Red Leaves" also connect to the story's main narrative and themes, the hunt for Issetibbeha's body servant so that he can be buried with his newly deceased master. As Moketubbe is carried by slaves during the pursuit, he clings to the slippers, but wearing them on his feet seems to drain him of life. As he lies nearly comatose, his slaves remove the shoes and he then begins "to pant, his bare chest moving deep, as though he were rising from beyond his unfathomed flesh back into life" (327). This curious development implies perhaps that the Native Americans, wearing "their stiff European finery" (331), in copying the institution of slavery from whites have also imported the moral decay that comes with the peculiar institution. Moketubbe can only wear the slippers on his "big, tender, dropsical feet" for short periods of time, and the shoes seem to actually be causing the diseased flesh, as both the slippers and his body appear frail and worn out: "He could not wear them very long while in motion, not even in the litter where he was slung reclining, so they rested upon a square of fawnskin upon his lap—the cracked, frail slippers a little shapeless now, with their patent-leather surfaces and buckleless tongues and scarlet heels, lying upon the supine obese shape just barely alive" (335). Just as clinging unnaturally to Caddy as replacement mother is unhealthy for Benjy, Moketubbe and the other Native Americans' adoption of white, European customs and values slowly rots at their culture and their selves, Faulkner implies. (Moketubbe's obesity and shabby dress recall the moral decay of Januarius Jones in *Soldiers' Pay*.) It is also unnatural and unhealthy to replace a woman with a thing, a fetishized object. Quentin and Jason want to control and contain women's bodies to keep them pure. Moketubbe and Benjy show that it is easier to possess and control the woman by simply replacing the actual person with an object.

These shoes also demonstrate actant functions of clothing, as "Red Leaves" does not show the shoes metaphorically weakening Moketubbe but actually draining the life from him. This may be one of the moments to risk appearing naïve or foolish, as Bennett and Latour suggest one must, by taking Faulkner seriously here. The story shows that the shoes have a measurable physical effect that is discernible to others. When Herman Basket first sees the motionless Moketubbe, he immediately asks, "He has worn them since daylight?" The responder says, "You can see," to which Basket replies, "We can see" (325). Later, Moketuube seems to know he is dying and to know "he could not wear them very long" or risk hastening his death, yet he longs to wear them at any opportunity, and when his feet are placed into them, his face immediately shifts to "that expression tragic, passive and profoundly attentive, which dyspeptics wear" (335). It is as if Moketubbe is ingesting something from the shoes into his body, as the reference to dyspepsia (or indigestion) suggests, linking clothing and death again, though in a different way than Caddy's muddy drawers. Moketubbe's physical response to donning the shoes is reminiscent of a drug addict, perhaps foreshadowing the morphine-addicted Uncle Willy in Faulkner's 1935 story of the same name. Like Willy, Moketubbe is addicted to the mental effects of the shoes no matter what effect they have on his body. The narrator of "Uncle Willy," in fact, uses a sartorial metaphor in describing the title character's death and to suggest an important division between the physical and metaphysical person: "the dying wasn't anything, it just touched the outside of you that you wore around with you for comfort and convenience like you do your clothes" (247).

Sanctuary

Uncle Willy marries a Memphis prostitute, whose appearance in a pink dress scandalizes the town, linking her to Caddy and Miss Quentin; and pink women's clothing again feature prominently with regards to a "fallen" woman in *Sanctuary*, Faulkner's salacious potboiler gangster story that is full of references to clothing.[4] The novel opens with Horace Benbow and Popeye facing each other across a

---

[4] Faulkner himself describes the novel as "a cheap idea" "deliberately conceived to make money" (*Essays* 176), though recent criticism has certainly challenged this view.

spring for nearly two hours, and their different clothing suggests an inverted pairing rather than mirror images. James Watson points out that Benbow's "gray flannel trousers" and "tweed coat" are more akin to Ivy League fashions[5], while Popeye's slim suit is more like the dandy clothing of the period: "Facing one another across the pool, Popeye and Horace are costumed as opposed aspects of the author, one with a gun in his pocket and the other with a book" (*Self-Presentation* 91). Popeye's "suit was black, with a tight, high-waisted coat" (4), about which Temple sarcastically asks, "What river did you fall in with that suit on? Do you have to shave it off at night?" (50). His outfit—"tight suit and stiff hat all angles, like a modernist lampstand" (7)—seems to be a nod to the young Faulkner's tailored tight clothing, though it may also be inspired by the most famous gangster of the 1920s, Al Capone, whose signature style "included his spats, his showy necktie, his fob watch and chain tucked into his vest pocket, his distinctive pin-striped suits—and, of course, the brimmed hat worn at an angle designed to cast a shadow over the scar on his cheek" (Herald 32).[6] Popeye's hat is repeatedly described as slanted throughout the novel, and Jay Watson points out that Popeye's style aligns him with modernity as it "projects the angularity already established among interwar painters, sculptors, and photographers as a key visual hallmark of speed." Benbow's style, on the other hand, is from "an older, slower era," helping to establish "two kinds of characters in *Sanctuary*: fast ones and slow ones, the latter hopelessly overmatched by the former" (*Modernity* 103). To this we might add that there are fashionable characters and unfashionable characters, the latter hopelessly overmatched by the former.

The possible Capone link is therefore interesting in the way that fashion signals modernity. Al Capone was the first modern, celebrity gangster. Whereas most gangsters tried to stay out of the news, Capone sought out publicity, giving an interview to *Cosmopolitan* magazine in 1927 and appearing on the cover of *Time* in March of 1930, just about eleven months before the publication of *Sanctuary* (Eig 105).[7] At a time when newspapers often still published two daily editions and therefore needed sensational news to sell, Capone was featured heavily in Chicago, with the *Tribune* publisher comparing him to Babe Ruth (Eig 108). This was also an era when newsreels and films ushered in the start

---

[5] Horace is described in nearly the same exact outfit in *Flags in the Dust* (180, 182).
[6] Faulkner references Capone by name (though not his clothing) in *If I Forget Thee, Jerusalem* (286).
[7] Another interesting, though perhaps entirely coincidental, Faulkner connection is the fact that "Scarface" claimed to have received his famous facial scars fighting in the First World War, though he was never actually in the Army.

of celebrity culture, and flashy Hollywood gangsters even dressed like Capone. His trademark white fedora was so copied by other organized crime figures that Chicago police began to pull over any cars carrying men in white hats (Valentini). The fedora for both Capone and Popeye becomes a symbol of manhood. It hides the real-life gangster's scars that might mark him as weak, while Popeye refuses to take off his hat while watching his surrogate Red with Temple at Miss Reba's, which could connect the hat with another object, the corn cob, which many critics have of course noted is a surrogate for Popeye's manhood. William Brevda analyzes Popeye's connections to Capone in detail in "'Without Even His Hat Took Off': Falkner's *Sanctuary*," noting that both men are known for owning large amounts of fashionable clothing (408). He argues for the importance of things, clothing, and, especially, hats in the novel, with Popeye's and Temple's headgear functioning as Freudian substitutes for missing or impotent genitalia. Temple's stylish cloche hat aligns her with modern fashion trends, just as Popeye and real-life gangsters were defined by their stylish suits and hats (410), while pink undergarments link Temple to Caddy, Quentin, and other Faulkner characters.

When Temple first arrives at the Old Frenchman Place, she sees "a woman's undergarment of faded pink silk" hanging on a clothes line that closely resembles those from *The Sound and the Fury*: "It had been washed until the lace resembled a ragged, fibre-like fraying of the cloth itself. It bore a patch of pale calico neatly sewn" (43). Later, we see Ruby wearing the same or a similar garment "of faded pink crepe, lace-trimmed, laundered and laundered until, like the garment on the wire, the lace was a fibrous mass" (37). The multiple washings suggest the repeated impurities of Ruby's prostitution history, sins in the eyes of society that cannot be washed away easily, while Ruby's and Temple's similar outfits at night of a raincoat over underwear posit a link between the two women and foreshadow Temple's fate. The 1924 silent movie *Sinners in Silk* "took the opportunity to show off 'prostitute pink' teddies of silk or rayon" (Herald 37), and so this particular garment may have carried for Faulkner and readers of the era the connotation of illicit sex. Faulkner's use of the garment in these two novels builds on the film's symbolism, while the worn state of the nightgown suggests the moral decay of its wearer or perhaps even a fraying of the fabric of society that has created bootlegger gangsters and whorehouses frequented by the supposed representatives of law and order. Temple's family is not unlike the Compsons, and so her story might be seen as one possible way that Miss Quentin's could go.

While the associations of laundry and washing with race are discussed in the next chapter, in these examples the more pertinent connection of laundering is with sexuality. The description of these pink undergarments insinuates that Temple and Ruby, like Caddy and Quentin, can never wash away their supposed sins (in the eyes of their society anyway), can never become clean or pure because of their sexual experiences.[8] Faulkner counterpoints these women with the cold, prim, and proper Nacrcissa Benbow who is almost always dressed in white (25, 26, 107), and this is perhaps representative of the other alternative for Miss Quentin, underscoring the impossibly limited choices of Southern white women: placed on a pedestal and held to unrealistic standards of femininity created by men or overly sexualized by men and consequently denigrated as not-quite white. Dilsey refuses to clean Caddy's muddy drawers, while Minnie, the Black hired hand at Miss Reba's, is tasked with cleaning Temple's bloody clothes. There is, in fact, a strange fixation on Temple's clothing throughout the novel, beginning with the high heels that make walking through the woods difficult (40).[9] While Jason complains that Quentin's sexuality is not suitably contained by her clothing, Temple can only wish her clothing could protect and cover her.

Over and over again, Temple is described as wrapping herself in her coat, a raincoat she finds in the house, or both (70, 74, 75, 80, 87, 90, 162, 181, 217). Clearly, she longs for some sort of protection against the menace she senses from the men around her, and the coat becomes almost talismanic before her assault, as she repeatedly clutches it, fastens it, and holds it closed. Meanwhile, Van forcibly rips open her coat (74), Goodwin demands she take off the raincoat she found (80), and Popeye twice gropes her underneath the coat (74, 218). When she later recounts her experience to Horace, she compares the coat to a chastity belt: "I thought about fastening myself up some way … That was why I got the raincoat and put it on" (217). Lee similarly gropes Ruby after forcibly opening her coat, again linking Ruby and Temple through an item of clothing

---

[8] These pink undergarments also recur in connection with illicit sex in *Light in August* when Joe Christmas hides among Ms. Atkins's clothing in "pinkwomansmelling obscurity" before he is caught (122).
[9] Faulkner refers to her high heels as "slippers" in the rest of the novel, though this seems to be not so much a mistake as a difference in usage during Faulkner's time. Slippers commonly referred to any shoe that could be slipped on without buckles or laces. Thus, Caddy's more well-known slipper may, in fact, be a high-heeled shoe, which would perhaps be more fitting as an emblem of the nascent sexuality that Benjy senses and that ultimately drives her from home.

but also through their treatment by men as sexual objects, things with no bodily autonomy. The exterior and interior become conflated, reversed, and mixed up. The coat (and clothing in general) is meant to be a protective barrier between the self and the world, but for Temple the coat offers no defense. Men can and do breach her defenses at will, and when she removes her dress for sleeping, she bares herself literally and metaphorically, as male behavior alters her interior self through the breach of her body.

When Ruby offers Temple the hope of leaving during the night, Temple wants to get her clothes first, to which Ruby replies, "Do you want your clothes … or do you want to get out of here?" (81). The clothing, though, is a part of Temple not so easily left behind; it represents the version of herself that she has inhabited, the coquettish and fashionable schoolgirl flapper, and one's self-image is not easily discarded. Temple stays the night, and without her dress under the coat, she is in a liminal state, half-naked and half-dressed in the corn crib: "[Temple] saw within her fallen coat naked flesh between brassiere and knickers and knickers and stockings" (87). Just as Mahon's scar was unsettling because it revealed the tenuous boundaries of the body, so the gap of naked flesh lays bare the fundamental permeability of the body but also the self, "semi-nudity as a signifier of intermediate states of being" (Cavallaro and Warwick 186). Temple is on the threshold of the person she was and the new, different person she will be after her rape.

Cavallaro and Warwick explain that because clothing is so bound up in the self we present to the world, the removal of it can be threatening to one's sense of self: "the presence of clothes/cloth as items detachable from the body underscores their role as social masks to be donned and discarded at will, rather than intrinsic properties of identity; it suggests that discarded items may be adopted again and that the garments presently worn may be cast off and deserted, equally arbitrarily" (186). Thus, when Temple leaves the crib (before reentering it for the last time), it is significant that she finds items of her clothing scattered about the floor of the house:

> She picked up the dress and hat and tried to brush them with her hand and with the corner of her coat. Then she sought the other slipper, moving the quilt, stooping to look under the bed. At last she found it in the fireplace, in a litter of wood ashes between an iron fire-dog and an overturned stack of bricks, lying on its side, half full of ashes, as though it had been flung or kicked there.
>
> (88)

This scattering of clothing and self relates to the effects of trauma, according to Eden Wales-Freedman, especially the state of "hyperarousal" that includes Temple's constant movement from room to room (232-3). Just before this, she had imagined her classmates "in their new Spring clothes" while she "clutching her coat about her ... lifted her foot and examined the soiled sole of her stocking" (87). These two successive images of just one foot reflect Temple's liminal position, one foot in the sordid underworld and one foot in the innocent, childlike world she has known. The single slipper in the ashes alludes to Cinderella (whose name comes from cinder or ash), though no prince will come to her rescue since the drunken lout Gowan Stevens has abandoned Temple. Faulkner's description of Temple in this scene as "no longer quite a child, not yet quite a woman" (89) underscores her liminal state, and the image of her "empty" slippers that recurs on the witness stand at the novel's end shows how her experiences leave her hollow inside, or perhaps more accurately, as suggested by clothing, more of a blank slate, not unlike a dress form or mannequin whose identity can be altered.

While the connection of an empty shoe to a hollow person seems superficial, Cavallaro and Warwick warn that "the shallowness of clothes" can mask their profound connections to "the broad cultural mechanisms through which subjectivity is structured and rendered both signifying and signifiable ... Dress, then, could be described as a *deep surface*, a system of signs that fundamentally relies on superficial modes of signification for the purposes of expressing the underlying beliefs of a given culture and the character of the subjects fostered therein" (135). In this sense Temple's empty shoe (and other clothing) is not only a reflection of her self-conception, but an indicator of how women are viewed more broadly in a patriarchal and phallocentric culture, as empty objects on display whose value resides in their relationship to men's sexual desires. Brevda, in fact, argues that *Sanctuary* is a novel of "Faulkner's depersonalization of his characters into things" (413).

Temple redresses before hiding again in the crib, and as she does, she intuits the connection between self and clothing: "she moved swiftly, smoothing her stockings and writhing into her scant, narrow dress. Now I can stand anything, she thought quietly, with a kind of dull, spent astonishment; I can stand just anything" (89). She can, indeed, stand anything, but the cost is a change in her very being, reducing her to a shell of the vibrant young woman she was at the beginning of the novel. She becomes, in essence, more like the clothes than the person who wears them. As Popeye drives her to Memphis after raping her, blood soils her clothes (echoes of Caddy's again), but he only tells her "I'll get you another coat tomorrow" (141), as if the outer stain on the garment were her biggest concern. At Miss Reba's, the sound of Minnie trying to clean the blood from her clothes is augmented by the sight of empty garments around her, a continuation of the empty shoes which visually capture her interior hollowness: "Her coat and hat hung on nails in the door, her dress and stockings lay upon a chair, and it seemed to her that she could hear the rhythmic splush-splush of the washing-board somewhere and she flung herself again in an agony for concealment as she had when they took her knickers off" (145). The scattered clothing again reflects her physical and mental states: fragmented and stripped of their integrity. This conflation and reversal of internal and external continues when Temple imagines becoming a man as defense against Popeye's assault. She imagines penetrating him with a spike (218), pictures herself dressed in a wedding dress lying in a coffin (219), sees herself as an older teacher "in a gray tailored suit" (220), and visualizes herself becoming a man: "Then I thought about being a man, and as soon as I thought it, it happened. It made a kind of plopping sound, like blowing a little rubber tube wrong-side outward" (220). These images and others like them in the novel illustrate Barnard's point that in traditional fashion, "masculinity becomes defined as the spectator or voyeur of femininity, and femininity becomes reduced to appearance or spectacle" (141). Barnard also contends that modern fashion has been used to reverse the identities and positions of men and women, and Temple's fantasy is about just this: a desperate desire to reverse positions and become the voyeur or actor rather than the watched object.

Soon after this fantasy, Temple attacks one of Popeye's signature suits, the object replacing the person in an attempt for violent revenge on her assailant:

> Temple turned over on the bed. When she did so she saw one of Popeye's innumerable black suits lying across a chair. She lay looking at it for a while, then she rose and snatched the garments up and hurled them into the corner where the hat was. In another corner was a closet improvised by a print curtain. It contained dresses of all sorts and all new. She ripped them down in furious wads and flung them after the suit, and a row of hats from a shelf. Another of Popeye's suits hung there also. She flung it down. Behind it, hanging from a nail, was an automatic pistol in a holster of oiled silk.
>
> (225)

It is as if she sees others as mere mannequins too, and since this clothing represents both him and her, she wants to destroy both, or at least obliterate the new Temple symbolized by the new dresses Popeye has purchased for her. The association of the gun with the clothes (it even seems to be wearing a garment, the silk holster) conveys the power that these objects have, while the phrase "furious wads" (as opposed to "She furiously ripped them down") imbues the clothes with her emotions and her rejection of her new self as she hurls her new cosmetics into the corner as well. Shortly after this, she looks at herself in the mirror, then takes out two dresses, as if deciding between two states of being, before putting both back where she got them. Then she gets out her watch "and propped it against the pack of cigarettes so she could see it from the bed, and lay down. When she did so she felt the pistol through the pillow" (229). The imagery here is akin to Ike McCaslin relinquishing the watch, gun, and compass in order to see the bear in *Go Down, Moses*. Here it is a watch, gun, and dress, with clothing replacing the compass as a way of orienting the self in the wider world. She is in the bear's den. Rather than relinquishing these objects, she is contemplating taking them up for the first time after her violent "initiation" into the world of men. Her entrance into the world of men is quite different from Ike's. She is the prey whereas Ike has the privilege of wrestling with the metaphysical question of whether he wants to be a predator or not as he watches the bear: men are voyeurs, women the watched. She is more object than subject, but here is deciding whether to take up arms and become an active, violent (male) predator herself, the gun "slid under her flank" (229) recalling her vision of growing a penis earlier. In these scenes, clothing acts to prompt Temple's behavior, Popeye's suit jolting her out of her passive state, while also signifying multiple meanings as multifaceted symbol.

Temple's relinquishing of these modern objects may also suggest she is not, after all, suited to be one of the modern characters associated with speed and fashion in the novel. Her movement all but stops once she reaches Memphis, a virtual prisoner at Miss Reba's and while she is given and buys new clothes, she mostly wears robes or exhibits an antagonistic relationship to the garments, trying to destroy them and dousing them in perfume (256).[10] Wales-Freedman suggests that Temple's trauma is linked in the novel to a more universal trauma of modernity: "agony and torment ... unnamed" (238–9), and this may speak to Faulkner's fears about what the fast modern world means for women in particular. Even Faulkner's Civil War-women enjoy more agency and power than the seemingly modern Temple.

[10] The imported "Chinese robe" that Temple owns recalls Estelle's habit of wearing kimonos and may be Faulkner's way of commenting uncharitably on his wife through his characters.

The Unvanquished

In *The Unvanquished* (1938), war allows for temporary suspension of many communal norms, affording women more freedom and agency, which is reflected in clothing. However, it is not a simple formula where Drusilla's masculine clothing gives her more freedom than women who wear conventional feminine attire. Granny exhibits as much, if not more, power, intelligence, and agency in her wartime exploits as Drusilla does as a member of Colonel John Sartoris's regiment. Both pay the price for their transgression of boundaries eventually, as Faulkner's nineteenth-century women characters meet a similar fate to those from the twentieth century, and the transformative power of clothing can only go so far.

Granny's first successful assertion of power in the male-dominated public sphere occurs when Bayard and Ringo hide under her voluminous skirts after killing a horse belonging to the Union army. The image here is of maternal protection, almost a return to the womb, as Black and white boys huddle beneath the dress of a protective white mother. It is nearly a reversal of the Black mother Dilsey embracing and protecting Benjy and Miss Quentin, as well as her own children, in *The Sound and the Fury*, and the racial implications are potentially retrograde though Ringo later joins Granny in her mule-trading adventures, similarly enjoying freedom from cultural norms during wartime. Granny takes advantage of patriarchal codes in a trickster fashion in this scene, daring the Union officer to violate a gentleman's code by touching her skirts or even mentioning what might be under them. This comic, almost cartoonish use of Granny's cliché hoop skirt, is at least somewhat redeemed by the level of winking ironic commentary on such moonlight and magnolias tropes baked into the scene. Granny repeatedly uses men's conventional attitudes about women and their underestimating a woman's shrewdness and business acumen to her advantage while bilking the US Army out of thousands of dollars that she largely redistributes to poor people (white and Black) ravaged by the war "in clothes made out of cotton bagging and flour sacks" (147). Ultimately, she pays a steep price for stepping outside her culturally sanctioned gender roles (as do many Faulkner women), murdered in cold blood by Grumby, whose band of irregulars "wore no uniform" (149), symbolically indicating their refusal to follow the conventions of war or even basic ethical standards. Granny's story is related to Drusilla's not only in the ways each are punished for transgressing gender boundaries, but also both make problematic moral pivots. Drusilla's shift to defender of an outdated, patriarchal revenge code is discussed below, and Yaeger points out that Granny and Faulkner turn away from the human drama of thousands of freed and fleeing enslaved people in order to follow the Sartoris family silver (205), an example of the power of things over people.

I do not discuss Drusilla's cross-dressing in terms of transvestism. This dated term and concept has been useful for past critics, but I think the notions of gender as performance and cultural construction from Judith Butler and others are by now so familiar and accepted that only to discuss how masculinity is privileged over femininity in the 1860s (or 1930s) adds nothing new to the critical conversation. Instead, I want to focus more on the clothes themselves as objects and actants. Drusilla is fond of wearing pants "like a man" and is the "best woman rider in the country" (89), perhaps modeled after Faulkner's aunt, Mary Holland Wilkins, who Blotner describes as "an accomplished rider, completely fearless" (One-Volume 14), adding in his research notes that she was "one of the first in Oxford to wear a divided skirt."[11] Her short haircut seems modeled on the popular and (at least initially) countercultural bob cut of the 1920s and 30s, and worn by Estelle and by other unconventional Faulkner women, such as Susan Reed in "Hair," whose bob cut, makeup, and clothing mark her as sexually promiscuous to the townspeople. The wearing of pants by women had a decidedly political meaning in the nineteenth and early twentieth centuries. As Fischer writes in *Pantaloons and Power*, "For women to take control of their appearance, to distance themselves from a primarily ornamental identity, primarily dependent on men and devoted to pleasing men, was intrinsically transgressive" (4). While Granny's protection of the boys in "Ambuscade" has a maternal quality to it, Drusilla's actions are clearly and repeatedly defined as masculine. Her short hair "looked like Father's," her "hands were hard and scratched like a man's that works" (91), she goes to war in Carolina "riding with the troop like she was a man" (149), and her mother believes "Drusilla had deliberately tried to unsex herself" (189). Aunt Louisa (the term Bayard uses to refer to Drusilla's mother) is shocked by her daughter's wearing of pants, just as the American public was shocked by the dress reformers of the era in which Faulkner's novel is set: "Gender distinctions were extremely rigid in the

---

[11] Blotner also notes that she would fly in Dean's airplane while Maud Faulkner would not (Blotner Papers, Box 2100, Folder 019).

nineteenth century, and when those distinctions were blurred, observers usually found the experience very upsetting" (Fischer 155). Drusilla does not attempt to pass as a man during the war, similar to the pioneering historical figure Mary Walker who wore "predominantly male garments" without trying to hide her sex while working as a Civil War battlefield surgeon in Tennessee (149). Rather, wearing of men's clothing as a woman is a way of claiming the agent/spectator role typically reserved for men and rejecting the traditionally female role of passive object.[12]

Like Walker, Drusilla continues to wear male clothing after the war, and she explains to Bayard that she wants control over her life without being forced to accept a stultifying reality because she is a woman:

> Living used to be dull you see. Stupid. You lived in the same house your father was born in ... and then you grew up and you fell in love with your acceptable young man and in time you would marry him, in your mother's wedding gown perhaps ... and then you settled down for ever more while your husband got children on your body for you to feed and bathe and dress ... and then you and your husband died quietly and were buried together.
>
> (100)

This vision of conformity is what impels Drusilla to rebel, to attempt to claim the power and agency men have to define their own lives by donning the outer wear that seems to aid their freedom. While it is true that clothing was one of the only ways to express a non-conforming gender identity for centuries, it could also be an expression of a desire for autonomy as opposed to nonbinary gender or sexuality. Aunt Louisa finds Drusilla's wartime clothing upsetting because she dresses "in the garments not alone of a man but of a common private soldier" (191), and she understands that clothing is the key to putting her daughter back in her "proper" place. The ornamental function of women like Drusilla is an intersection of gender and class, and traditional women's clothing helps enforce the status quo, as Barnard demonstrates, citing Veblen: "Women's hats or bonnets, shoes, skirts ... and their long hair, all hamper women and leave them completely incapable of 'useful exertion.' They all prevent a woman from doing

---

[12] It is possible for women to wear men's clothes with no radical or transgressive critique of the gender binary ascribed to the act. For example, in *Intruder in the Dust*, country women preparing for hog butchering are described as wearing "men's old felt hats and long men's overcoats" while the men wear "crokersack aprons" (4). The intent of wearing the clothing and whether that intent subverts communal norms can be just as important as the articles of clothing.

anything remotely like work, and are therefore part of the process of signalling that her class position allows her not to work" (Barnard 116). While Barnard emphasizes how clothing reinforces class, it is also true that corsets, crinolines, skirts, and dresses make certain kinds of physical activity impossible for women, thereby restricting them to the domestic sphere, not because they are incapable of thriving in the public spheres of commerce and government, but because their culturally imposed clothing makes their participation impossible. The clothing that is available and acceptable for women to wear determines their social roles as an actant, as well as helping justify those roles as natural, and this helps expose that limiting gender discourses rely on things, not innate truths.

Louisa begins crying again when she sees her daughter working at the mill "in the muddy brogans and the sweaty shirt and overalls and her hair sunburned and full of sawdust," but when she forces Drusilla to wear a dress, Bayard proclaims, "She was already beaten" (201). John tries to espouse the position that clothing has no real power (perhaps because as a man he is not judged for his clothing in the same way), but the dress has already exerted its influence on Drusilla, almost immediately altering her personality and behavior:

> So Father came out too and we went down to the spring and found Drusilla hiding behind the big beech, crouched down like she was trying to hide the skirt from Father even while he raised her up. 'What's a dress? he said. 'It dont matter. Come. Get up, soldier.' But she was beaten, like as soon as she let them put the dress on her she was whipped; like in the dress she could neither fight back nor run away."
>
> (201)

She is defiant until she puts on the dress that she has not worn in three years, and the dress is more than a symbol of traditional femininity; it is the thing that causes Drusilla to acquiesce, recalling the shoes that drain the life from Moketubbe. Thus, we see clothing's role as an actant, both enabling Drusilla's sense of power and freedom during the war and also extinguishing that spark after it. It is not that her clothes reflect an already existing gender identity, but the garments actually constitute that identity, the costume creating the persona. The dramatic change in her personality in "An Odor of Verbena" is not due to mental breakdown or illness, but because she now fully inhabits the role she earlier scorned of "bride-widow of a lost cause" (191) while constantly wearing a "yellow ball gown" (219, 230, 233) that seems almost a caricature of the Southern belle outfit, a return to Granny's traditional skirt of the novel's opening. A frivolous and decorative dress produces a frivolous and decorative person.

Michael Williams, in his article "Cross Dressing in Yoknapatawpha County," rejects Cleanth Brooks's classic reading of Drusilla as having "forgotten pity, compassion, and even her womanhood" as she becomes obsessed with "some abstract conception of masculine honor" (Brooks 335) and instead counters that she is now married and a widow dressed in traditional feminine attire: "she could just as easily be described as most fully *remembering* her womanliness" (Williams 382). Williams describes Drusilla as "completely in masquerade" (335), which helps to emphasize the role playing and costume wearing, though it also deemphasizes the influence of the clothing itself. Rather than donning a costume that fits the part she is playing, I would argue that wearing the dress pushes her into the persona she inhabits at the novel's end. Patricia Yaeger brings an intersectional reading to the novel, arguing that the ways Drusilla and Ringo fade into the background of the novel reveals the impossibility of "any dream of cross-racial or cross-sectional collectivity … as if supporting new forms of oppression for African Americans must also result in new constellations of gender oppression" ("Verbena and Violence" 220). Yaeger notes that in the scene where Drusilla is forced to change clothes, she runs to Louvinia for comfort, "another marked woman," and that this scene is part of "Faulkner's profound if conflicted sense of the inadequacy of the roles allotted Southern women" (216). That is, neither the soldier's uniform nor the ball gown fit Drusilla's true gender identity, but in this time and place, there are no other, nonbinary choices available. The ball gown also links her to two traditional female symbols, the Statue of Liberty and Miss Columbia, "a combination of Indian princess and classical goddess" popular in the media of the early twentieth century (Elahi 51–2). Both women were symbols of national identity and were always depicted in draped dresses to link them to tradition, "robed in the draperies of a specifically Western and eternal antiquity" (52). This makes her a fitting emblem for a nation that forsakes its avowed principle of equality for both women and African Americans. Thus, Drusilla's change of clothing represents continuity with the past and tradition, while her earlier clothing, like that of Faulkner's more modern and progressive women, indicates a rupture with the past, as exemplified by Charlotte Rittenmeyer in Faulkner's next novel, again featuring the containment of a modern woman as the trauma of modernity continues.

If I Forget Thee, Jerusalem

Clothing is much more prominent and important in "The Wild Palms" section of Faulkner's 1937 novel *If I Forget Thee, Jerusalem* (originally published as *The Wild Palms*) than in the "Old Man" section. Of course, since "Old Man" focuses on a "tall convict" who unintentionally runs away from prison and spends most of the novel navigating treacherous flood waters far from civilization in his prison uniform, this is perhaps unsurprising. However, just as scholars have found thematic and other connections between the two counterpointed sections of the novel, certain aspects of clothing resonate as well.

Charlotte Rittenmeyer and Harry Wilbourne's first meeting is heavily influenced by objects. The birthday telegram that Harry receives from his sister is an actant that affects everything that follows since it is, in a very real sense, the cause of his meeting Charlotte. Certainly, the sister's action of sending the telegram (as opposed to, say, choosing to use a different object like a telephone) might be seen as the real catalyst, but I would suggest otherwise, again at the risk of appearing foolish or naïve. The telegram as a thing also influences human behavior; it need not be the only influence in order to be an actant, and which actors and actants have more or less influence than others is beside the point. If the telegram did not exist as an object, then Harry's roommate, Flint, would not have found it lying on his (Flint's) pillow by mistake, and he never would have invited Harry out of pity to the party where he meets Charlotte. Although Flint suggests Harry will not need "dress clothes" because the host "will probably be wearing a bathrobe" (31), they both don tuxedos before heading out. It turns out that the host is, in fact, wearing a bathrobe (32), and Harry is conspicuously overdressed, his attire, rather than his personality, prompting Charlotte to flirtatiously ask if he is "slumming" (34) at the party "in a borrowed costume such as he had never worn before" (31). Here again, the object, this time the tuxedo, instigates the action, initiating a chain of events that will end in Charlotte's tragic death. Charlotte seems to recognize the power of clothing to influence the wearer as well as the viewer—in this case, the "costume" turning him into someone he is not—telling him to come to dinner two nights later in his own clothes: "And dont wear that. Wear your own clothes. I want to see" (36). She wants to see who he really is, not only in terms of his personal fashion choices, but what he might be like free from the influence of his fancy dress. Flint corroborates the idea of clothing as costume when Harry is nervous about meeting Charlotte at a hotel for their first assignment and he advises his roommate to become a character and use a fake name while carrying a brick-filled bag and raincoat as props in order to make people see what you want them to see (38).

Charlotte's clothing changes are noted far more than any other character, and she is the opposite of Drusilla in that she refuses to let the clothes define her. After the simple "print cotton dress" (33) of their initial meeting, she selects more of a couture outfit for dinner at her apartment, "something he knew had been purchased as a semi-formal garment and which she wore with the same ruthless indifference as she had the garment in which he had first seen her, as if both of them were overalls" (36). Even as she changes from these clothes to "a cheap coverall" (76) to an apron to "a pair of trousers and an old sweater" (98) to the sheep coats and wool underwear in Utah (150) to the "worn sweater and a pair of faded jeans pants" (5) at the beach, Charlotte's personality and her devotion to her and Harry's doomed dream do not waver. Patricia Gantt argues that her wearing of both men's and women's clothes is associated with her art and reflects her freedom from society's strictures (420). The reference to jeans is especially appropriate for the couple's attempt to reject capitalist bourgeois normalcy. Fred Davis, in *Fashion, Culture, and Identity*, describes jeans in the United States and Europe as a "sartorial symbolic complex at war … with class distinctions, elitism and snobbism" (70). The first people to wear jeans outside of a work context were US artists in the 1930s and 40s, and the garment maintained a counter-cultural cache into the 1960s when they were adopted by hippies as part of their rejection of middle-class values and consumerism: "Jeans, then, were used by those critical of the prevailing, or dominant, ideology of the time to construct a position from which that ideology could be criticised and opposed; they constituted a site of resistance to that dominant ideology" (Barnard 135). Similarly, Davis says that jeans, given their origin as work clothes in the American West and later associations with countercultural artists, motorcycle gangs, and hippies, are visible markers of "antiestablishment sentiments" (70).[13]

Despite her and Harry's commitment to living a life of love free from the materialist and consumer trappings of mainstream society, their relationship is severely tested when they move to an isolated mine in Utah. While the adornment function of clothing was preeminent in their initial courtship, the protective function becomes dominant here, and the literal and figurative

---

[13] Davis goes on to note the ironic and dialectical movement of jeans in the late twentieth century to markers of status, wealth, and distinction with the rise of designer jeans (75–7).

aspects of protection are indelibly mixed. Fleeing bourgeois conformity both symbolically and materially denoted by modern things—their "suburban bungalow full of electric wife-saving gadgets" (112)—Harry and Charlotte convince themselves that a spontaneous move to a remote mining operation will protect their relationship from becoming stale and conventional. Their ill-planned departure sees them greeted at their snow-covered new home with, "Is them all the clothes you brought out here? You'll freeze" (153). The reality of their situation demands some conformity, and they accept the same clothing from the commissary that everyone else wears, "the sheep coats and woollen [sic] underwear and socks" (150).

The cold climate and extra layers of protection underscore the importance of nonhuman things and also presage symbolically how their relationship will grow colder as the two of them are pushed farther apart: "now they had both become profoundly and ineradicably intimate with cold for the first time in their lives, a cold which left an ineffaceable and unforgettable mark somewhere on the spirit" (153). They are forced to sleep in the same room as another couple, the Buckners, so they cannot talk privately at night nor have sex for six weeks (165), though the Buckners seem less inhibited (161–2). If the doffing of clothing represents a shedding of social norms, particularly sexual ones, as we have seen in *Soldiers' Pay* and *Mosquitoes*, then the fact that Harry and Charlotte refuse to remove their clothes and have sex in this setting suggests they are less free from social restrictions than they like to think. While Harry and Charlotte find the extra layers of clothing "felt like ice, like iron, stiff" (155), mirroring their increasingly arduous relationship, the more weathered Buckners maintain a warm and comforting marriage and try to pass on advice about the climate that doubles as advice for enduring a long-term union that is bound to lose some of its initial heat and passion over time:

> You wont never get warm out here ... The thing is, to make up your mind you will always be a little cold even in bed and just go on about your business and after a while you will get used to it and forget it and then you wont even notice you are cold because you will have forgotten what being warm was ever like.
>
> (154)

Faulkner himself was in the middle of an icy relationship with Estelle around the time of beginning work on this novel. The couple were on the verge of a divorce, even filing initial legal papers against one another in October of 1936 (Rollyson, Vol. 2 57–8). Faulkner's passionate affair with Meta Carpenter, which Estelle knew about, was coming to an end around this same time, and Meta married Wolfgang Rebner on April 5, 1937, despite Faulkner's attempts to dissuade her (102–3). He began work on *If I Forget Thee, Jerusalem* in August of 1937 realizing he would now be stuck in an increasingly acrimonious marriage. Harry and Charlotte try to counter the increasingly cold and stiff nature of their relationship when the Buckners leave the mine, immediately shedding the protective layers to have sex (166). However, now unprotected and naked, Charlotte becomes pregnant when her douche bag freezes (for unexplained reasons, Harry never contemplates donning a protective condom, despite their adamant opposition to having children together). Again, we see an object not only influencing human behavior, but actually precipitating the death of Charlotte and lifelong incarceration of Harry, as the loss of functionality of the douchebag is caused by another object, the heater that stops working, and these two objects affect the couples' lives much more than their well-meaning intentions, their choices, and their feelings of love. Charlotte thinks that "passion" will suffice as birth control (172), but material and nonhuman entities (weather, the heater, the douche bag) prove more influential than human intention or feelings.

Arriving on the Mississippi Gulf coast for Harry's ill-fated attempt at a home abortion, the landlord/doctor and real estate agent judge them immediately by their clothing. Harry's "disreputable khaki slacks" (5) mark him as pretentiously poor, "like he was Vanderbilt or somebody, in them dirty fishing pants and nothing but an undershirt under his coat" (6), but Charlotte's garments are viewed through the lens of sexuality rather than class: "She's got on pants," the agent said. "I mean, not these ladies' slacks but pants, man's pants. I mean, they are too little for her in just exactly the right places any man would want to see them too little but no woman would unless she had them on herself" (5). The potential threat of Charlotte possessing masculine power is neutralized and contained by the male gaze imposing feminine sexuality on men's clothing. In fact, Faulkner shows in microcosm how fashion rebellion is appropriated and co-opted to reinforce existing paradigms. Barnard uses the example of feminists in the 1960s and 70s rejecting makeup, bras, high heels, and other items of fashion that they saw as constructing limiting gender identities for women (142). However, each of these rejections were fairly quickly appropriated by the fashion industry as new trends to be sold to the very women who challenged the industry's status quo in much the same ways that punk and hip-hop fashions that began as rejections of corporate and consumer ideology were quickly co-opted, repackaged, rebranded, and sold to mostly white, middle-class consumers

(136–41). Charlotte's wearing of men's pants as a rejection of traditional feminine dress and identity immediately becomes a new way to make her into a sex object. The degree to which her rebellious feminism is coopted into a story of traditional patriarchal morality is revealed in a glimpse of yet another pink garment when Harry briefly remembers a fictional counterpart to the dying Charlotte: "He was trying to remember something out of a book, years ago, of Owen Wister's, the whore in the pink ball dress who drank the laudanum and the cowboys taking turns walking her up and down the floor, keeping her on her feet, keeping her alive" (241). The individuality and nonconformity Charlotte displays in her clothing is perhaps admirable, and she even throws Harry's new crossing guard hat into the fire, rejecting a uniform that represents conformist lives. However, Charlotte ends up in the uniform and feminine garment of a hospital nightgown that does not even cover her exposed and vulnerable dead body after Harry's attempted abortion fails horribly. This feminine garment, "which she had never owned, never worn before" (238), symbolizes her defeat, Gantt argues: "For this final time she appears in women's clothes, a visible indication of her inability to subvert society's role for her life" (421). Her blood has perhaps even turned her nightgown pink, linking her to Faulkner's other rebellious women whom men seek to punish. Richard Godden counts clothing among many markers of "gender switching" (*Fictions* 180), and Diane Roberts links Charlotte to Faulkner's other women who are punished for asserting male privilege through dress and action: "Cross-dressing in Faulkner's fiction always leads to dangerous undifferentiation that the culture always seeks to correct" (208). My emphasis on clothing does not upend these readings, but it could suggest how a novel often taken to be about the couple's ideas, principles, and values is also very much about physical objects and nonhuman things. They are doomed by things as well as by vague notions of social norms, patriarchal discourse, or culturally sanctioned roles.

In the novel's counterpointed sections of "Old Man," the flood is also connected to birth and blood, but the convict swept by floodwaters away from his prison and captors clings to an identity established through uniform clothing. An overflowing of feminine forces connects the two sections, as masculine counterforces try to contain the feminine power that threatens to erase boundaries. The unnamed tall convict desperately clings to his identity as a prisoner, preferring the "incontrovertible passivity" of solid earth and fixed identity to the "substanceless and enveloping and suffocating" flood waters of a fluid, shifting selfhood aligned with the feminine that could "snatch you violently out of all familiar knowing and sweep you thrall and impotent for days against any returning. *I dont know where I am and I dont reckon I know the way back to where I want to go*" (195). The "striped garments" (61) of his prison uniform mark him as a pariah of society such that he is shot at by lawmen he has never seen only because of the clothes he wears (146, 192). When asked why he was not spotted as a prisoner due to his clothes during his sojourn, the tall convict suggests that the reason is deeper than the mud and soot that disguised his uniform: "it's being scared and worried and then scared and then worried again in clothes for days and days and days that changes the way they look" (207). Again, we see here the idea that clothing can contain some actual essence of its wearer, not unlike John Sartoris's coat discussed in the "Clothing and Class" chapter. This same idea might be applied to Charlotte and Harry, whose appearance devolves from tuxedos and evening gowns to shabby secondhand sweaters to hospital nightgowns and prison jumpsuits. The association of cotton with Parchman prison (here and in *Go Down, Moses*, and *The Mansion*) also suggests that Charlotte's original cotton dress functions as a uniform of the personal prison she seeks to flee. Even when he gets a change of clothes while living in the Cajun's shack, the tall convict keeps his prison-issued uniform safe and hidden, bringing it with him everywhere just like the prison-issued boat, until he can wear it again. His Cajun clothing and his adventures with the pregnant woman are just temporary flights from his true self and his true home, and the tall convict embraces his identity through his clothing, preferring the fixed stability of prison life to the fluctuating chaos of life outside. Ironically, Harry's quest to reinvent himself and to prize love, freedom, and nonconformity above all lands him in the same prison in the end.

The Hamlet

While Flem Snopes's rise to prominence and power using clothing is discussed in the chapter "Clothing and Class," *The Hamlet* also uses clothing in the context of gender, particularly with the characterization of Eula (Varner) Snopes. Eula is raised to fulfill very traditional, stereotypical feminine roles: "Mrs Varner did not particularly care whether the daughter went to school or not. She was one of the best housewives in the county and was indefatigable at it" (108). Her father provides her with toy versions of "housekeeping implements" (107), as if trying to indoctrinate his daughter through the power of objects into a cult of domesticity in which she plays the role of dutiful, doll-like wife: "All we want anyway is to keep her out of trouble until she gets old enough to sleep with a man without getting me and him both arrested. Then you can marry her off" (109). Eula is primarily described by the narrator in terms of her body and the sexual arousal that men attribute to it. Her objectification includes the comparison of her body to furniture and to a superfluity of meat: "there was too much—too much of leg, too much of breast, too much of buttock; too much of mammalian female meat" (111). Echoing multiple earlier novels, this excess can barely be contained by her clothing, and her brother Jody is consistently outraged by the exposure of her body while she rides behind him on his horse to school, "the incredible length of outrageously curved dangling leg and the bare section of thigh between dress and stocking-top" compared to the modesty of "the other children in overalls and coarse calico and cast-off adult shoes" (112). Jody's role as brother is a curious combination of Quentin and Jason Compson: he feels compelled to protect the body and sexual purity of his sister, yet his relentless noticing—and occasional groping (145, 148)—of her clothing and body, as well as his consequent anger, "impotent and outraged" (159), aligns him more with Jason's fury at his sister and her daughter.

Labove, the football-playing schoolteacher of Frenchman's Bend, is also obsessed with Eula's body, and he apparently has the chance to move up the social and economic ladder with Eula before Flem ever does. The shoes that Labove receives as payment for each game the football team wins are the main actant affecting his decision to play, a choice which, in turn, leads to his accepting the schoolteacher job instead of returning to the family farm. He aims to be the governor someday (116), but his ambitious plans do not come to fruition, when his sexual desire for Eula washes away all else while Flem sees her as part of a much larger transaction. The loud "clattering scraping noise" (114) of his football cleats contrast with Flem's stealthy sneakers, foreshadowing sartorially Labove's impending failure. In his initial encounter with Will Varner, Labove's clothing fails to make the initial impression that Flem's does: "Labove stood quite still, in a perfectly clean white shirt which had been washed so often that it now had about the texture of mosquito netting, in a coat and trousers absolutely clean too and which were not mates and the coat a little too small for him and which Varner knew were the only ones he owned" (118). Just as Labove's dress exudes a certain interior quality of himself, Eula does the same without any exertion, "emanating that outrageous quality of being, existing, actually on the outside of the garments she wore" (113). Thus, her family's repeated attempts to cover her seemingly always-exposed body by lengthening the hems of her dresses and forcing her to don corsets are doomed to fail (144), the ability of clothing to protect, mask, and contain utterly useless. The family's efforts to use clothing in this way helps clarify a strange memory of Labove's about a Black man shot on a train station platform whose multiple layers of garments stop the bullet from harming him: "he remembered the peeling away of the jumper, the overalls, a ragged civilian coat … beneath that a shirt and a pair of civilian trousers. The waist of them was unbuttoned and the bullet rolled out onto the platform, bloodless" (139). Labove longs for a protective barrier between himself and Eula, but he feels drawn back to her against his own will, his football uniform and graduation cap and gown affording him no protection.

Eula's supposedly innate sexuality is defined not so much by her body as by the relationship between her body and her clothes: "not like a girl of sixteen dressed like twenty, but a woman of thirty dressed in the garments of her sixteen-year-old sister" (147). It is as if the failure to properly match clothing and person makes her more alluring. It is not simply that more skin/less clothing results in more sexual stimulation in viewers. Rather, it is the interplay of concealing/revealing and protecting/uncovering that creates interest, stimulation, and even meaning. Eula's "bare section of thigh between dress and stocking-top" (112) recalls Temple Drake[14] and is a perfect example of Barthes's explanation of the erotic in dress: "the intermittence of skin flashing between two articles of clothing … between two edges … it is this flash which seduces, or rather: the staging of an appearance-as-disappearance" (*The Pleasure of the Text*, 9–10). The liminal space "between two edges" creates arousal, a visual corollary to Eula's status as betwixt and between girlhood and adulthood, innocent and vixen, proper and naughty, and forbidden and available. All of the outfit changes and attempts to protect and contain her excess only result in premarital sex, an unplanned pregnancy, and a missing would-be father/husband. Only able now to save appearances, the family enlists Flem to dress up a bad situation, so to speak, putting Eula "in her Sunday clothes and put the rest of her things—the tawdry mail-order negligees and nightgowns, the big cheap flimsy shoes and what toilet things she had—into the tremendous bag and took her to town in the surrey and married her to him" (163). By the novel's end, Eula has finally been put under wraps, fulfilling the traditional roles of wife and mother while wearing an "expressionless mask-face" and "the first tailored suit ever seen in Frenchman's Bend" (402), as she and Flem pack up and leave for Jefferson to start the next act of their rise, Eula at least temporarily contained in marriage if not clothing.

---

[14] Roberts notes that Eula's and Temple's threatening sexualities are both safely contained by and within motherhood in their later novels (214).

The Town and *The Mansion*

Eula's sex appeal in the second installment of the Snopes trilogy is again described as stemming from the interplay of body and clothing:

> [J]ust moving, walking in that aura of decorum and modesty and solitariness ten times more immodest and a hundred times more disturbing than one of the bathing suits young women would begin to wear about 1920 or so, as if in the second just before you looked, her garments had managed in one last frantic pell mell scurry to overtake and cover her. Though only for a moment because in the next one, if only you followed long enough, they would wilt and fail from that mere plain and simple striding which would shred them away like the wheel of a constellation through a wisp and cling of trivial scud.
>
> (10)

It is the mystery of Eula that is so alluring, the unknown that is veiled underneath her enigmatic façade and her clothes that seem to fit just perfectly, revealing by concealing. The specific garments that Eula wears are rarely mentioned in *The Town*, reflecting the male narrators' and observers' infatuation with Eula as a symbol rather than as an actual human being, "an invention of testosterone, not a person" (Roberts 215). Gavin Stevens, for instance, cannot be bothered to describe Eula's dress in any detail and can only project his own feelings onto her clothing:

> [T]he dress which was not a morning gown nor a hostess gown nor even a house dress but just a simple cotton dress that was simply a dress and which ... appeared not so much as snatching in desperate haste to hide them but rather to spring in suppliance and adulation to the moving limbs, the very flowing of the fabric's laving folds to cry *Evoe! Evoe!*
>
> (230)

The archaic "Evoe" is a Bacchanalian exclamation, an ecstatic howl of joy that Eula is a goddess figure to Gavin and the town's men, a representation of Lust and Sex. Chick compares her to "Fate" (15) and to Juno and lauds her as virtually the Platonic ideal of woman, again emphasizing excess and containment: "there was just too much of what she was for any just one human female package to contain and hold ... forever after nothing less would ever do" (6). The garments of a goddess are irrelevant, it seems.

Eula's daughter, Linda Snopes Kohl, is not held in quite such exalted esteem, and her clothing choices are the male narrators' focus in *The Mansion*. Linda has as much in common with Charlotte Rittenmeyer from *If I Forget Thee, Jerusalem* as with her actual mother. She has traditionally masculine qualities, works to support herself, is sexually frank, tough, even ruthless, is injured in war, and wears androgynous clothing. With twenty years separating the publication of the two novels, it is perhaps not surprising that Linda's donning of "masculine" clothes is much less shocking and transgressive. The overalls she wears to work in the aircraft factory get noticed by Gavin, though only in an offhand way that denies their masculinity: "Anyway, she could wear overalls again, once more miniscule in that masculine or rather sexless world engaged, trying to cope with the lethal mechanical monstrosities which war has become now" (273). Even a machine-dominated factory of war is defined here as sexless rather than masculine, and when the pair go to dinner at a modern "joint," Gavin somewhat prudishly notes that "she could have worn anything beyond an ear trumpet and a G string, and even then probably the ear trumpet would have drawn the attention" (275–6). Linda is a fully modern woman, even as Gavin remains more traditional in his sensibilities. For all the talk of Charlotte's pants, Linda's choice to wear pants is presented simply as one of several options rather than as a daring and provocative protest:

> [D]ressed as usual in the clothes she seemed to spend most of her time walking around the adjacent countryside in—the expensive English brogues scuffed and scarred but always neatly polished each morning, with wool stockings or socks beneath worn flannel trousers or a skirt or sometimes what looked like a khaki boiler-suit under a man's stained burberry; this in the fall and winter and spring; in the summer it would be cotton—dress or skirt or trousers, her head with its single white plume bare even in the worst weather.
>
> (398)

Linda needs no protection from clothing nor from men, and she does not pay with her life for transgressing traditional gender roles, though she does, like Charlotte, experience grief.

The more noteworthy instance of cross-dressing in *The Mansion* occurs when Flem tricks his cousin Mink into trying to escape from Parchman prison disguised as a woman. The sunbonnet and dress he dons for his ill-fated escape attempt is treated more as a joke than a transgressive moment. Flem sets Mink up with a ridiculous and obvious costume so that he will be caught easily and have his prison sentence extended. This is not a cross-dressing moment that suggests change or progress or transformation. Instead, the clothing cements the status quo just as Mink's primary character trait—his desire to kill Flem for revenge—remains unchanged over nearly forty years, while Flem, too, wants to keep things static and, as discussed in the "Clothing and Class" chapter, has stagnated in his life, ossified by material success. Nonetheless, this would-be jail break perhaps entrenches Mink's loathing of his cousin even further, as he is publicly emasculated through both his failure and his cross-dressing. Flem's all-too-easy manipulation of Mink feminizes him by traditional standards, so that wielding the phallic gun and penetrating Flem with a bullet is the only possible way for Mink to reclaim his manhood. Ironically, it is Linda's subtle machinations that allow Mink to kill Flem, perhaps suggesting that Faulkner is consciously punning on the notion of who wears the pants in the Snopes family.

One final story should be mentioned that relates to both cross-dressing and the motif of pink women's undergarments. "Divorce in Naples" was likely written soon after Faulkner's return from Europe in the mid-1920s, and it is his "most overtly gay story," as Gordon calls it (85). The story details the tribulations of a homosexual relationship between two sailors, the older George and the younger, less experienced Carl—whom the other sailors refer to as George's "wife." While on shore leave, Carl sneaks away from George and has sex with a female prostitute, angering George and threatening to tear the couple apart. At the end of the story, the lovers are reconciled after Carl performs what Gordon calls "a kind of purification ritual" (89), tearing off all of his clothes, taking a long shower, and then disposing of his dirty underwear out of a ship's porthole. Again, we have unclean undergarments associated with sexual sin or wrongdoing, and Gordon reads this scene as Carl's rejection of his heterosexual experimentation and embrace of his homosexual identity. As a replacement for the discarded underwear and discarded heterosexual identity, Carl asks George to buy him "a suit of these pink silk teddybears that ladies use. A little bigger than I'd wear, see?" (893). While Blotner reads the request for a pink teddy as a signal that Carl will continue to sleep with women in the future, Gordon persuasively argues that, together with his purifying shower, the desire for women's underwear indicates Carl's reconciliation with George and a declaration of his future fidelity: "he wants a pink teddy. He wants his lover to buy it for him. He wants one that will last as he grows up and stays with George" (89). Far from presenting Carl's desires or the pair's relationship as deviant, wrong, or sinful, Faulkner uses a detached narrator to neutrally report on the couple's travails from the point of view of their shipmates who seem to accept them and their sexuality. The symbolic importance of clothing that matches one's interior self-conception on display in "Divorce in Naples" runs throughout Faulkner's fiction, and the significance of dress goes beyond only symbolic value, though that is certainly important.

Interestingly, there is no need for symbolic containment of male desire—even desire for another man—in "Divorce in Naples." Only women's sexuality must be contained through clothing, while men in Faulkner's works use clothing to enhance their appearance, assertiveness, and attractiveness. Donald Mahon, Quentin, Popeye, Moketubbe, and Harry all use clothing to mask, enhance, or even replace their missing virility, while for women like Drusilla, Quentin, Temple, and Charlotte, clothing must contain the sexuality that threatens to exceed "proper" boundaries. It is the individual's place within their culture and their relationships to the power structures within that culture that dictate the social function of clothing. The use of clothing as exterior expression of inner identity is distinct but not entirely free from this social function. That is, there is a strong and mutually constitutive connection between one's internal identification of the true self and its expression through clothing, but women are often punished for pushing that identity and its sartorial expression beyond culturally sanctioned boundaries. Eula's treatment over the course of the Snopes Trilogy is emblematic of this difference: as she gradually becomes redefined as a mother, her sexuality, body, and clothing are less and less remarked upon. The threatening (to men) excess of sexuality that could not be contained by clothing in *The Hamlet* is contained and hidden through motherhood and death in *The Mansion*. Even if her affair with de Spain is known, it is unspoken.

The increased attention to garments as things in the final two installments of the Snopes Trilogy will be discussed at more length in the Clothing and Class chapter, but the importance of clothing as object and actant is significant in relation to gender as well. Clothing acts on people and affects their behavior in a variety of ways. The sight of articles of clothing triggers strong reactions in *Soldiers' Pay*, *Mosquitoes*, *The Sound and the Fury* (particularly for Quentin and Jason), and for numerous characters in *Sanctuary*, *The Unvanquished*, and *If I Forget Thee, Jerusalem*. The touch and physical presence of clothing evokes visceral reactions in Benjy, Moketubbe, Drusilla, and Temple. It is perhaps in "The Wild Palms" that the importance of objects, including clothing, is the most pronounced, as things influence human actions and outcomes as much as people do, a trend that continues when clothing is examined through the lenses of race and class.

2

Clothing and Race

The intimate connections among clothing, the body, and identity have been explored in the previous chapter, and Black bodies in the United States have always been subject to the control of others:

> The bodies of slaves (and later of free blacks) were contested terrain, the sties on which a struggle between racial groups was often destructively played out … Yet within the confines of an oppressive social system, African Americans have been able to develop and give visual expression to cultural preferences that were at variance with those of the dominant racial group.
>
> (White and White 4)

Faulkner follows Mark Twain's *Pudd'nhead Wilson* in suggesting a complicated and potentially subversive connection between racial identity and clothing. In that novel, Twain demonstrates "that neither clothing nor race is an essence or part of an unchangeable ethnic identity, that each is a supplement that can be destabilized, and that the category of gender can complicate this even further" (Elahi 55). Thus, clothing can be the site of ideological battle, both as a stand in for the Black body and in terms of contested symbolic meanings.

Clothing was one mechanism of control during slavery, with South Carolina's Negro Act of 1735 actually listing suitable materials for slave clothing: "it was clearly intended that slaves would wear loose-fitting garments made of the coarsest available cloth" while the genteel of society were meant to wear more tailored, tight-fitting garments with soft, brushed cloth (White and White 8–9). In *Stylin': African American Expressive Culture from Its Beginnings to the Zoot Suit*, Shane White and Graham White marshal multiple instances of slave owners blaming fine clothing for unruly slave behavior (6–10, 29–30), and they show how slaves made their own clothing, creating innovative styles and fashions to proudly wear on Sundays: "If the intention of slaveholders was, as one of them asserted, to forbid their slaves 'to do anything for themselves in order to cultivate attitudes of absolute dependence,' then clothing proved to be a lapse of some significance" (36). While auctions dehumanized enslaved people by putting their unclothed bodies on display like farm animals, creating clothes and even fashionable styles allowed slaves to reclaim some degree of humanity.

While a preference for stylish clothing and bold colors is certainly not monolithic, such a predilection did persist in significant parts of the African American community after emancipation, with the finest outfits usually worn on Sundays. Wearing fashionable clothing could provide a sense of dignity often not afforded to people of color by white society, as well as provide a sense of identity as something other than a worker. During Reconstruction and the Jim Crow era, wearing clothes that were deemed by whites to be too fancy, expensive, or showy could be dangerous: "African Americans were required to dress, walk, comport themselves, and direct their gaze in a manner that registered uncomplaining subservience. Blacks understood, for example, that it could be dangerous to wear expensive clothes or, particularly in rural areas, to don Sunday attire during the week" (154). White and White detail how Black men were frequently assaulted for dressing too well or were required to change clothes under threat of arrest. Mobs would literally cut the uniforms off Black soldiers returning from the First World War at the train stations, sometimes forcing them to walk away in their underwear (154–5), a far cry from Faulkner's own experience returning home on the train in full (and fake) military regalia that he knew would impress rather than infuriate those who saw him.

These restrictions and recriminations on dressing fashionably may have deterred some people from doing so, but they also made the subversive, rebellious element of stylish clothing more alluring to others. In both rural and urban Black communities, Sunday was a day for dressing in one's most elegant outfit and going out in public to be seen and to see what others were wearing.[1] Driven by the rise of the department store in the early twentieth century, the fashion industry was the spearhead of a consumer boom, according to historian William Leach: "the engine of fashion existed now in thousands of cities at the heart of everyday life, churning up desire for commodities that carried with them the promise of personal transformation" (328). All-Black fashion shows and beauty pageants were popular in major American cities (White and White 208–11), while more informal fashion shows took place on streets like Beale

---

[1] Wearing fancy Sunday clothes was certainly not limited to African Americans in Faulkner's real and fictional worlds. Digital Yoknapatawpha's keywords include references to "Sunday clothes" in fourteen different short stories and novels, in reference to both Black and white characters.

Street in Memphis, Seventh Avenue in New York (called the African Broadway), and Chicago's State Street, which was known as the Stroll (225). "Every northern city had its equivalent of the Stroll," but Chicago's was the king of them all, with Harlem's Seventh and Lenox Avenues the only real rival (234). Black Southerners would have read about the fashion parades on the Stroll in Black-owned publications like the *Chicago Defender*, which was often read far to the south of the Windy City (225). A 1931 *New York Times* article "suggested that, rather than being followers of fashion, young African Americans were its cutting edge" (235), and Black musicians were front and center, creating eclectic styles that hearkened back to slaves' patching, reworking, and mixing of various styles: "The constructed appearance of these musicians was, in time-honored African American fashion, an act of *bricolage*, a creative combination of clothes (many with small adjustments here and there), textures, and colors that frequently belied the origins of its constituent elements" (243). Fashions like the zoot suit that Cab Calloway helped popularize were made to stand out rather than blend in or imitate more staid mainstream and white styles, though, again, it should be stressed that not all Black Americans dressed stylishly and not all white Americans conservatively. As I will discuss at the end of this chapter, the zoot suit was a clothing choice that intentionally challenged the racial status quo with its bold and brash fashion statement. While this particular sartorial choice is designed to call attention to the wearer and the message of the clothing, other outfits are useful for their ability to deemphasize the wearer while both of these dressing choices can allow the wearer to participate in the African American traditions of masking and performing.

My subject in this chapter, then, is not so much the realities of African American fashions in the early twentieth century, but rather Faulkner's particular and subjective perceptions and depictions of them. According to Blotner, Faulkner admitted throughout his life his difficulties in understanding the "thoughts and feelings" of the Black Mississippians among whom he lived (Vol. 2, 1038–9). Some early Faulkner critics on the issues of race are still some of the most valuable, with *Faulkner and Race* a notable collection of insightful essays. Craig Werner echoes Blotner's point, arguing that "while Faulkner was a good observer, he consistently interpreted Afro-American behavior in static rather than kinetic terms" (37) and agreeing with James Baldwin's assessment that "Faulkner could see Negroes only as they related to him" (473). Thadious M. Davis depicts how Black people become more "visible" in American culture during the period of Faulkner's youth and into the 1920s, resulting in "changes in artistic images of blacks" ("From Jazz" 72). Thus, Faulkner's portrayals of clothing and fashion in relation to Black characters is perhaps a reflection of what aspects of actual African American fashion were most visible and most notable to him. Faulkner's own admittedly limited understanding of Black Americans combined with the masking inherent in African American culture mean that Faulkner is less attuned to how clothing reflects and creates inner identity, a prominent theme in the chapter on clothing and gender. Instead, the focus is more on the pubic-facing identity created by clothing, the connections between fashion and larger cultural issues, and what James A. Snead claims is "the main lesson of Faulkner's novels," the futility of racial division (152). Davis's later work, *Games of Property*, is an important one in Faulkner studies, and her analysis of *Go Down, Moses* influences my readings of Faulkner's use of clothing in not only that novel, but other works as well. Clothing's status as an actant and importance as a thing are still prominent in relation to race, though it is almost always complicated by the symbolic meanings of garments in relation to the racial and racist systems of Faulkner's time and place.

The Sound and the Fury

If there is one aspect of the African American experience that Faulkner *can* identify with and understand to some degree, it is surely role playing. In *The Sound and the Fury*, Quentin repeatedly comments on Deacon's clothing, suggesting that what he wears is part of a larger acting job meant to deceive others and enhance his own position. He thinks of Deacon as something of a clown, or at least imposter, who dresses up for and marches in every parade, including "in a stovepipe hat, carrying a two inch Italian flag" for Columbus Day and a G.A.R. uniform (Grand Army of the Republic, a Union Army veterans group) on Decoration Day (82). Quentin also recognizes the way Deacon plays a role in order to benefit from the white students at Harvard, not only in his oft-cited quote about race as behavior ("a sort of obverse reflection of the white people he lives among" [86]), but especially when he notes Deacon's penchant for ingratiating himself with white Southerners the minute they arrive in Boston: "He had a regular uniform he met trains in, a sort of Uncle Tom's cabin outfit, patches and all" (97). Quentin describes Deacon's minstrel show dialect and manner that he uses "until he had you completely subjugated … though his manner gradually moved northward as his raiment improved, until at last when he had bled you until you began to learn better he was calling you Quentin or whatever, and when you saw him next he'd be wearing a cast-off Brooks suit" (97). Deacon's outfit (and the behavior that goes with the costume) is what initially prompts arriving freshmen to trust him, while his dressing up for different parades reveals all of his outfits to be theatrical. Quentin's attitude toward Deacon displays his condescension toward all people of color, but his awareness of Deacon's use of costumes and acting comes from his own similar experiences, as discussed in the previous chapter. Deacon's deftness at playing roles for his white audience illustrates how Black men are able to hide within their clothing, hiding their true selves behind the mask and costume they know whites will see, as when in *The Town* "two white men discussing in a store full of Negroes a white woman's adultery" causes the shrewd Black crowd to disappear within their clothing: "a few of the Negroes still lingered, the arms and faces already fading back into the darkness behind the lighter shades of shirts and hats and pants as if they were slowly vacating them" (329). Deacon's costuming is not mere minstrelsy. He uses clothing and role playing to subvert racial categories and hierarchies. The crowd in *The Town* rightly intuits that using clothing to disappear is advantageous in their particular situation, but Deacon understands that using clothing to stand out can put him in a position of power relative to his white audience. Through his depiction of Deacon, Faulkner demonstrates his awareness of how masking and costuming conceal the inner self from a white audience, as well as admits his own limitations in seeing beyond the surface of Black Americans.

Deacon's uniform recalls similar scenes with Caspey Strother in *Flags in the Dust* and shows why masking can be important for self-preservation. Once he has worn the uniform during his First World War service in Europe, Caspey returns to Mississippi espousing ideas of racial equality: "I dont take nothin' fum no white folks no mo' … War done changed all dat. If us cullud folks is good enough ter save France fum de Germans, den us is good enough ter have de same rights de Germans is" (58). This overt threat to white supremacy is negated in multiple ways, including Faulkner's exaggerated use of dialect in this early novel to render Caspey's words somewhat comical, underscored by his clearly exaggerated war stories. When sixteen-year-old Isom dresses up in Caspey's uniform, Miss Jenny experiences a moment of "brief, cold astonishment" (49), before resorting to ridicule and belittlement of both Isom and Caspey's war service. Finally, when

Caspey directly challenges Old Bayard by disobeying one of his commands, the white man assaults him with "a stick of stove wood" (80), knocking him to the ground and effectively quelling his talk of equality for the remainder of the novel. Deacon's more subtle strategies are perhaps understandable.

Both Deacon and Dilsey use clothing to counter the tendency of African Americans being seen by the dominant culture as either childlike or elderly, as discussed by Habiba Ibrahim in *Black Age: Oceanic Lifespans and the Time of Black Life*. Of course, both of these cast Black people as powerless, so dress and fashion can assert agency wordlessly, perhaps avoiding the direct conflict Caspey faces. Just because Quentin sees Deacon's performance as faintly ludicrous does not mean that is the only way to interpret it. Thadious Davis argues that Tomey's Turl uses Sunday clothes to recast his identity and his place in the social hierarchy: "Producing through clothing an image of himself that is different from his everyday, asexual, subjugated self, Tomey's Turl suspends the boundaries and codes of that life and rewrites the script for the black male body" (54). The economic gains that come at least in part from Deacon's use of clothing do something quite similar for him, allowing for a sense of self constructed on his own terms regardless of what Quentin and a white audience may think of him.

The fact that Dilsey is only seen clearly through the final third-person narrator section of *The Sound and the Fury* is another self-conscious admission on Faulkner's part of the inability of white people to see accurately their fellow Black citizens. Dilsey's clothing is similar to Deacon's in some ways, but contrasts with the outfits of Faulkner's white women. Many critics have commented on the regality of her purple Easter outfit, and this aligns her with Deacon's ability to project a self apart from her economic and racial subjugation to white people. The fashion parade of Sunday clothes on the way to church (291) recalls the Stroll and allows for a communal expression of dignity and flamboyance so often suppressed in the everyday life of the Jim Crow South. In some ways, Dilsey's garments break down the barriers of this society. The man's hat that she wears (266) is perhaps a subtler version of the gender nonconformity discussed in the previous chapter, and her placing of the hat on Benjy's head goes beyond a blurring of gender lines to a radical if temporary acceptance of the Other across lines of gender, race, class, and neurodiversity. Her many layers of clothing reinforce her difference from the many white women who wear flimsy or revealing garments, like the women of *Mosquitoes*, Miss Quentin, Temple, Charlotte, and even Caroline Compson.

"That Evening Sun"

The activity and business of laundry has historically been racially charged in Southern society. With whiteness defined in opposition to blackness, who cleaned whose clothes was one of many markers to delineate racial groups and hierarchies. Black women for decades did the laundry of white families as socially permitted remunerative labor that also served to reinscribe boundaries of race and class, as Colonel Sartoris does so blatantly in "A Rose for Emily" when he decrees that "no Negro woman should appear on the streets without an apron" (119–20). Ike McCaslin, for instance, only realizes Roth's mistress is mixed race because she mentions "taking in washing" (*Go Down, Moses* 343). Disruptions to that entrenched system, then, are both symptomatic of and causes of changes that those in power may find threatening. The opening of "That Evening Sun" mentions not only the new electric streetlamps, "bloated and ghostly bloodless grapes" (289), but also the fact that there is now a city laundry that gathers dirty clothing on the traditional Monday morning. "[T]he soiled wearing of a whole week" is still sometimes collected by individual black women, though now they retrieve their loads in cars instead of on foot (289). This modernization in how laundry is done portends a wider shift in race relations concomitant with the decline of prominent old families like the Compsons. It is appropriate, then, that Quentin's narration quickly shifts in the second paragraph to fifteen years earlier, a safer time for white people anxious about their social standing, though the story shows cracks in the systemic structures of racism in that earlier time as well.

In this earlier time, Black women would carry the white families' laundry on "their steady, turbaned heads, bundles of clothes tied up in sheets, almost as large as cotton bales" (289). Faulkner makes explicit the link between cotton as an agricultural product and the consumer commodity of clothing, suggesting a link between the menial domestic labor of twentieth-century Black women and the back-breaking work of enslaved field hands. This implicates (largely white) consumers of clothing as well in this history of oppression. Similarly, white men like Mr. Stovall who are consumers of the commodity of Nancy's body are implicated in the oppression, violence, and terror inflicted on her domestically. The metaphor of laundry indicates the desire on the part of the white community to have their sins washed away by scapegoating African Americans as the agents of sin. Mr. Compson, for example, tells Nancy, "if you'd just let white men alone … If you'd behave yourself, you'd have kept out of this"

(295). As Ren Denton comments on this scene, "In other words, he blames her, or he exposes white culture's tendency to blame black women for anything amiss within their homes … Mr. Compson's words imply that Nancy has earned Jesus's wrath because of her sexual promiscuity, rather than the white man asserting his need for sexual gratification" (103).

The way that Nancy and the other Black women carry the bundles of laundry on their heads suggests a continuity with their bodies and with their selves similar to clothing worn as garments. In fact, Nancy puts the bundle of laundry on her head, "then upon the bundle in turn she would set the black straw sailor hat which she wore winter and summer" (289–90). This positioning of the laundry between head and hat makes the bundle an adjunct of her body and head, thereby suggesting the laundry is an important part of who she is, perhaps even a way of saying she is not to be reduced to only a prostitute and victim. On the other hand, extending Brevda's argument about hats as genital substitutes in *Sanctuary* could indicate the interpolation of commodified, white, male desire between her self and her body. Doing laundry provides at least some degree of economic freedom, though it also emphasizes her subjugated racial and class status. The act of hanging herself with her own dress, then, takes on added significance as a statement of selfhood and bodily autonomy while also adding a new twist to the idea of clothing as actant. Using her own dress as a noose exposes the hidden reality of her pregnant body and likewise exposes the sins of whites that had been covered, from the "respectable" white father of her child to the flimsy pretense that her suicidal tendencies are merely the result of drug use. Quentin's infamous final question, "Who will do our washing now, Father?" (309), carries all the connotations and meanings of laundering clothing. Black people, and Black women in particular, are needed to launder the sins of whites off-stage, as it were, in order to maintain an illusion of whiteness as clean and free of sin.

This story also highlights the challenges of applying object oriented ontology (OOO) to Faulkner's Black characters. If Nancy's suicide attempt is one of her only recourses to bodily autonomy, then her dress is the physical object or actant to facilitate the act. However, the incident and the story as whole, if not Faulkner's entire oeuvre, reveal how African Americans are positioned culturally as things themselves, most obviously in the "logic" of slavery, but continuing in twentieth-century racist discourse and practice. It is potentially problematic, then, to argue that objects like clothing should be understood as actants when actual people are struggling to define themselves legally and culturally as fully human actors. Faulkner's focus on this struggle perhaps explains his limited use of clothing as actant in relation to Black characters. As discussed in the "Clothing and Gender" chapter, clothing's status as an actant is often linked to the prominence of objects in modernity, yet his Black characters are rarely positioned as fully modern subjects. Black characters who challenge the status quo or push contemporary boundaries are most often consigned to the past narratively: Ringo, Charles Bon, Tomey's Turl, Percival Brownlee, and Ned McCaslin, to name a few. While there are some instances of clothing's importance as an object or thing in relation to race, Faulkner more often uses dress in connection to themes of identity, particularly the creation of public personae.

For example, in *The Sound and the Fury* Dilsey and her clothing are characterized quite differently from Nancy and hers. Disley's Easter Sunday outfit, "a stiff black straw hat perched upon her turban, and a maroon velvet cape with a border of mangy and anonymous fur above a dress of purple silk" (265), seems to signify on Nancy's "turbaned" washerwoman outfit ("Evening" 289). John T. Matthews's comments on Dilsey's ensemble in a way that recalls White and White's description of slaves proudly altering their cast-off garments into expressive fashion: "The stiffness signals her fortitude, the purple the royalty of her personal dignity. She accepts the hand-me-down clothes of her white 'betters,' learning how to arrange them into a style of her own" (106). Dilsey's outer appearance fits the character traits that Faulkner emphasizes in a character drawn from his complicated relationship with Caroline Barr: inner strength, compassion, and endurance, the traits that hold together the Compson family that is disintegrating like so much cheap fabric. When Quentin tries to launder his own clothing in *The Sound and the Fury*, it does not go well. He tries to use gasoline to remove the blood stains from his shirt (172, 178), but without Dilsey around to do his washing, Quentin cannot remove the stain of blood that suggests his sister's loss of virginity. The sin remains his for failing to do his "duty" and protect his sister's honor, as well as Caddy's for violating communal norms through premarital sex and pregnancy. Dilsey makes a point of not cleaning Caddy's soiled underwear; instead, she "wadded the drawers and scrubbed Caddy behind with them" (74) in a vain attempt to clean her. This failure to clean or launder is thus a failure to reinscribe whiteness, recalling Caroline's admonition that her daughter does not want to "look like a washerwoman" (63), as well as Jason's later racializing of her daughter Quentin's sexual behavior. Another scene of failed laundering occurs in *Sanctuary*, when Minnie attempts to clean the blood from Temple's clothes on her first night at Miss Reba's brothel. Again, using Black women to cleanse the sins of whites will not work, as Minnie comments that hymenal blood is "the most hardest of all" to get clean (147), echoing the social condemnation of women's sexuality, even when raped.[2]

Light in August is the only Faulkner text where a white person does the laundry of a Black or mixed-race person—and even this instance is questionable due to the undetermined race of Joe Christmas's father. When Joe is described as being dressed "in a clean white shirt now and the serge trousers creased now every week" (233), the phrasing suggests the Joanna has begun to do his laundry. This is an interesting reversal of the traditional racial dynamic of laundry that makes Black male characters like Jesus in "That Evening Sun," as well as Sykes in Zora Neale Hurston's "Sweat" (1926), decry and forbid their wives taking in white families' laundry. While this traditional arrangement makes clear the lower standing of Black women, it also reinforces the emasculation of Black men who are doubly dependent for money on their wives' labor and the bounty of white families who paternalistically provide the possibility of earning money. Joe ultimately proves he is similar to Jesus and Sykes in terms of masculine pride and misogyny. Standing in his cabin on the Burden place, he remembers when "a woman" (presumably Mrs. McEachern) would do his laundry and replace any missing buttons on his clothes. Unable to accept help or kindness from a woman, Joe would use his (overtly phallic) "pocket knife" to "cut off the buttons which she had just replaced" (107). This memory is enough to cause him to repeat the action on the shirt he wears before heading out naked into the night where car headlights cause his body to "grow white out of the darkness like a Kodak print emerging from the liquid" (108). The image here is one of rebirth, naked body emerging from liquid, although in Joe's case it is a rebirth into the calcified attitudes of maleness/whiteness in order to reject the threatening softness of female/Black.

---

[2] In *The Reivers*, there is also a scene of laundering in a brothel, though in this more lighthearted novel it is the white Everbe/Corrie who insists on washing Lucius's clothes in an apparent attempt to assuage her guilt over the "stains" of sexual (and other sinful) experience that Lucius has gained under her watch (206). Like Caddy's and Temple's stained underwear, though, the loss of innocence cannot be undone; unlike those two characters, however, Lucius's (male) experiences are largely played for laughs, making this scene more like that of Houston washing Ike Snopes's "stained foul" overalls after sex with the cow (*Hamlet* 194–5).

Light in August

While clothing is not prominently described throughout most of *Light in August*, its absence may be instructive as well. That is, in his depictions of Joe Christmas, Faulkner could choose to suggest racial coding through clothing. Instead, he seems pointedly not to racialize Christmas's clothing in keeping with his character's ambiguous racial status and the ways his skin color destabilize the binary racial categories of the South and United States of the early twentieth century. That is, clothing is not used in connection to his inner identity, but to emphasize his public identity and appearance to others. When Joe first appears, the narrator and other characters describe his serge trousers, white shirt, and straw hat as creating the impression of a tramp or a hobo (31) wearing "city clothes" (32) or "Sunday clothes" (34), with no one suggesting his clothes mark him as potentially Black even though the job he is hired for is referred to as one for Black men and his coworkers speculate that "he was a foreigner" (33). When he makes enough money working to afford new clothes, he "came to work in new overalls" (35), a change that allows him to blend in as white to an even greater degree. Christmas's clothing, the few times it is remarked upon, is described as being similar to that of other white men, specifically Lucas Burch, whose new hat is "like Christmas' but with a colored band" (40) and Byron Bunch, who also wears "cheap serge which is not new" (48). This visual similarity with white men in terms of clothing, as well as skin color, underscores the arbitrariness and irrationality of the racial categories that dictate Christmas's life. It also extends Davis's point in *Games of Property* about how the "shadow" of race mixing and racial hybridity hangs over Isaac McCaslin's life in *Go Down, Moses* (145). Joe's indeterminate, even white, clothing foreshadows the threat to the "game of boundaries," as Davis calls it, that enforces segregation between white and Black.

Joe's white appearance is reinforced by repeated references to the clothing of multiple characters as soiled, a description that references the human condition as much as anything or perhaps the stain of original sin with more of a Calvinist bent. The term "soiled" is used to refer to the clothing of Christmas (31, 227), Lucas Burch/Joe Brown (41), and Gail Hightower (308, 403), while Doc Hines's garments are "dirty" (342). This same term, "soiled," is used for Caddy and her daughter Quentin's clothing in *The Sound and the Fury*, so an element of sinful, if not sexual, impurity is perhaps hinted at in such references. McEachern, Joe's adoptive father, whips his son for not learning his catechism, but pointedly tells Joe to remove his trousers first: "Take down your pants … We'll not soil them"

(149). Changing from soiled garments to new or clean ones is also a repeated image that obviously suggests purification but also a change in identity (not necessarily purer). Joe as a teenager trades the cow that his adopted father McEachern has given him for a new suit which he hides in the barn. McEachern rightly intuits that the only need for such flashy garments (as opposed to his own "suit of hard, decent black" [141]) is as "some adjunct to sinning" (201), specifically pursuing the waitress Bobbie Allen for a sexual relationship: "What else would you want with a new suit if you were not whoring?" (164). The feel of his new garments reflects Joe's inner duality and his inability to accept pleasure: "The new cloth, after his soft, oftenwashed overalls, felt rich and harsh" (171). The suit behaves as actant both in how it entices Joe into surreptitiously buying it, as if maturing to a sexual relationship would be impossible without it, as well as in how it prompts McEachern's anger and violence. As with the soiled garments of Caddy and Temple, each of these soiled males is an outcast in the community. Deviation from communal standards—regardless of how warped or irrational those standards are—results in ostracizing, at least when that deviation is known publicly, a visible stain on the exterior that reveals inner corruption.

We might expect Joe to change his clothing when he lives as a Black man in Chicago and Detroit, but Faulkner makes no mention of his fashion choices in those scenes. It is only after he has killed Joanna and is a fugitive that he stops in Mottstown at a "white barbershop" for a shave and a haircut before buying "a new shirt and a tie and a straw hat" (349–50). This fact infuriates the white public who want Joe to perform the roles of both Black man and fugitive from the law:

> That was what made folks so mad. For him to be a murderer and all dressed up and walking the town like he dared them to touch him, when he ought to have been skulking and hiding in the woods, muddy and dirty and running. It was like he never even knew he was a murderer, let alone a nigger too.
>
> (350)

Joe's multiple instances of undressing in the novel reinforce this notion of his being unable to match his interior and exterior. The community wants him to look and act as they expect him to, to conform to preordained cultural roles, but because he does not know who he is in fundamental ways, Joe can never simply wear the mask and costume that his society thinks he should. His most vulnerable moment comes when he lies naked with Bobbie in her bed (removing his ill-gotten new suit) and confesses that he is (or thinks he is) part Black

(195–6). The rejection he experiences from Bobbie then guides his reaction to Joanna baring herself to him later. He conflates vulnerability and openness with weakness that, in his mind, must be eradicated. In fact, as he approaches her house for the last time, Joe is following Joanna's orders in a note telling him to come to her, but he has already decided that he will not change who he is by admitting his blackness and going to school: "He would not change his clothes now. In his sweatstained overalls he would traverse the late twilight of May and enter the kitchen" (278). His refusal to adopt a new identity from one of the very few available to him is reflected in his refusal to change clothes, while after he kills Joanna, his purchase of a new suit and public parading of it again signals a refusal to adhere to societal expectations of what role he should inhabit. Joe is unable to indulge the clothing/identity connection in the same ways the white women examined in the first chapter often can. Faulkner focuses more on the exterior image, the role-playing aspect of clothing with Black characters with whose internal struggles he cannot identify with as readily as with his white characters.

Earlier in the novel, Joe finds that the men in Max's restaurant are impossible to identify because they do not wear clothing that identifies their place in the world, as virtually everyone else does: "The men were not in overalls and they all wore hats, and their faces were all alike: not young and not old; not farmers and not townsmen either. They looked like people who had just got off a train and who would be gone tomorrow and who did not have any address" (174). This lack of identity attracts and repels Joe, as it speaks to the fundamental instability of his own identity. In a society where nearly all of the men dress in overalls for work and then change into similar outfits of white shirts and black or khaki pants afterward, clothing is shown as a way to blend in as well as to stand out. Joe makes repeated attempts throughout his life to blend in with various communities, reflected in his conventional dress, but he never does feel that he belongs. The similar clothing and similar mundane lives of the white people Joe lives among suggests that uniform dress begets uniform behavior, a communal norm from which deviance is established to mark outsiders. Joe's deviant actions and mixed-race background mean that he never truly fits in, regardless of his external appearance. Rather than Joe's indistinct clothing reflecting his inner liminality, following OOO, it is perhaps *because* he does not dress the part that he can never mentally create and accept a stable, integrated, and productive identity. The unreliability of clothing as marker of race also suggests the unreliability of skin color as marker of race, and Rebecca Nisetich shows how whiteness is contingent on other factors in the novel (such as gender, class, and sexuality) so that whiteness must be reinforced irrespective of skin color, as when Brown must question Christamas's racial makeup in order "to reify his white racial identity by defining himself in opposition to his partner" (5). The inability of uniform clothing to reveal inner realities also coincides with the indeterminate, possibly queer, sexualities of numerous characters in the novel, including Christmas, Hightower, Brown, Joanna Burden, and Byron Bunch, as explored in more detail by Nisetich.

Percy Grimm favors uniform dress and uniform belief. We are told that Grim was lazy, directionless, and "had shown no ability in school" as a young man, sounding, in fact, much like Christmas: "a man who had been for a long time in a swamp, in the dark" (450–1). The "civilian-military act which saved him" allows him to wear a uniform like those from the First World War, for which he was born too late and "he would never forgive his parents for that fact" (450). The appearance of the uniform is matched by the appeal of uniform thought that it signifies, the freedom "of ever again having to think or decide" and a "blind obedience, and a belief that the white race is superior to any and all other races and that the American uniform is superior to all men" (451). Although the narrator mocks Grimm's "self-conscious pride of a boy," his fellow citizens are impressed by his "captain's uniform" that he struts through downtown wearing "each national holiday that had any martial flavor whatever" (451). This militaristic costuming is quite similar to that of Deacon in *The Sound and the Fury*, but whereas Deacon's blackness makes him an object of derision for white onlookers, Grimm's whiteness lends him instant credibility with his audience. Grimm's attitude and beliefs affect the men around him, even if the sheriff tells them not to wear uniforms and guns in public: "They now moved in a grave and slightly aweinspiring reflected light which was almost palpable as the khaki would have been which Grimm wished them to wear, wished that they wore, as though each time they returned to the orderly room they dressed themselves anew in suave and austerely splendid scraps of his dream" (457). Are clothes the actant here? As with Joe's identity, it is as if clothing is motivating not merely reflecting behavior. Instead of uniforms mirroring unanimity of thought and purpose, here it is the beliefs that create solidarity, namely a belief in white supremacy that must be enforced violently, until the men's external appearance finally matches their internal conformity: "And they now wore uniforms. It was their faces" (457). While Faulkner later identified Grimm as a precursor to the Nazi storm trooper (Blotner and Gwynn 41), he is also a predictor of twenty-first-century neo-Nazis who have adopted a modified version of Grimm's uniform. At the infamous 2017 clash in Faulkner's sometime home of Charlottesville, Virginia, far-right groups adopted a uniform of white polo shirts and khaki pants in what *The Guardian* described as an attempt "to cultivate an aesthetic that could appear non-threatening, even aspirational."[3] The same article quotes Andrew Anglin, founder of the Daily Stormer, a white supremacist website, as telling his followers, "We need to be extremely conscious of what we look like, and how we present ourselves." While the twenty-first-century neo-Nazis want to tone down militaristic associations, Grimm calculates correctly that paramilitary dress will tap into feelings of patriotism and white supremacy among his 1930s audience.

Gail Hightower also has a visceral experience with a military uniform, but it plays out quite differently for many reasons, not the least of which is the fact that his father's garment is more important as an object than as a symbol. Actually, his father's coat is not technically a military uniform but a "somber frock coat" that he preached in and "wore instead of uniform" (468). Nonetheless, the wartime artifact is an object of awe and wonder to the eight-year-old Hightower, who is particularly enamored of the Union patch that darkly hints at killing his father must have done. More than what it represents in relation to the war and history, the coat is a tangible link to his distant parents:

> Then the garment, the neat folds. He did not know what it was, because at first he was almost overpowered by the evocation of his dead mother's hands which lingered among the folds. Then it opened, tumbling slowly. To him, the child, it seemed unbelievably huge, as though made for a giant; as though merely from having been worn by one of them, the cloth itself had assumed the properties of those phantoms who loomed heroic and tremendous against the background of thunder and smoke and torn flags which now filled his waking and sleeping life.
> (468)

The young Hightower, who "grew to manhood among phantoms" (474), finds a stronger, more tangible connection to this article of clothing than to his actual parents, recalling Johnny Sartoris's coat discussed in the following chapter. The fact that the coat symbolizes the war is also significant, and Hightower can

---

[3] Gavin Haynes's article documents the history of the polo shirt's political associations while a 2019 piece by Cynthia Miller-Idriss analyzes the adoption of the Fred Perry brand and other mainstream fashions by alt-right groups as part of a strategy to normalize their radical, racist beliefs: "in the days leading up to the Unite the Right rally in Charlottesville, a prominent neo-Nazi blogger instructed marchers to dress respectably, noting that their appearance was more important than their ideas in getting people to listen."

consequently attach all sorts of abstract meaning to it, qualities of honor, courage, and pride that he associates with the war and with his father and grandfather. However, the coat as an actant has the power to affect his physical behavior and wellbeing. He is unable to eat or sleep the night he discovers it, and then he has "one of his intestinal fits" the next day as he feels "that horrified triumph and sick joy" when contemplating the Union Army patch (470). The uniqueness of this garment is also significant, suggesting the singularity of its wearer. His father was a self-taught doctor and an abolitionist who nonetheless fought with the Confederacy in the Civil War, and Hightower's choice to devote his life to his grandfather's image perhaps suggests the inadequacy he feels in his father's shadow, his inability to follow in his footsteps—or to fit into the coat of "a giant" (468). The smells and feel of the object almost literally infect Hightower, and the combination of the literal and the metaphorical overwhelm him to the point that he orders his entire life around the feelings generated by that coat. Without finding, touching, and smelling the coat, Hightower likely would not have had the same obsession with his grandfather's war legacy (which was apparently at odds with his father's lack of militarism), and therefore he would not have doggedly insisted on moving to Jefferson, subsequently forsaking his marriage and leading to an ascetic life that is only derailed by Byron's intrusion. Were it not for the coat in the attic, Lena's infant would perhaps die instead of living as a symbol of hope in an otherwise bleak novel.

Absalom, Absalom!

Just as clothing is associated with identity, or lack thereof, in *Light in August*, so is it used by Faulkner in *Absalom, Absalom!* Although not all instances of clothing connect to race directly or primarily in the novel, the specter of race hangs over the book and dominates the critical conversation surrounding it, and I think it is more effective to discuss the novel as a whole here, including examples where clothing is not implicated in the novel's racial politics, rather than splitting discussion of the novel over three chapters. Thomas Sutpen's rise is defined by his acquisition of objects and possessions, including clothing. Faulkner's use of clothing in *Absalom, Absalom!* reveals the complicated and nuanced ways in which race and class intersect in the novel, in Faulkner's body of work, and in the United States of Faulkner's lifetime. Moreover, gender complicates the intersections of class and race still further so that *Absalom!* illustrates how the concerns of each of my three chapters cannot easily be separated and how clothing is a site of intersectionality, and I hope that placing this discussion in the middle of the book will gesture to the intersections of gender, class, and race on the canvas of clothes.

Young Thomas Sutpen's nascent class consciousness associates "fine clothes" with wealth, idleness, and slaveholding (177), with an emphasis on the leisure part of Thorstein Veblen's leisure class. Illustrating Veblen's point that the rule of "conspicuous waste of goods ... finds expression in dress" (167), the plantation owner for whom Sutpen's father works mystifies the young Sutpen because he is a "man who not only had shoes in the summertime too, but didn't even have to wear them" (184). The boy's ill-fated errand to the big house when he is turned away from the front door is imprinted on Sutpen's psyche as much because of clothing as anything else. He approaches the front door "in garments his father had got from the plantation commissary and had worn out and which one of the sisters had patched and cut down to fit him and he no more conscious of his appearance in them than he was of his skin" (185). His awakening to class consciousness is catalyzed by race and clothing, specifically the slave who opens the door "who wore every day better clothes than he or his father and sisters had ever owned and ever expected to" (184), and who greets the boy by disdainfully "looking down at him in his patched made-over jeans clothes and no shoes ... who had never thought about his own hair or clothes or anybody else's hair or clothes until he saw that monkey nigger" (188).

Race and class are deeply intertwined in this scene as Sutpen begins to understand that his position is even lower than the Black people he has understood to be automatically and inherently beneath him. Instead, his family is looked down upon both by white women with parasols riding in fancy carriages (187) and by the Black butler in his "better clothes" (188). Standing there "outside the barred door in his patched garments and splayed bare feet," Sutpen can suddenly see himself and his family's poverty differently and specifically in terms of their dress:

> [S]eeing his own father and sisters and brothers as the owner, the rich man (not the nigger) must have been seeing them all the time—as cattle ... a race whose future would be a succession of cut-down and patched and made-over garments bought on exorbitant credit because they were white people, from stores where niggers were given the garments free.
>
> (190)

The clothing itself, and its purchase price, drives home the fact that they are even beneath slaves in the social pecking order (at least in some sense, though clearly not in others), and that they, like slaves, are treated by the planter class as things and objects. As his sister does the hard manual labor of washing clothes (with its associations with Black women), Sutpen cannot help now but to notice her garments and see her as cattle: "her back toward him, shapeless in a calico dress and a pair of the old man's shoes unlaced flapping about her ankles and broad in the beam as a cow" (191). Their lack of control and agency over their own lives makes the Sutpens no better than inanimate objects existing only to be tossed around by the forces of history and economics or to be exploited like livestock by those who own things. Even their move from the western Virginia mountains to the Tidewater has no motivating reason or purpose but is merely the family being acted upon rather than acting, "sliding back down out of the mountains and skating in a kind of accelerating and sloven and inert coherence like a useless collection of flotsam on a flooded river moving by some perverse automotivation such as inanimate objects sometimes show" (180–1).

Deposited like so much glacial silt at the doorstep of a wealthy Tidewater plantation, Sutpen fixates on the objects the planter possesses, perhaps because he has been positioned as a thing himself:

> [H]e did not even imagine then that there was any such way to live or to want to live, or that there existed all the objects to be wanted which there were, or that the ones who owned the objects not only could look down on the ones that didn't, but could be supported in the down-looking not only by the others who owned objects too but by the very ones that were looked down on that didn't own objects and knew they never would.
>
> (179)

It is not the wealth per se that Sutpen covets; rather, the money is a means to acquire the objects that are his true desire. It is not only the insult of being turned away from the front door that motivates him toward his grand design, but also the insult of not being allowed to see all of the mysterious and wonderful objects that he knows are in the house, as well as the knowledge that one man can hoard so many objects for himself: "he still didn't envy the man he was watching. He coveted the shoes" (184). Three years after completing his mansion, "he wanted a wife" (29), and he obtains at roughly the same time a wife and four wagons full of expensive furniture and other objects. His lifelong quest for a male heir is not about having a son but rather the need to have somewhere for his objects to go, someone to inherit them. The objects he pursues are like Lacan's *objet a*, vain attempts to fulfill a primal lack that cannot be filled (notably, his mother dies when he is a child).

Sutpen's tale illustrates Veblen's contention that "The motive that lies at the root of ownership is emulation" (25), and several Faulkner characters exhibit Veblen's notion of invidious comparison whereby they are made to feel insignificant and demeaned by their lack of possessions. Things and objects prominently displayed, Veblen says, are more important than wealth itself: "In order to gain and to hold the esteem of men it is not sufficient merely to possess wealth or power. The wealth or power must be put in evidence, for esteem is awarded only on evidence" (36). Sutpen's fixation on the material trappings of wealth is reminiscent of Sarty Snopes's fascination with the objects in Major De Spain's house, and in both cases the poor boy and his family are identified with blackness and also with things that are less than fully human. Faulkner repeats a similar scene yet again in *The Mansion* when Mink Snopes becomes outraged that Houston's Black hired hand has a nicer house than he and "wore warmer clothing than any he or his family possessed" (12). Mink's sense of insult and injustice is compounded by his own patchwork outfit: "the slicker held together with baling wire and automobile tire patching which was the only winter outer garment he owned over his worn patched cotton overalls … cursing the Negro for his black skin inside the warmer garments than his, cursing the very rich feed devoted to cattle instead of humans" (12–13). Again, we see people figured as objects with Mink's garments an assemblage of textiles, farm implements, and car parts that lower him beneath a person who is constructed socially as less than human, as well as beneath a cow. Rather than using his resentment to fuel a socioeconomic rise the way his cousin Flem and Sutpen do, Mink takes violent revenge by murdering Houston, succeeding in changing his outfit in a different way: "His familiar patched faded blue overalls and shirt were exchanged now for the overalls and jumper of coarse white barred laterally with black" (54). The examples of Sutpen, Sarty, and Mink all show how class resentment is inextricably bound with racial identity and that clothing is the most visible—and therefore most important—marker of difference and rank. In each case also, there is a profound connection articulated between the exterior image of clothing and the interior image of the self in ways that Faulkner is unable to express for Black characters.

Sutpen's success at moving from shirtless and mudcovered to "fine clothes" (193) is not quick, and the fact that he one day appears in town "in the same garments in which he had ridden into town five years ago" (31) indicates that although he may understand the importance of clothing, he sees its value only in its ability to conceal his unchanged interior. To him, the house and even his marriage to Ellen serve the same purpose as the clothes, dressing him up to create an illusion of respectability for the townspeople:

> Being men, these spectators did not realise that the garments which Sutpen had worn when he first rode into Jefferson were the only ones in which they had ever seen him, and few of the women in the county had seen him at all yet. Otherwise, some of them would have anticipated Miss Coldfield in this too: in divining that he was saving his clothes, since decorum even if not elegance of appearance would be the only weapon (or rather ladder) with which he could conduct the last assault upon what Miss Coldfield and perhaps others believed to be respectability.
>
> (28)

Sutpen understands only that he needs the veneer of respectability, but he does not change who he is. Even when he wears "a new hat now, and a new broadcloth coat" (35), they are the same style of garments as before, just new items that polish some of his roughness but do nothing to effect any real change. As we will see, Flem Snopes in *The Hamlet* understands the transformative power of clothing much better than does Sutpen, and Flem's climb up the social ladder is more successful as a result. Sutpen does intuit that the wealth needed to purchase the "right" objects and clothing is enough to demarcate his racial differences from Black people, but he fails to see that that alone cannot confer class respectability.

The end of Sutpen's life demonstrates again through clothing and objects how little he has changed from his youth. Wash and Milly Jones are, like Sutpen was, reduced by poverty to a lower level than the Black people who "were better found and housed and even clothed than he and his granddaughter" (226). Rather than recognize or empathize with people living as he once did, Sutpen reduces Milly to the state of livestock, "a mare" (229), as he did with his sister, "a cow" (191), years before. Her status as an object fit only for breeding is underscored by Sutpen's courting of her with ribbons taken from the display case in his store and a new dress, which also recalls the "flutter of cheap ribbons" (9) adorning Sarty Snopes's objectified sisters in "Barn Burning." The baldly transactional nature of these "gifts" aligns with much of the themes of critic Caroline Miles's Marxist scholarship on Faulkner, particularly her article, "Yankee Dollars: The Challenge to Southern Values in 'Two Dollar Wife' and *The Sound and the Fury*." Miles details how Caddy Compson is reduced to "a marker of economic exchange" that loses value once her pregnancy is discovered (53) and Herbert Head "discards her like a worthless piece of machinery" (55), which parallels Milly's treatment by Sutpen, as does Jason's relationship with the Memphis prostitute Lorraine in other ways. The obscure short story "Two Dollar Wife" makes this reduction of women to commodities whose value is determined by their sexuality and their desirability even more overt, and Miles's analysis can be applied to Sutpen's valuing of Milly's body as worth a dress and a few ribbons and beads, before discarding her altogether like a useless mare or "a worthless piece of machinery." This incident gestures backward to the chapter on gender and forward to that on class while also revealing the falsity of the racial hierarchy that Wash assumes will afford him and his granddaughter humane treatment by Sutpen.

Faulkner uses other characters to parallel Sutpen's lack of change in fashion and in character. The obdurate Goodhue Coldfield wears the same "decent and heavy black coat in which he had been married" every Sunday "until he put it on for good the day he climbed to the attic and nailed the door behind him and threw the hammer out the window and so died in it," apparently to avoid having to fight for the Confederacy to defend slavery (52). His unchanging moral character is indicated by his uniform clothing, and his failure to provide adequate parenting is reflected in his daughters' sartorial choices. Rosa meets Quentin in "the eternal black which she had worn for forty-three years now" (3), though Faulkner later describes Rosa wearing—or at least owning—other clothes that are always secondhand garments from her aunt or sister. In fact, these old clothes are basically all she inherits from her father and aunt. She is never taught to cook or sew or "to do anything practical" (65), so she crudely cuts the aunt's dresses down to fit her, accurately reflecting her inherited moral and social positions that she perhaps alters slightly but does not fundamentally change. Rosa has no real identity of her own; a forgotten daughter, spurned niece, overshadowed sister, and rejected bride, she is herself a castoff forever trying to inhabit someone else's clothes:

> She wasn't jealous of Judith. It was not selfpity either, sitting there in one of those botched-over house dresses (the clothes, castoff sometimes but usually new, which Ellen gave her from time to time were always silk, of course) which the aunt had abandoned when she eloped with the horse- and mule-trader, perhaps in the hope or even the firm intention of never wearing such again, blinking steadily at her sister while Ellen talked.
>
> (59)

Ellen's castoffs are at least silk, but they are still someone else's clothes. Rosa cannot dress for her part because she has no part to play. Her aunt has the character and wherewithal to run away from the clothes and identity that has been imposed upon her, leaving her costumes for her understudy, as it were, as she elopes to escape her part in this family drama leaving Rosa "the spinster doomed for life at sixteen" (59), a misfit in "*fitless garments*" (199). The references to clothing highlight the similarities between Rosa and Thomas Sutpen, both fumbling their lines and failing to dress or convincingly inhabit the characters and roles to which they aspire.

Her sister Ellen similarly inherits a dubious legacy from her father with no evidence that she benefits from any better parenting than her younger sister. When Charles Bon visits the first time, Ellen is coldly calculating in trying to maneuver him and Judith together:

> She spoke of Bon as if he were three inanimate objects in one or perhaps one inanimate object for which she and her family would find three concordant uses: a garment which Judith might wear as she would a riding habit or a ball gown, a piece of furniture which would complement and complete the furnishing of her house and position, and a mentor and example to correct Henry's provincial manners and speech and clothing.
>
> (59)

Bon is treated as a thing rather than a person, though it has nothing to do with race in this instance. It is more of a trait of Coldfields and Sutpens to use people as tools to further an end. The comparison of Bon to a garment demonstrates how he (like Ellen was for Thomas) is a prop to complete a scene, a costume to complete a character, and Ellen would like to arrest time so that all of them will be "like painted portraits hung in a vacuum … the originals of which had lived and died so long ago that their joys and griefs must now be forgotten even by the very boards on which they had strutted and postured and laughed and wept" (59). Again, a lack of change is what defines the characters and leads to their pathetic fates.

Charles Bon and the French architect are defined as different by their similarly unusual clothing, but neither changes (as a character or sartorially) throughout the novel. The French architect arrives in fashionable clothing, "a frock coat and a flowered waistcoat and a hat which would have created no furore on a Paris boulevard, all of which he was to wear constantly for the next two years" (26). The contrast between his Parisian fashion and Sutpen mudcovered and shirtless is stark and telling. When the architect runs away "in his embroidered vest and Fauntleroy tie" (177), his fancy clothes offer him no protection, and when he is caught, his tattered clothes mirror the frazzled emotional state of "a little harried wild-faced man" who has been hiding in a cave:

> [A] little man with one sleeve missing from his frock coat and his flowered vest ruined by water and mud where he had fallen in the river and one pants leg ripped down so they could see where he had tied up his leg with a piece of his shirt tail and the rag bloody and the leg swollen, and his hat was completely gone.
>
> (206)

Bon's son, Charles Etienne St. Valery Bon, also wears "expensive esoteric Fauntleroy clothing" (157)[4] which aligns him, his mother, his father, and the French architect on one side of a divide, but not exclusively a racial one. It is also an urban/rural divide between these cosmopolitan, multicultural, and fashionable types, on the one hand, and the uncultured, provincial Sutpens and Coldfields, on the other.

Judith's clothes are most often described as "shapeless" calico, often paired with a faded bonnet (151, 157, 163), while Bon's octoroon mistress/wife wears fashionable clothes, even when dressing the part of the grieving widow in "new lace and silk and satin negligees subdued to the mauve and lilac of mourning" (157). When she too passes away and Clytie brings the young Charles Etienne St. Valery Bon back to Sutpen's Hundred, she intuits that changing his dress is a necessary aspect to make the boy one of them, perhaps even sufficient on its own. Upon arriving back in Mississippi, Clytie has already covered his fashionable clothes with rustic overalls, symbolically burying his former self in the garb of a new identity: "the boy of twelve now and looking ten, in one of the outgrown Fauntleroy suits but with a new oversize overall jumper coat which Clytie had bought for him (and made him wear, whether against the cold or whether not your grandfather could not say either) over it" (159). Part of the motivation for this change—or at least part of the effect—is racial in nature, as his new clothing immediately aligns him with blackness, as well

---

[4] Frances Hodgson Burnett's popular children's novel *Little Lord Fauntleroy* (1886) kicked off fashion fads in both Europe and, especially, the United States based on the descriptions of children's clothing in the text and the accompanying illustrations by Reginald Birch. Dorothy and Saxe Commins actually called Faulkner (at least among themselves) "Little Lord Fauntleroy" (204, 217, 218), as related in her memoir *What Is an Editor? Saxe Commins at Work*.

as ruralness: "the delicate garments of his pagehood already half concealed beneath that harsh and shapeless denim cut to an iron pattern and sold by the millions—that burlesque uniform and regalia of the tragic burlesque of the sons of Ham" (159-60). Uniforms often "give an indication of economic worth or status" (Barnard 64), though in this case class and race are bound up together, as the new clothing is necessary to signal Bon's status as both economically and racially subservient. This clothing change is important not only as a reflection of Bon's new status, but as a way of creating that new reality, as Barnard explains:

> [I]t is not the case that there is already in existence a society with different cultural groups, who are already in positions of relative power, who then use fashion, clothing and dress to express or reflect those positions. Fashion, clothing and dress are signifying practices, they are ways of generating meanings, which produce and reproduce those cultural groups along with their positions of relative power.
>
> (38)

Barnard is essentially describing clothing's role as an actant in helping to shape the identity of individuals, as we have seen to varying degrees with Christmas, Grimm, and Hightower in *Light in August*. Here, whether intentionally or not, Clytie reinforces the hegemony of whiteness by neutralizing the transgressive potential of Bon's mixed race by placing him in his "natural" subservient racial category by means of a visible uniform or costume. Indeed, Bon's demeanor and sense of self seem to shift dramatically after his move (though the novel does not narrate much of what happens to him nor why).

The "half concealed" outfit of his youth suggests the interplay of exterior and interior, just as the coldness and impassivity of his new guardians are reflected in "that gaunt and barren household where his very silken remaining clothes, his delicate shirt and stockings and shoes which still remained to remind him of what he had once been, vanished, fled from arms and body and legs as if they had been woven of chimaeras or of smoke" (160). Years later, he seems to cling to his former identity, even as he accepts his fate, living sequestered in the attic and occasionally donning his former clothes, "the rags and silks of broadcloth in which he had arrived," and looking at himself in a "shard of broken mirror … in the delicate and outgrown tatters in which he perhaps could not even remember himself" (162). Bon's broken sense of self leaves him clinging to bits of his old clothing and identity, as if they still contain some of who he once was. In fact, Faulkner hints at that being the case when the French architect uses clothing to give Sutpen's pursuing hounds the slip:

> [T]hey had to drag the dogs away from the tree, but especially away from the sapling pole with the architect's suspenders tied to it, as if it was not only that the pole was the last thing the architect had touched but it was the thing his exultation had touched when he saw another chance to elude them, and so it was not only the man but the exultation too which the dogs smelled that made them wild.
>
> (196–7)

Something of the architect himself is embodied in the suspenders, and the dogs sense this in a very real way, refusing to leave the spot. Bayard's embrace of his dead brother's coat in *Flags in the Dust* and Hightower's obsession with his father's coat in *Light in August* convey this same idea, which also helps explain Bon's clinging to the tattered remains of his former dress and former life. The symbolism of the garments is powerful, but there is also something concrete in the objects themselves that affects these people.

The degrading of the younger Bon's clothing and reshaping or fragmenting of his identity parallels the degeneration of the Sutpen line over time. There is change rather than the stasis described above, but it is decay rather than growth. The elder Bon's clothing is described much like his son's, walking around in a "slightly Frenchified cloak and hat … reclining in a flowered, almost feminised gown" (76). It is the indeterminacy of race and gender identity reflected in the clothing that becomes so threatening. The linking of blackness and femininity here is similar to that in *Light in August* where Christmas identifies both with weakness that he must purge from himself. In both novels, the liminal threat must ultimately be contained and put in its place in order to reaffirm hegemonic discourses of race and gender, reinforcing Davis's point about white fears of racial hybridity (146). Bon's urbane clothing and elegant mannerisms dazzle Henry and other students at the University of Mississippi who "aped his clothing and manner and (to the extent which they were able) his very manner of living" (76). Although we are told multiple times that Henry imitates Bon in superficial ways (81, 85, 254), we never actually see Henry changing his style of dress because clothing is not superficial. Instead, a stubborn resistance to change defines both Henry and Bon. Bon would rather die than change his mind about forcing Henry's hand, even stubbornly suggesting that if Henry will simply say he wants Bon to go to Judith, then he will not go through with it (275). Henry, too, would rather murder his brother than seek a solution or confront Bon and his father directly, a stubbornness that Mr. Compson detects when he imagines Henry resisting the truth of Bon's identity: "*I will believe; I will. I will. Even if it is so, even if what my father told me is true and which, in spite of myself, I cannot keep from knowing is true, I will still believe*" (72). Unyielding in their choices, Henry kills Bon, effectively ruining the lives of at least half a dozen people in the process.

Ultimately, the recurring imagery of scraps and rags is perhaps what best defines the legacies of the ruined Sutpens and the defeated South, the tattered remains of once-glorious plans.[5] Judith and Clytie make the former's wedding dress from "rags and scraps" (81), while Rosa attempts to sew garments "for her niece's trousseau," scrounging bits of cloth stolen from her father's store to make "intimate young girl garments" though she sadly has no experience with such things thanks to her neglected upbringing: "you can imagine too what Miss Rosa's notion of such garments would be, let alone what her notion of them would look like when she had finished them unassisted" (61). Oddly, Mr. Compson links Rosa's sewing of these garments to the Civil War:

> [S]ewing tediously and without skill on the garments ... whipping lace out of ravelled and hoarded string and thread and sewing it onto garments while news came of Lincoln's election and of the fall of Sumpter and she scarce listening, hearing and losing the knell and doom of her native land between two tedious and clumsy stitches on a garment which she would never wear and never remove for a man who she was not even to see alive.
>
> (61)

This connection gains some clarity with the revelation that the Sartoris women have sewn a regimental battle flag out of silk dresses (63), riding around the state to allow "the sweetheart of each man in the company" to add a few stitches to the flag (98). With both the flag and the poorly made garments, we see people trying desperately to stitch together an identity—on both personal and national levels—but the efforts are doomed to fail: cheap articles made with stolen goods and stitched together with no skill for no good purpose. At the end of the war, Henry kills Bon and runs upstairs to find Judith clad only in her unfinished wedding dress and Rosa's clumsily sewn undergarments made from flour sacks

---

[5] Besides the passages discussed, other images of scraps and rags of clothing occur on pages 61, 63, 82, 105, 108, 162, and 206.

and curtains (108, 139). These images give new meaning to Sutpen pontificating about destiny and fate:

> [H]e said how he thought how there was something about a man's destiny (or about the man) that caused the destiny to shape itself to him like his clothes did, like the same coat that new might have fitted a thousand men, yet after one man has worn it for a while it fits no one else and you can tell it anywhere you see it even if all you see is a sleeve or a lapel.
>
> (198)

By the end, Sutpen and the South have come undone, victims of their own poor construction, reduced to rags and scraps of a vainglorious vision.

Go Down, Moses

Go Down, Moses opens with a hunt that is more performance than actual pursuit, and the participants dress in costume to play their roles, Tomey's Turl, the not-quite white half McCaslin brother donning "his Sunday shirt that was supposed to be white but wasn't quite either, that he put on every time he ran away just as Uncle Buck put on his necktie each time he went to bring him back" (29). These references point toward the performative nature of all the action of "Was," and if this hunt is largely social theater or playful game, then we might also question just how natural the other hunting scenes are in the novel. The opening pursuit of Tomey's Turl takes on a farcical quality as the dogs tracking the scent of his coat are so friendly with their quarry that they allow themselves to be locked in a cottonhouse (17), while the hunters make bets about how and when they will catch Tomey's Turl this time. Of course, the hunt turns out to be more of a courting ritual with Tomey's Turl and Sophonsiba Beauchamp both in pursuit of a spouse. Sophonsiba also dons a faintly ludicrous plantation mistress costume, pretentiously dressed up to convey glamor and nobility where there is none, just as she insists on calling her spartan Mississippi farm Warwick to intimate the family's supposed connections to English aristocracy: "Her hair was roached under a lace cap; she had on her Sunday dress and beads and a red ribbon around her throat and a little nigger girl carrying her fan" (12).

All three characters use clothing to redefine and reinvent themselves, and Davis argues that this is liberating for Tomey's Turl since the playful, sporting nature of the activities in "Was" allows for "freedom from the normal social order and its dehumanizing boundaries" (45–6). As Davis says, Tomey's Turl dressing "white" (and appearing white) reveals the "porous nature of racial barriers and caste, class, and economic boundaries" by transforming the wearer into a "gentleman" who looks like his sibling Buck: "Turl announces that a different set of rules are in motion from those that obtain while he remains on the McCaslin place" (53–4). The clothing change is integral to the shift in identity and agency that Tomey's Turl undergoes on the excursion to Warwick, and Davis points out that Buck, too, changes when he dons his necktie: "Buck's tie and Turl's white shirt become more than articles of clothing; they are signifiers of the social status, economic worth, and gender identity of the two men" (54). Davis also essentially argues that clothes are actants in "Was," aiding Tomey's Turl in his acts of resistance to the confining ideologies of race: "In their disguises, they become different men acting outside of their typical social and cultural realities. Producing through clothing an image of himself that is different from his everyday, asexual, subjugated self, Tomey's Turl suspends the boundaries and codes of that life and rewrites the script for the black male body" (54). This function of clothing is similar to what we have already seen in relation to Deacon, as well as to the self-definition of characters like Lucas and Butch Beauchamp. For each, clothing is important in terms of asserting a masculine gender identity in addition to the racial meanings, and although Buck's tie also asserts a particular masculine authority, it is different for Tomey's Turl since, as Davis says, the male slave's masculinity "is a buried and less accessible marker of his identity" (12). While Buck's tie may ornament his already acknowledged masculinity, Turl's clothing must act to bring forth what is buried and denied by his culture.

At other points in *Go Down, Moses*, clothes act more as markers of hierarchy instead of actants of transformation. In most of the hunting scenes at Major de Spain's camp, clothing is hardly mentioned at all, a technique that lends an aura of equality to the hunters, as if tracking and shooting abilities are all that matter in the wilderness. As I have argued elsewhere, this natural and egalitarian space in the woods is a pastoral pose that Faulkner questions and subverts (*Clear-Cutting Eden* 150–1). The Black cook Ash, for instance, is always stuck in the kitchen and cleaning, begging for one opportunity to actually hunt (308). When local swampers show up to watch the hunt for Old Ben, clothing suddenly takes on importance for demarcating these poor whites' social position, their "clothes but little better than Sam Fathers' and nowhere near as good as Tennie's Jim's" (210), including "their worn hats and hunting coats and overalls which any town negro would have thrown away or burned" (224). As Davis notes, whiteness is an unstable category that must be reinscribed, but here the white men's garments threaten to reveal the arbitrary and permeable nature of the color boundary. These poor white swampers are, in a sense, doing whiteness wrong, an example of what Jay Watson calls the misperformance "of social subjects or groups that don't seem to get their whiteness right" (xv). This quote comes from the introduction to *Faulkner and Whiteness*, a collection that emphasizes a "performance-based approach to whiteness" (xvi), and this scene from *Go Down, Moses* shows how even in the wilderness, clothing is being used to perform whiteness and demarcate proper whites from white trash who misperform their racial identity. Even the better clothing of the principal hunters shifts in meaning when the context is altered on Ike and Boon's trip to Memphis for whiskey:

> It was as if the high buildings and the hard pavements, the fine carriages and the horse cars and the men in starched collars and neckties made their boots and khaki look a little rougher and a little muddier and made Boon's beard look worse and more unshaven and his face look more and more like he should never have brought it out of the woods at all.
>
> (218–19)

Placed in a new setting, the men and their clothing appear as uncouth rubes instead of mythical woodsmen in a majestic drama, and their appearance even threatens their white identity. The costumes, the setting, and the characters all help Ike maintain his pastoral fantasy of untainted wilderness which results only in his beloved Big Woods being sold off to a lumber company and cleared for profit. Before his last trip to the hunting cabin, Ike visits Major de Spain in his office, "the short plumpish gray-haired man in sober fine broadcloth and an immaculate glazed shirt whom he was used to seeing in boots and muddy corduroy" (302). The hunting clothes have fooled Ike and allowed him to sustain his belief in an unchanging natural world beyond the reach of crass capitalism, but de Spain's dress in his office drives home the fact that he is a businessman more interested in profit than mystical communion with spirit animals. Juxtaposed with Tomey's Turl's use of clothing to reconstitute himself "as empowered to act and to be a subject" (Davis 45), these incidents emphasize the work and intentional effort of Turl to resist his confinement. Simply changing outfits is not enough.

Clothing also flatters to deceive in the more comical episode of Lucas Beauchamp and the metal detector salesman. The urban salesman assumes his urbane bearing reflects an interior difference between himself and Lucas. Like a trickster figure, Lucas uses the presumptions of his adversary against him, rejecting the authority of his white skin and fancy clothes: "He was young, not yet thirty, with the assurance, the slightly soiled snap and dash, of his calling, and a white man. Yet he even stopped talking and looked at the negro in battered overalls who stood looking down at him not only with dignity but with command" (76). Similar to the previous examples, the supposedly simple pastoral haven turns out to be much more complex than the outer appearance would suggest, and the young salesman's internal defeat is registered in his clothing: "the dashing city hat crumpled beneath his cheek, his necktie wrenched sideways in the collar of his soiled white shirt, his muddy trousers rolled to his knees, the brightly polished shoes of yesterday now two shapeless lumps of caked mud" (86). Ultimately swindling the salesman into renting his own metal detector, Lucas effects a telling costume change once his victory is complete and he no longer needs to play the role of a simple Black farmer in battered overalls: "in threadbare mohair trousers such as Grover Cleveland or President Taft might have worn in the summertime, a white stiff-bosomed collarless shirt beneath a pique vest yellow with age and looped across by a heavy gold watchchain, and the sixty-dollar handmade beaver hat which Edmonds' grandfather had given him fifty years ago" (94). This episode connects Lucas to Tomey's Turl, who, it must be remembered, is Lucas's father, in the way that Lucas harnesses the power of clothing, using it rather than being acted on by it, causing the salesman to alter his thoughts and actions because of what he thinks he sees in front of him. The metal detector affair illustrates what Ringo means in *The Unvanquished* when he suggests and dismisses to Bayard the idea of killing Redmond to avenge Colonel Sartoris's death: "But I reckon that wouldn't suit that white skin you walks around in" (218). Skin color, in a very real sense, is like clothing: it is a performative outer façade that creates a certain persona for the wearer and certain expectations for others that may not accurately reflect the inner person.

Just as the salesman's nice clothes and white skin fail to protect him, other characters exemplify the protective element of dress. The removal of clothing, as seen in other chapters, indicates vulnerability, and in *Go Down, Moses* we see this when Buck undresses in Sophonsiba's bedroom (21) and when Ike's wife undresses in front of him for the first and only time (298–9). Both examples involve dropping one's guard, lowering protective barriers resulting in intimacy with another person. We see Ike do something similar when he relinquishes the compass, watch, and gun in a bid to demonstrate his vulnerability and to commune with another creature, Old Ben the bear. Although these items are not clothing, their power as actants means that Ike must discard them in order to strip down to his essence and be able to truly see another living creature. Rider conveys a similar vulnerability in "Pantaloon in Black" when he briefly returns to work through his grief at the sawmill: "stripped to the waist now, the shirt removed and the overalls knotted about his hips by the suspender straps, his upper body bare except for the handkerchief about his neck and the cap clapped and clinging somehow over his right ear" (137). Later that night, Rider displays clothing's power to conceal when he uses a razor hidden inside his shirt to kill the crooked nightwatchman Birdsong. Finally, "Pantaloon" also exhibits the power of clothing as a thing. The story's opening line emphasizes the chain of physical connection from Mannie to clothing to Rider: "He stood in the worn, faded clean overalls which Mannie herself had washed only a week ago, and heard the first clod strike the pine box" (129). The overalls are like the coats that Bayard and Hightower use in an attempt to connect with the dead, as well as the scraps of cloth and self that Charles Etienne Bon clings to, and the narrator of "Pantaloon" voices the feeling of a remnant left behind: "the dead who either will not or cannot quit the earth yet although the flesh they once lived in has been returned to it" (130). The overalls that Mannie handled and cleaned contain actual traces of her, faint though they may be, just like her footprints in the dust that Rider knows are still there and provide a real, if ghostly, trace of her:

> [T]he pale, powder-light, powder-dry dust of August from which the long week's marks of hoof and wheel had been blotted by the strolling and unhurried Sunday shoes, with somewhere beneath them, vanished but not gone, fixed and held in the annealing dust, the narrow, splay-toed prints of his wife's bare feet where on Saturday afternoons she would walk to the commissary to buy their next week's supplies while he took his bath ... his body breasting the air her body had vacated, his eyes touching the objects—post and tree and field and house and hill—her eyes had lost.
>
> (131)

Just as Bayard burns his brother's coat because the object brings more suffering than comfort, so Rider destroys his own life unable to bear the absence of his loved one.

Throughout "Pantaloon" there is an opposition between physical objects and abstract emotions/ideas. The loss of Mannie's physical presence and the anguish caused by the physical remainders cause the emotional and psychic suffering that prompts Rider to forfeit his own life. The physical is given primacy by the narrative, as Rider seeks to use physical feats using the objects of the log and the razor to somehow compensate for the loss of Mannie's physical being. The memory of her simply will not do. This connects "Pantaloon" to the rest of *Go Down, Moses* as Ike unconvincingly tries to suggest the primacy of abstract ideas over physical reality when he indignantly rejects his inheritance to take a supposedly principled stand. He fails to see that his abstract principles do nothing to materially help actual people like Fonsiba and Roth's mistress, the unnamed granddaughter of Tennie's Jim and the great granddaughter of Tomey's Turl.

The cotton that is grown on the McCaslin-Edmonds plantation is sent to be turned into textiles and clothing, the same clothing sold in the commissary store. In this sense, clothing is implicated in the history of slavery, oppression, and racism that defines the world of *Go Down, Moses*. The worldwide demand for cotton drives the exploitative economic engine that keeps first slaves and then sharecroppers and tenant farmers in thrall to the plantation: "the whirling wheels which manufactured for a profit the pristine replacements of the shackles and shoddy garments as they wore out and spun the cotton and made the gins which ginned it and the cars and ships which hauled it" (270). According to Gene Dattel's *Cotton and Race in the Making of America*, cotton was "America's most important foreign export from 1803 to 1937," and it was always an industry "characterized by a racial caste system" (293, 294). As the demand for cotton clothing grew throughout the nineteenth and early twentieth centuries, more and more laborers were shackled to this global industry. While 8.6 million acres in the United States were dedicated to cotton in 1870, that number had grown to almost 46 million in 1925 (296). In Mississippi 92 percent of farms in the Delta in 1910 were operated by tenants, and on those farms 95 percent of the tenants were Black (322). Despite the continued use of traditional farming techniques in Mississippi well into the twentieth century, the technological innovations throughout the global cotton and textile industries meant that objects were increasingly exerting influence over these poor farmers' lives: "Although we may not wish to acknowledge it, the cotton boom was a perfect example of how machines and technology control human destiny" (30). The economic significance of cotton needed for an ever-expanding clothing market thus keeps Black farming families tied to the land and its crop, even forcing them to buy back the products of their labor when it returns in garment form to the commissary store: "the cheap durable shirts and jeans and shoes and now and then a coat against the rain and cold" (*Go Down, Moses* 253). The ledgers that Ike reads reveal the plantation to be one of Timothy Morton's hyperobjects referenced in the Introduction:

> [A] whole land in miniature, which multiplied and compounded was the entire South … that slow trickle of molasses and meal and meat, of shoes and straw hats and overalls, of plowlines and collars and heel-bolts and buckheads and clevises, which returned each fall as cotton—the two threads frail as truth and impalpable as equators yet cable-strong to bind for life them who made the cotton to the land their sweat fell on.
>
> (279)

The importance of objects of clothing is central to the entire system. Demand for garments fuels demand for cotton, and market pressures to keep both of these things as cheap as possible help create an oppressive, exploitative labor system with human victims.

While Lucas resists the institutionalized racism that he lives under and Roth's mistress and child offer a hopeful alternative to historical segregation, a more rebellious figure emerges at the very end of the novel: Samuel Worsham "Butch" Beauchamp, the great-grandson of Tomey's Turl. He is banished from the McCaslin-Edmonds plantation, joins the Great Migration to Chicago, and is convicted of killing a policeman and sentenced to death. Butch follows a similar path to that of Joby Strother who, we are told in "There Was a Queen," has left Jefferson and "gone to Memphis to wear fine clothes on Beale Street" (727) and of TP Gibson, who, according to "Appendix: Compson 1699–1845," also makes it to Beale Street wearing "the fine bright cheap intransigent clothes manufactured specifically for him by the owners of Chicago and New York sweatshops" (270). Leaving rural Mississippi, each gains a degree of agency and modernity they were previously denied. Nonetheless, the cotton in his outfit, as well as its "fawn" color, links Butch back to the land of his birth and the other stories of *Go Down, Moses*. Dattel details the slow demise of cotton as an industry in the first half of the twentieth century as market forces and technological changes severed the cable-strong ties that yoked Black workers to cotton farms. Butch, kicked off the McCaslin-Edmonds plantation, evokes the plight of many displaced and suddenly adrift Black Southerners: "The displacement of workers changed the labor dynamic. No longer did white cotton planters need blacks as laborers; they were jettisoned without even a nod to paternalism" (Dattel 360). Moving north to Chicago, Butch becomes a consumer of cotton rather than a laborer working under slave-like conditions to produce it. While his freedom and defiance seem better than the plight of many who remained, his incarceration and death also arguably mark him as another victim: "The reign of King Cotton as an economic juggernaut ended, but its ugly human legacy remains among a great many Black citizens who are unprepared to function effectively in the modern world" (361).

When questioned by a census worker in his jail cell, Beauchamp answers sardonically "in a voice which was anything under the sun but a southern voice or even a negro voice" (351), suggesting how much he has rejected his adolescent identity as rural, Southern, Black farm worker. Wearing "fine Hollywood clothes and a pair of shoes better than the census-taker would ever own," he tells the white questioner that his occupation has been "getting rich too fast" (352). His outfit is likely a zoot suit, a cutting-edge item of fashion at the time: "He wore one of those sports costumes called ensembles in the men's shop advertisements, shirt and trousers matching and cut from the same fawn-colored flannel, and they had cost too much and were draped too much, with too many pleats" (351). Zoot suits were associated with "young urban Black and Hispanic males who were fascinated by jazz music" (Walford 84), and Elizabeth Wilson explains that zoot suits connoted a sense of rebellion and racial protest: "The zoot suit is an especially clear example of a symbolic counter-cultural style that caused a moral panic and led to actual violence in the streets. The zoot suit was defiance, a statement of ethnic pride and a refusal of subservience" (198). In June 1943, one year after the publication of *Go Down, Moses*, there were week-long "Zoot Suit Riots" on the West Coast ignited by Black and Latino youths wearing zoot suits which servicemen thought flouted both racial hierarchies and rationing regulations, and so they retaliated by cutting off the offending youths' hair and clothing (Walford 89, Wilson 198, Baker 44). Butch Beauchamp's clothing indicates simultaneously his membership in a youth subculture, a Black subculture, and an urban subculture—a rejection of traditional white authority in the rural Jim Crow South, though also a rejection of allegiance to the United States, especially in the eyes of the soldiers who initiated the riots: "Instead of fighting for America and democracy, the youths chose to hang around on city streets, flaunting their indifference to the war effort by wearing clothing that outrageously broke the newly introduced rationing regulations" (White and White 249). Butch has less in common with his grandfather Lucas than he does with Malcolm X, both in attitude and style, who describes in his autobiography his transformation into his "Detroit Red" persona in 1942, wearing a "sharkskin-gray 'Cab Calloway' zoot suit, the long, narrow, knob-toed shoes, and the four-inch-brimmed pear-gray hat over my conked fire-red hair: it was just about too much" (89). Malcolm X uses the same phrase, "too much," that Faulkner uses repeatedly in reference to Butch's clothing (351), but the meaning is not quite the same.

The white perspective in *Go Down, Moses* judges his clothes as "too much" in a derogatory sense, applying white notions of propriety, aesthetics, and style to his outfit, while Malcolm X uses the term to connote a positive outlandishness to an intentionally performative and over-the-top style. As discussed at the beginning of the chapter, Faulkner sees Black people and clothing in limited ways, very often only when they loudly deviate from white norms. Davis argues that "Faulkner can only envision Butch Beauchamp as the bad seed of a bad father, who must be punished for leaving the south and transgressing its political economy and arbitrary morality" (232). Butch uses his flashy clothing to demand recognition and assert his value, or as Davis puts it, "His flashy clothing is a marker of his individual and racial visibility, and a sign of his reclaiming his body and expressive culture as his own" (223). If Davis is right that Faulkner is unable to imagine a future for Butch in the South and "exploits Butch's failed migration as an opportunity to celebrate traditional ties of blacks to the South and to create an elegy to the old paternalistic virtues" (236), he also exposes how the South has failed to allow for Black men to become fully modern subjects and citizens, so constricting their lives and opportunities that they must either lash out or flee—or both, as Butch does. His clothing both facilitates and symbolizes his transgression, so it is sadly fitting that his executioners shave his fashionable hairdo and cut his zoot suit from his body before taking him to his death (352). The other descendant of Tomey's Turl at the novel's end is Roth Edmonds's unnamed mistress, and she, like Butch, speaks and embodies Turl's original acts of rebellion and agency. Wearing "a man's hat and a man's slicker and rubber boots" (339), she intrudes on the masculine domain of the hunting camp and perhaps succeeds where Butch fails. She rejects the "old paternalistic virtues" now embodied by Uncle Ike, and she and her child will continue to live on their own terms. She is able to speak not only for Tomey's Turl, but also for the silenced Tomasina, and in the process, as Davis argues, "[S]he transfigures her lineage from the paternal past (the law of the father) into the maternal present" (226).

Intruder in the Dust

When Lucas reappears in Faulkner's next novel, *Intruder in the Dust*, published six years after *Go Down, Moses*, his clothing is integral to his racial identity. Whereas in *Go Down, Moses*, Lucas repeatedly uses his connection to his white grandfather, L. Q. C. McCaslin, to assert his equality to or superiority over the Edmonds, female-descended line, in the latter novel Chick Mallison repeatedly links Lucas's dress to his own grandfather:

> a broad pale felt hat such as his grandfather had used to wear (6);

> a gold toothpick such as his grandfather had used: and the hat was a worn handmade beaver such as his grandfather had paid thirty and forty dollars apiece for (12);

> the boiled white shirt of his own grandfather's time ... and the gold toothpick like the one his own grandfather had carried in his upper vest pocket
>
> (24)

All of these references early in the novel establish the racial conflict at the heart of the narrative stemming from the opinion of Jefferson's white community that Lucas is not properly deferential: "We got to make him be a nigger first. He's got to admit he's a nigger. Then maybe we will accept him as he seems to intend to be accepted" (18). The insinuation through clothing that Lucas might be the equal of Judge Stevens, and therefore all white men, is also a reminder of Lucas's racial hybridity.[6] Davis makes a similar point about Lucas in *Go Down, Moses* acquiring equality with white people through a nonhuman thing, a marriage contract. This document is a sign of freedom, manhood, and equality under the law, and objects of clothing function similarly in this later novel. In contrast to *Go Down, Moses*, the physical and abstract are brought together in *Intruder in the Dust*, with justice prevailing to save the physical body of a Black man, as Faulkner moves from Ike McCaslin's "principled" withdrawal from the world to protest injustice to Chick's decision to do something about it.

There is a narrow range of roles that Black men are expected to play, and Lucas's failure to conform puts his life in danger. His connections to whiteness

---

[6] Chick also compares Miss Habersham's black hat to what "his grandmother had used to wear" (73). Her connection to the grandmother and Lucas's to the grandfather strengthens the case for his equality with white people through clothing—and not poor whites. The few other mentions of Miss Habersham's clothing in the novel emphasize her bespoke gloves from New York up to $40 a pair (75) and her "flat-heeled thirty dollar shoes" (217).

make him more of a threat in the eyes of whites, and Chick's repeated comparisons to his grandfather help explain why he sees this Black man as an authority figure who deserves his help. The comparison to a grandfather might potentially negate his threat, to return to Ibrahim's point about blackness being figured as extremely old or infantile, but Lucas's use of clothing counters the positioning of him as elderly and ineffectual. Not only Lucas's behavior, but his choice of raiment is part of the problem, a failure to dress the part in which white people have cast him, threatening to expose "the porous nature of racial barriers" (54), to use Davis's phrase:

> [Lucas visits the Square] on weekdays like the white men who were not farmers but planters, who wore neckties and vests like the merchants and doctors and lawyers themselves, as if he refused, declined to accept even that little of the pattern not only of Negro but of country Negro behavior, and always in the worn brushed obviously once-expensive black broadcloth suit of the portrait-photograph on the gold easel and the raked fine hat and the boiled white shirt of his own grandfather's time and the tieless collar and the heavy watch-chain and the gold toothpick.
>
> (24)

When Lucas is initially arrested and brought to jail, the protective nature of his defiant clothing is revealed when his hat falls to the ground as he emerges from Sheriff Hope Hampton's car and Chick realizes that the people gathered to watch "were probably the only white people in the county who had ever seen him uncovered" (43). The use of the word "uncovered" here suggests Lucas's vulnerability to both the white-dominated justice system and the extra-judicial lynch mob gathering on the Square. When the sheriff returns his hat, the item seems to take on agency and an almost totem-like significance: "in a motion not quite sweeping he set the hat back on his head at the old angle which the hat itself seemed to assume" (43). The gathered crowd does not take kindly to this moment nor to Lucas walking "erect now" (43), seemingly unafraid of vigilante justice, and they yell at the sheriff, "Knock it off again, Hope. Take his head too this time" (44). Lucas remains defiant, though not confrontational, "looking not at them but just toward them" as he strides into the jail, "the hat arrogant and pale in the sunlight" (44). Recalling Brevda's psycho-sexual reading of hats in *Sanctuary* underscores why the white crowd might feel so threatened at this Black man's hat cocked at a provocative angle.

Lucas's hat is not the only nor the most important clothing that operates as an actant. In fact, Chick's clothing is, in a sense, responsible for all of the events in the novel. In the tale's opening scenes, Chick falls into an icy creek while hunting with Aleck Sander, and Lucas helps pull him out before bringing Chick to his cabin and warming him in front of the fire.[7] The fall into the creek literally upends the white-Black relationship, putting a white male at the mercy of a Black male and destabilizing by making fluid the traditional Southern racial binary. Chick's clothes are "like soft cold lead which he didn't move in but seemed rather to mount into like a poncho or a tarpaulin" (6). These altered, frozen garments must be removed, and in his now vulnerable state (without his protective layers), Chick feels the smell of the quilt—"that unmistakable odor of Negros"—envelope him "like a cocoon" and permeate his very being so that "it would be four years more before he would realise the extent of its ramifications and what it had done to him" (11). This unnerving change effected by an object he only dimly senses in the moment and his naked feeling of exposure result in his trying to combat his sudden vulnerability by clumsily attempting to pay for his food and hospitality, boorishly dumping the coins on the floor when Lucas does not take them. This error in judgment haunts Chick throughout the novel, one that he returns to in his mind over and over; it is the catalyst for everything he does afterward, the frozen clothing setting in motion the chain of events that culminates with Lucas's acquittal. Acknowledging that a nonhuman object is an actant does not minimize the importance of choices and actions of humans, like Chick and Miss Habersham, but I want to emphasize the significant effects of nonhuman things on the events of the novel. Chick's uncle, Gavin Stevens, says as much when he notes that Crawford Gowrie would have gotten away with the murder of his brother, but he was "foiled here by the fact that four years ago a child whose presence in the world he was not even aware of fell into a creek" (223).

This incident with the frozen clothes is an appropriate beginning for a novel in which objects and non-human things play significant roles. The coins and their insulting symbolic implication are tied directly to the clothes and the quilt, two objects that initiate Chick's decision. Guns are instrumental to both the murder and how it is solved, since Lucas's Colt pistol could not have been the gun that killed Vinson Gowrie while a First World War-era German luger—an object well-known to the whole county—matches the bullet wound. Horses, mules, and trucks (as well as their prints in the dirt) affect the actions of multiple

---

[7] Oddly, *The Town* includes a scene in which Aleck Sander jumps in an icy creek on a bet and has to remove his clothes and be warmed by the hunting coats of Chick and his other white playmates (56).

characters, and their use is dictated by two dead bodies, while pieces of lumber are the catalyst for the initial murder.

The ending of *Intruder in the Dust* shows progression from *Go Down, Moses* in Faulkner's world, with Butch Beauchamp's dead body replaced by Lucas Beauchamp's defiantly alive one. If the prospect of Butch Beauchamp in the South was "too difficult and upsetting for Faulkner to imagine" in *Go Down, Moses*, as Davis argues (255), then he seems more open to the idea in the post-Second World War landscape of *Intruder*. The rebelliousness of Butch's life and zoot suit, which seemed contained to far-off Chicago, have now arrived visibly in Yoknapatawpha County with Lucas's haughty defiance and Aleck Sander's "flash Saturday shirt and a pair of zoot pants" (232). Not only Aleck Sander, but the whole of the younger Black generation seems attuned to fashion and the meaning of clothes:

> [T]he young ones with straightened hair and makeup in the bright trig tomorrow's clothes from the mailorder houses who would not even put on the Harper's Bazaar caps and aprons until they were inside the white kitchens and the older ones in the ankle-length homemade calico and gingham who wore the long plain homemade aprons all the time so that they were no longer a symbol but a garment.
>
> (118)

Domestic help jobs may still be one of the only forms of employment, but this passage reveals a split between old and young, past and future, a harbinger of more changes to come. These changes in clothing style are certainly about the self-image of the wearers, but they can also affect that of the mostly white observers as well. A study published in 2020 in the *Journal of Social Psychology* found that clothing choices can either evoke or attenuate negative racial stereotypes toward Black men. A group of mostly white and female participants were able to counter their implicit biases when viewing photographs of Black men in more formal attire, while models wearing athletic uniforms or sweatpants and sweatshirts were both rated significantly lower for attributes like intelligence, trustworthiness, and warmth (Gurung et al.). Perhaps the much-remarked upon fact in Faulkner's novel that the gathered would-be lynch mob never actually attempts to kidnap, lynch, and murder Lucas can be explained by his somewhat formal, expensive clothing that complements his proud bearing. Arguably, clothing in more than one way actually saves his life.

Although the language of containment is not used in the same ways it is in relation to women's clothing and bodies, the importance of maintaining social boundaries of race is comparable in Faulkner's fiction. Similar to some of Faulkner's rebellious women, he creates multiple Black male characters who attempt to rewrite the script of their stifling cultural narratives, including Tomey's Turl, Lucas Beauchamp, Deacon, Charles Bon, and Butch Beauchamp. For each of them, clothing plays an integral role in making themselves visible to the dominant white culture and asserting their own agency, subjectivity, and manhood. Black women and their dress are almost entirely ignored by Faulkner, figuring most prominently in their connections to laundry. The drama of creating one's internal identity, and how clothing both reflects and helps forge that identity, is largely missing for Black characters, as Faulkner provides more of an onlooker's view, a white outsider's perspective. Thus, the emphasis is on the visibility of African American clothing, and how it does or does not conform to cultural racial boundaries. While race may at times be an element of the struggle for identity for white characters, it is always pertinent, if not dominant, for Black characters. In *Games of Property*, Davis cites the work of legal scholar Patricia J. Williams who, in *The Alchemy of Race and Rights*, describes slavery as based on a reductive "vision of blacks as simple-minded, strong-bodied economic 'actants'" (220), denying them their full range of potential humanity. Faulkner shows how Black Southerners are able to redefine themselves from less-than-human things to autonomous actors, partly by using the power of actual objects to act on other human subjects in ways that empower rather than dehumanize. The example of Lucas's and Mollie's marriage license is a succinct illustration because of the binding legal nature of the object, but clothing does similar work for, say, Lucas in *Intruder in the Dust* as his clothing and hat reinforce and legitimize the abstract qualities of dignity and equality he projects. In this way, the racial and gendered aspects of clothing do share some commonality: both Faulkner's female and Black characters use clothing to counter (or attempt to counter) their own relegation to the status of commodity or object.

3

Clothing and Class

In his discussion of how wealth confers honor on its possessor in *The Theory of the Leisure Class* (1899), Thorstein Veblen elucidates his famous concept of conspicuous consumption. While we might normally think of wealthy people, or the "leisure class" to use Veblen's term, parading the sidewalks in expensive furs or three-piece suits, Veblen argues that it "becomes incumbent upon all classes lower in the scale" to adopt the standards of those above them (84). Not only that, but conspicuous consumption works with working-class garments as well, and Veblen specifically notes how "uniforms, badges, and liveries" begin as marks of honorifics but become the opposite when associated primarily with menial labor (79–80). In this sense, the lower classes are motivated to dress more like the leisure class in order to demonstrate their belonging: "With the exception of the instinct of self-preservation, the propensity for emulation is probably the strongest and most alert and persistent of the economic motives proper" (110). Published just thirty years before *The Sound and the Fury*, many of the concepts in Veblen's best-known work play out in Faulkner's fictional fashions.

Veblen also links conspicuous consumption to gender, since as the wealth of a society progresses, women come to be seen as status symbols (148–9). The clothing of women and of household servants functions in the same way to confer prestige on their male heads of household: "In both there is a very elaborate show of unnecessary expensiveness, and in both cases there is also a notable disregard of the physical comfort of the wearer" (182). A fashionably dressed wife would, therefore, be better evidence of wealth and status for a husband than a less fashionable one, particularly since the changing whims of fashion make clothing a particularly wasteful and visible sign of wealth. Clothing, in fact, is the most significant of material goods for Veblen:

> [N]o line of consumption affords a more apt illustration than expenditure on dress. It is especially the rule of the conspicuous waste of goods that finds expression in dress ... [E]xpenditure on dress has this advantage over most

other methods, that our apparel is always in evidence and affords an indication of our pecuniary standing to all observers at the first glance.

(167)

Although Veblen's ideas first published in Faulkner's childhood are still useful for examining class and consumption in his fiction, one problem or limitation with Veblen's model of fashion is that it presumes a top-down structure; that is, he suggests that fashion originates with the leisure class who must constantly change styles when the lower classes begin to copy them so that they may reinscribe social boundaries visually. This model fails to account for the fact that American fashion trends also originate in the lower and middle classes (especially as the twentieth century goes on), while the increasing prevalence of popular media means that new fashions are often consumed by all levels of society at the same time, rather than simply trickling down from the upper to lower rungs. We see fashion influences moving in both directions in various Faulkner texts. Issues of class also intersect and interweave with gender and race in many instances, making neat divisions impossible, though I try to focus mainly on economic themes in this chapter. Faulkner's emphasis on class consciousness and class mobility as embodied in clothing runs through multiple texts, while issues of personal and social identity recur from previous chapters, and clothing acts on people in powerful ways. Richard Godden in particular has argued that Faulkner's focus shifts in his later novels away from race and toward class as his primary concern. It is useful to examine some of Faulkner's early works to see how these class concerns are being worked out prior to the late-career Snopes Trilogy.

Flags in the Dust

In *Flags in the Dust*, young Bayard Sartoris returns home from military service by train, as Faulkner did, but his actual combat experiences, especially witnessing the death of his twin brother in aerial combat, have left him empty and numb, exemplifying the Lost Generation who populate many novels of the time. Instead of being greeted at the rail depot as a returning hero, Bayard jumps off the slowing train and runs into the woods, foreshadowing his later retreat to the MacCallum's wilderness refuge. Simon, the Sartoris's Black servant, dressed up "in his linen duster and an ancient top-hat" (5), tells old Bayard that his grandson was not even wearing his military uniform when he leapt from the train "like a hobo," and he presciently wonders whether "dem war folks is done somethin' ter him" (7). Bayard's reluctance to wear his uniform indicates his guilt and shame at having failed to protect his brother Johnny in the war and for surviving when his brother did not. Multiple instances of false soldiers and fake uniforms reinforce young Bayard's imposter feelings and suggest a self-conscious mocking of Faulkner's own R.A.F. experiences, his own foolish "being taken in by a uniform," as Miss Jenny says (50–1). As discussed in the previous chapter with regards to race, sixteen-year-old Isom dons his uncle Caspey's war uniform to the "cold astonishment" of Miss Jenny (49). Isom as a "play soldier" (53) finds an echo in the blind musician outside Rogers's restaurant: "he too wore filthy khaki with a corporal's stripes on one sleeve and a crookedly-sewn Boy Scout emblem on the other, and on his breast a button commemorating the fourth Liberty Loan and a small metal brooch bearing two gold stars, obviously intended for female adornment. His weathered derby was encircled by an officer's hat cord" (118). Like Faulkner, the musician is an imposter in a fake uniform, the Boy Scout emblem seemingly a reference to the author's brief stint as a scoutmaster in 1924, and this notion of war veterans (real or fake) trying to elevate their status or class standing in a post-war society is also explored in the First World War short stories discussed below.

Horace Benbow, in "his clean, wretchedly-fitting khaki" (156), enjoys wearing the uniform he feels entitled to, and he is a bit insulted when his sister wants him to change out of it after picking him up at the depot (156). Soon enough he is dressed in a different sort of uniform, "flannels and a blue jacket with his Oxford club insignia embroidered on the pocket" (182), one that marks him as different from the Black veterans, common farmers, and county dwellers, whose clothing Faulkner uses to characterize them succinctly:

> [C]ountry people—men in overalls or corduroy or khaki and without neckties, women in shapeless calico and sunbonnets and snuff-sticks; groups of young girls in stiff mail-order finery, the young heritage of their bodies' grace dulled already by self-consciousness and labor and unaccustomed high heels and soon to be obscured forever by childbearing; youths and young men in cheap tasteless suits and shirts and caps, weather-tanned and clean-limbed as race horses and a little belligerently blatant.
>
> (118)

A group of African American people described earlier in this same paragraph has no commentary on dress at all, so Faulkner seems to intentionally call attention to the connection between class and clothing in this passage, pointedly ignoring clothing as a racial marker. The fact that only white people are designated by class distinction speaks to Faulkner's relative lack of insight into Black life discussed previously, as well as the economic oppression in Faulkner's Mississippi that squeezes all Black citizens into a lower economic bracket. The drab, predictable clothes augur drab, predictable lives—or are the clothes perhaps helping shape their destinies, locking the wearers into permanent roles so that neither their social betters nor they themselves can envision them as anything else? Warwick and Cavallaro apply Foucault's ideas about discipline and punishment to clothing to show how dress plays an important role in maintaining division between upper and lower classes: "From this perspective, society can be seen to be organized through clothing into a series of observable boundaries; those erected on the single body by separate items of dress, those existing between bodies, and those serving to distinguish groups of bodies from other groups" (78–9). This is the class divide that Flem Snopes seeks to bridge in *The Hamlet* and that Byron Snopes cannot cross in *Flags*, only managing to rob the bank and flee town, clutching an upper-class garment in the form of Narcissa's stolen underwear as he goes.

Surratt's "neat tieless blue shirt" (134) falls somewhere in between these two groups, and he relates that he swore to himself as a child "that I wouldn't never plant nothin' in the ground, soon's I could he'p myself" because his tenant farming family's labor never improved their socioeconomic position: "ever' time we made a furrow, we was scratchin' dirt fer somebody else" (137). Surratt dresses differently from his country customers who are beholden to the likes of the Sartorises, the de Spains, the first families of Yoknapatawpha, while he sells them sewing machines that might allow them to make their own clothes which might help them become someone else, to escape the destiny of their birth. This is not to say that the clothes necessarily exert a force on the wearer that traps them in a certain occupation or socioeconomic bracket. It may be, for instance, that those who feel destined (or doomed) to be farmers unconsciously select the uniform of the farmer in order to assert membership in a group. The meanings of dress, like literary texts, are not solely a function of the wearer or author, though. The disdain evident in the narrative voice in the above passage suggests how viewers interpret and assign meaning to clothes, and the perception of individuals by others certainly can limit or impact their socioeconomic successes and failures.

Fashion is always associated with the new, with change, and with the modern by its very nature. Warwick and Cavallaro point out how in each decade of the twentieth century, the rhetoric of fashion repeats the same tropes of reinvention, breaking with the past, unprecedented change, new freedom, etc. (105–7). Young Bayard Sartoris, especially, finds it nearly impossible to move on from the past, engaging in a series of self-destructive behaviors because of his feelings of guilt for his brother's death, as well as his more general post-traumatic stress from the war, what was then called shell shock. The Sartoris family as a whole is tied down by the past, and Faulkner paints a contrast between the modern country-club set and the old-timers for whom life barely changes, "the brisker urbanites weaving among their placid chewing unhaste" (161). Old men dressed in confederate gray lounge "unhurried" on the square where "the young men loafed also" (161), while the edges of the town sport a more modern feel, "definitely urban presently," with a movie theater, garages, and "small new shops with merchants in shirt-sleeves" (160). Harry Mitchell is a cotton speculator, working in the international market of cotton rather than the fields, and his modernity is exemplified by clothing that contrasts with the overalls of the farmers, "tight flannels and white silk shirt and new ornate sport shoes that cost twenty dollars per pair" (188). People like Harry play tennis, have tea, go to piano recitals, and wear fashionable clothing, all of which emphasize their modernity and separate them from the country farmers in overalls and shapeless calico or the men in Civil War uniforms pining idly for the past.

Young Bayard straddles this divide: he embraces the new technology of automobiles and airplanes, yet these become symbols for his desperate and futile attempts to outrun the past (like his search for solace in the timeless pastoral haven of the MacCallums). Besides cars and planes, other objects are also important as actants in Bayard's life. He opens a chest in his room late in the novel, an echo of Old Bayard's rusted chest that contains relics of the family past including what seems to be a wedding dress (88–9)[1]. Young Bayard's chest also contains clothing among its mementos, his brother's old hunting coat, which he "defiantly and deliberately" holds against his face, "its fading stale acridity drifting into his nostrils with an intimation of life and warmth. 'Johnny,' he whispered, 'Johnny'" (221). He literally breathes in particles of "what had once been blood" (221), and the coat provides both a literal and metaphorical connection to the past when his brother was alive, though it is also a reminder that his twin is gone forever. Peter Stallybrass writes of how clothing, particularly through smell, provides a connection across death "because cloth is able to carry

---

[1] Faulkner's description of this dress seems to indicate his familiarity with clothing and fabrics with its reference to "fine Mechlin" (88), which is a specific type of Flemish lace known for floral patterns, usually transparent and therefore worn over other clothes.

the absent body, memory, genealogy, as well as literal material value" (45). He details how Vladimir Nabokov, Philip Roth, and the poet Laurence Lerner each write about the powerful need to get rid of clothing that belonged to loved ones after their deaths, describing "the terror of the material trace ... because the trace seems empty, a reminder of all that has been lost ... There is an important sense in which the clothes *are* the pain" (40–1). Bayard takes the coat and other mementos from the chest, including a photograph of John, and burns them: "he laid the coat and the bible and the trophy and the photograph on the flames and prodded them and turned them until they were consumed" (222). The things themselves exert too much power over him, and it is both a symbolic purging of what they represent, but also, importantly, a need to destroy the physical objects that contain actual traces of his brother.

This incident connects to other moments across Faulkner's canon that highlight the power of clothing as object, but two in particular already discussed use the same idea of clothing's connection to a deceased loved one. Each of these examples relates more to gender than to class, which underscores the intersectionality of clothing as object. Rider's overalls that had been cleaned and handled by his dead wife Mannie and the frock coat of Hightower's father are powerful as physical things, although they also clearly have symbolic meanings. Faulkner's narratives, however, stress the importance of touching and smelling the clothing and how those actions generate physiological and mental responses which then significantly impact characters' actions. All three of these connections to the dead could also be related to sexual desire, illicit and unspeakable for Hightower and Bayard. Alfred J. López calls the coat of Hightower's father "[t]he trigger for Hightower's primal scene, the irreducible ground and pathogenic nucleus of all that troubles and besets him for the rest of his life ... [t]he very seed of Hightower's lifetime of psychic suffering" (62). López argues that Hightower's nauseous reaction to the garment links the incident to the novel's multiple examples of vomiting linked to "repressed sexual content" (63) and that his repressed homosexual and incestuous desires are channeled into the coat (66). As discussed below in relation to the First World War stories, John Duvall similarly argues that Johnny Sartoris experiences homoerotic and repressed homosexual desires, so that it is perhaps not a stretch to read Bayard's overwhelmed response to his brother's coat in comparable terms. Though López and Duvall make persuasive arguments, ultimately, it does not much affect my reading whether the desire in these examples is sexual and repressed or familial and open. The clothing as object is the conduit for that desire and quite literally replaces the person for the grieving person. Perhaps because articles of clothing are inherently transgressive—acting as both extensions of the body and shields of the body—these garments become a safer site for forbidden desire, one that allows the subject to deny the existence of the desire by projecting it onto the clothing instead. These three examples highlight the difference between the seeming triviality of things/objects/clothing as consumer goods (which Faulkner associates with the present/the future/the modern) versus the deep, psychic meaning of things/objects/clothing associated with the past and with people who are gone, compelling Rider, Hightower, and Bayard each to stoke and indulge their respective death wish to join the departed.

At the end of *Flags in the Dust*, Horace has moved to an unnamed new town, later identified as Kinston in the Mississippi Delta in *Sanctuary*, another novel whose modern characters are more fashionably dressed than those stuck in the past, as discussed in the Clothing and Gender chapter. This new town is the antithesis of the staid, tree-lined neighborhood in Jefferson that Horace has left behind, and it is defined by its relationship to things as consumer goods. The people have "chopped all the trees down and built themselves mile after mile of identical frame houses with garage to match," using their wealth to buy "cars and imported caviar and silk dresses and diamond watches" (373). This precursor to the suburban boom presages a modern world where the familial and personal relationships have been replaced by a devotion to material goods, a place where "the very air smelled of affluence and gasoline" (373). Young Bayard may not be cut out for such a world, and indeed many of Faulkner's men are not, especially those damaged by the war.

The First World War Stories

Faulkner's First World War stories capture the disillusionment, cynicism, and despair of the soldiers who make up the Lost Generation. The uniforms that so enthrall Lowe in *Soldiers' Pay* and Isom in *Flags in the Dust* are presented in these stories more as elaborate but meaningless costumes.[2] The opening lines

---

[2] Interestingly, Faulkner's Second World War stories, "Two Soldiers" and "Shall Not Perish," are devoid of any references to uniforms, despite their more overtly patriotic themes, perhaps indicating that Faulkner was not interested in exploring the hypocrisy of war and the sometimes-contradictory interior/exterior themes of his First World War stories in these later more sentimental tales originally published in *The Saturday Evening Post*.

of "Ad Astra," for instance, emphasize a loss of identity for Americans who, like Faulkner, have joined the British air force: "I dont know what we were ... we had started out Americans, but after three years, in our British tunics and British wings and here and there a ribbon, I dont suppose we had even bothered to wonder what we were, to think or to remember" (407). The clothing, the uniforms that are meant to mark a fixed identity, cannot overcome the existential lack of identity that consumes the soldiers. One of the pilots, Monaghan, has ripped off the identifiers of rank and achievement leaving "flapping" shoulder straps and holes "above his left pocket where his wings and ribbon had been" and this destruction reflects his inner lack: "'I'm not a soldier,' Monaghan said. 'I'm not a gentleman. I'm not anything ... I dont know what I am. I have been in this damn war for three years and all I know is, I'm not dead'" (414–15). Later, Monaghan clarifies that defacing his uniform is a disillusioned rejection of "all your goddamn twaddle about glory and gentlemen," and his drunken musings juxtaposing his father's manual labor with his own experiences at Yale and as an officer imply that he now sees as futile his attempts to rise socially and delude himself into thinking that in the war he was the equal of "them that owned the peat bogs" where his father used to work (416). Faulkner takes aim in these stories at the notion of war as a great societal equalizer that can enable upward mobility.

"Turnabout" opens with a description of the American Bogard's mismatched, hodge-podge uniform, as well as an emphasis on clothing's connection to military and social status. Bogard notices Claude Hope's "pea-coat buttoned awry and stained with recent mud, and upon his blond head, at that unmistakable and rakish swagger which no other people can ever approach or imitate, the cap of a Royal Naval Officer" (475–6) and later his "soiled silk muffler, embroidered with a club insignia which Bogard recognized to have come from a famous preparatory school" (481). As Zeitlin says of this story, an instantaneous glance "is sufficient for hyperalert, status-conscious men to size each other up on the basis of their respective 'insigne' of military rank and personal style, in keeping with the WWI tradition in which pilot-officer uniforms in all the major national services were always individually stylized and never in fact *uniform*" (*Aviation* 67). These insignia and clothing certainly represent status and position, but the war is making those things insignificant, even obsolete. They do not reveal the true courage and character of the men who wear them, just as the casual observers of these drunk soldiers assume they use their boats to "go back and forth fast when they forget napkins or something" ("Turnabout" 477), as if they are not real men, but "a male marine auxiliary to the Waacs" (481). Only by riding along with them is their true character revealed through action rather than appearance. The British seaman who rides with Bogard gains a new appreciation for aerial combat and bombing after a harrowing flight that ends with the men nearly being blown up by landing the plane without realizing an unreleased bomb is still clinging to the undercarriage. Bogard likewise understands the true heroism—foolhardy and suicidal though it may be—that the midshipmen exhibit every day on incredibly dangerous torpedo runs that leave them so drained and traumatized that they drink themselves into a stupor every night.

The class concerns in these stories are often tangled up with gender, and the masculinity issues raised about the boat crews by ignorant soldiers in "Turnabout" become more prominent in "All the Dead Pilots." Johnny Sartoris engages in a homosocial, if not outright homoerotic, battle with the English Captain Spoomer, an officer who has no flying experience and only achieved his rank through family connections. This idea that a family's class position outweighs performance in wartime relates directly to the concerns of "Victory," the story I will take up as an extended example below. Sartoris is emasculated by a woman in favor of a pilot with no combat experience (himself emasculated by that lack of war action and compensating through sexual conquest). Sartoris uses a garter to create a fake captain's insignia on a stolen captain's tunic and makes a corporal wear it while they box so he can fantasize about beating up Spoomer (514), a scene Duvall reads as part of the story's "symbolic equivalence of fighting and fornicating" ("Crying Game" 59). For Duvall, this homoeroticism continues from "Ad Astra," which reveals the "homoerotic element … integral to aerial combat" as Bayard lures German pilots with a decoy plane in order to ambush them and penetrate them "from the rear" with bullets (55). An incident in *The Town* recalls this moment, when Chick loans his hunting coat, "the best hunting coat in Jefferson" (57), to another boy to protect him from being penetrated from behind by the buck shot that Aleck Sander fires at the boy to satisfy a bet (57–8). In both cases, the hyper-masculine garments of the military uniform and the hunting coat afford protection against the potentially emasculating homoerotic feelings at play.

Sartoris's homoerotic fascination with Spoomer's clothing as stand-in for Spoomer the man continues in "All the Dead Pilots" when he goes to the woman's room knowing Spoomer is there with her. Instead of confronting the couple in flagrante delicto, he steals Spoomer's uniform and, on the way out, breaks the hand of a French corporal in a fight, making "the corporal scream like a woman" (525), feminizing him, Duvall says, before emasculating Spoomer with his own uniform ("Crying Game" 59). Dressing an unconscious ambulance driver in Spoomer's clothes (525), Sartoris forces Spoomer to return to the base dressed in "a woman's skirt and a knitted shawl" (527), an incident that sends Sartoris's rival scuttling back to England with his proverbial tail between his legs. It is as if shedding the uniform, with its inherent associations of traditional masculinity, allows Sartoris to reveal the less-than-masculine, even feminine "reality" underneath. The issues explored in these stories show how gender and sexuality overlap with class in Faulkner's uses of clothing. The ways that Sartoris's desire for Spoomer is mediated by a woman—and by clothing—aligns this early story with the later masterworks *The Sound and the Fury* (Quentin-Dalton Ames-Caddy) and *Absalom, Absalom!* (Henry-Judith-Charles Bon), as discussed in previous chapters.

I want to analyze more closely a final First World War story that dwells more extensively on the connections between clothing and class, "Victory." Originally published in the collection *These Thirteen* in 1931 and likely composed in the late 1920s, "Victory" develops many of the issues raised by the other war stories while also presaging Faulkner's later treatments of class and clothing in several novels. It is the story of Alec Gray, a Scotsman who eagerly enlists in the war, finds success on the battlefield, and then experiences a series of setbacks after the war until he is left destitute and homeless. Gray's refusal to return to his home and to his family profession of shipbuilding is tied by Faulkner to his burning ambition to improve his class standing. His taste of upper-class life as an officer proves too compelling for him to consider a return to his humble roots. Even while selling matches and begging for spare change on the streets at the story's end, Gray still dresses like a gentleman, maintains his waxed mustache, and employs a decorative walking stick, not unlike Faulkner himself at the time.[3]

Edmond Volpe speaks for many critics when he claims that the story was weakened when Faulkner removed a large portion of it to publish separately under the title "Crevasse," a story that Volpe considers the best of the First World War stories:

> Had Faulkner left in "Crevasse" there would have been good and convincing evidence that Captain Gray had under-gone a horrifying experience ... that

---

[3] Perhaps not coincidentally, in a 1929 article titled "Oxford, Mississippi," published just after *The Sound and the Fury*, Medford Evans says that Faulkner "walks a great deal by himself, carries a cane, and wears a moustache" (58).

made him a psychological cripple ... An unappeasable hunger for social status is hardly a credible vehicle to dramatize the malaise of a war-induced trauma ... The problem, I believe, is that Faulkner is mixing up his wars. The postwar trauma of lost social status and poverty belongs to the post-Civil War South, not post-World War I Europe.

(172)

This idea of Faulkner conflating the two wars is an interesting one but need not be seen as a flaw or weakness. Rather, it suggests that Faulkner's story is a commentary on war in general and the toll it takes on soldiers. The disconnect between Gray's war experiences and his class obsession that Volpe rejects as unmotivated may, in fact, be intentionally so—a lack of logical cause and effect, a lack of rational explanation pointing to something disturbing and unexplainable beneath the surface, a common response to the horrors of the First World War. Faulkner also takes aim at the persistent idea that wartime exploits and heroism can be an avenue for improving one's position in the postwar world, a meritocratic battlefield where one's actions count more than one's family, name, or identity. It also indicates how the issue of class continues to be bound up with war in Faulkner's mind, extending the connections established in *Flags in the Dust*.

Alec Gray does find temporary freedom and enhanced status in "Victory," yet he cannot accept a return to prewar conditions. His consuming desire to break free permanently from his inherited class position links him with characters like Thomas Sutpen and Flem Snopes. Volpe cleverly connects Gray to Sutpen through a scene in which Gray as a traveling salesman is sent to the side entrance of a house and then turned away by a servant (172), mirroring the primal scene in *Absalom* where Sutpen feels the shame of his class standing and begins his grand design for revenge. Surprisingly, this taciturn son of a Scottish shipbuilder resembles Sutpen in terms of ruthlessness as well. Alec Gray's first moment of class consciousness and shame comes when he is sentenced to seven months in a penal battalion by his sergeant-major for insubordination and not shaving. Gray repeatedly refuses to say "sir" to an officer, as if he refuses to accept the fact that he is below others in the hierarchy. Upon his return to his old platoon after completing his sentence, Gray uses the chaos of battle to murder coldly and brutally the sergeant-major with a bayonet in the anonymity and chaos of the trenches. Gray's subsequent daring and heroism in the battle earn him a medal and the chance to train as an officer. His father's reaction to this news, however, is a letter castigating his son for trying to rise above his station: "*for that way lies vainglory and pride. The pride and vainglory of going for an officer. Never miscall your birth, Alec. You are not a gentleman. You are a Scottish shipwright*" (447–8).

Gray's ruthless determination makes him a different version of Sutpen or perhaps a distant cousin of those ever-multiplying, ever-striving Snopeses. Like Sutpen and Flem, Gray knows to acquire all the trappings of the class to which he aspires, to dress the part, that is, but he similarly fails to be accepted in the way he desires. The story opens a few years after the war with Gray returning to visit the battlefields, and the narrator's focus is on the link between outward appearance and class from the opening lines. The French citizens who see him in the train station assume he is a British lord, "remarking his sober, correct suit, [and] his correct stick correctly carried" (431). The repetition of the word "correct" here suggests a Gatsby-esque attention to the trappings of class, the performance aspect, which Gray achieves with his manner, his clothes, and his perfectly waxed moustache (commented on many times by the narrator throughout the story). For Gray, his rise to the officer ranks gives him the illusion that a concomitant rise in civilian society is possible, a dream he stubbornly clings to despite repeated rejections after the war.

On his only trip home after the war, Gray's father does not recognize his son at first, due to the son's now white hair (apparently from the shock of war), his waxed moustache, and his "city clothing" (453) in lieu of his military uniform. While his father thinks he is being modest by not wearing his uniform, his refusal is in reality related to his insistence that he has a job arranged for him in England by his officer friends. That is, he is desperate to see his new, higher class standing *not* as a residual effect of his military promotion but as a permanent elevation earned through his wartime service, a new existence into which he is reborn through the trauma of the war. His father rightly intuits that the new clothes signal an attempt to cast off his former identity and heritage, telling Alec "the proper uniform for a Gray is an overall and a hammer" (454), but Alec will hear nothing of returning home and he goes to London, living in "the proper quarter with ... his waxed moustaches, his sober correct clothes, and his stick carried in a manner inimitable, at once jaunty and unobtrusive" (455).[4]

---

[4] Faulkner seems drawn to this character type as Gray finds an echo in *Sanctuary* in the form of a taxi driver who meets the trains in Kinston: "He was thin, with gray eyes and a gray moustache with waxed ends. In the old days, before the town boomed suddenly into a lumber town, he was a planter, a landholder, a son of one of the first settlers. He lost his property through greed and gullibility, and he began to drive a hack back and forth between town and the trains, with his waxed moustache, in a top hat and a worn Prince Albert coat, telling the drummers how he used to lead Kinston society; now he drove it" (297–8).

In "Victory" we see Faulkner working out this connection between clothing and class mobility that later becomes an extremely important aspect of Flem's rise through the ranks of Jefferson. Both Flem and Alec Gray, then, are attempting to break free of the confines of the class in which they were born, and both use clothing as a statement of intent to move up, as well as a vital component that makes that move possible: dressing for the job they want, not the one they have, as it were. The Snopes proliferation, of course, cannot be stopped, with Flem's ascent emblematic of the larger spread of Snopesism throughout Yoknapatawpha County. Gray's rise, by contrast, is only temporary, a by-product of the war, and his ultimate failure is surely due, at least partly, to the generational disillusionment in the aftermath of the First World War. Yet, there is more than the loss of faith engendered by the war at work in the story. It functions as a dry run, a rehearsal of the burning class ambitions crystallized later in Thomas Sutpen and Flem Snopes. The themes of gender and sexuality so prominent in Faulkner's First World War novel *Soldiers' Pay* and repeated in "All the Dead Pilots" are completely absent in "Victory." Gray shows a similar ruthlessness as Sutpen and Snopes during the war, but his quick flameout to joblessness and poverty is also related to the conflict. Sutpen and Snopes play a long game, beginning their rise near the bottom of the social order and climbing the rungs through a variety of ethically questionable means. While Gray's rapid descent might be attributed to Faulkner commenting on the relative rigidity of the British class system in relation to the American, more important is the fact that Gray's ascent comes through battlefield exploits, within the closed society of the military. He then attempts to shift his new rank into civilian society but finds that he and many other veterans are not credited in the civilian arena for their military achievements. It is, in fact, another failure of the war: men who served their country in desperate times have no skills to transfer to the post-war world, and the promise of improving one's lot in life turns instead into homelessness, destitution, and debasement, the final insult of a horrific war.

The numerous veterans seen begging on the streets in "Victory" suggest that these men have been left behind in an old world, unfit for a new modern one. Flem's stacks of identical white shirts and his "patented necktie" (*The Hamlet* 173) that is "made for him by the gross" (64) suggest machine-made, modern clothing, as opposed to the hand-made, home-spun goods of the past, which most of his fellow Frenchman's Bend residents still use. He is emblematic of the machine-made, mass-produced, profit-driven future. Gray's stodgy old uniform of the upper class may have been proper and *de riguer* before the war, but his waxed moustache and white hair mark him as a relic in modern London. When he is recognized at the end of the story by a well-off war buddy, it is significant that the friend and fellow former soldier has just come from an upscale tailor and is walking the streets of London to show off his fashionable "new clothes" (463). It is perhaps little wonder that Gray is mistaken by villagers for the father of a First World War soldier when he revisits the battlefields where he saw action, all of them assuming he is much older than he actually is.

In this sense, Gray is not unlike Southerners in the aftermath of the First World War, including Faulkner himself. As David Davis details in *World War I and Southern Modernism*, the war is the beginning of modernity and modernism in the South. Prior to the war, "Modernity was a foreign element" (20) in the region, while the war itself, Davis says, "brought the region into contact with modernity before the region actually modernized" (25). Thus, the sense that Gray has been left behind and is unable to find a place in the modern world expresses an anxiety common in the post-war South. While Faulkner himself never saw combat or the front, he could at least identify with the experiences of having left the South for the war, encountering urban and foreign cultures, and returning home to feel unsettled and outcast, derided by those in Oxford as Count No' Count. Struggling to hold a job while constructing a persona of a combat-injured war veteran walking the streets in his fancy store-bought R.A.F. uniform, Faulkner surely identifies with Gray's plight in "Victory."

A story within "Victory" provides an apt metaphor for the experiences of Gray and many other veterans. As Gray joins a group of homeless veterans under a bridge, one of them tells a story by the firelight. The man was blinded during the war, and his fiancée visits him in the hospital, and for eight days, he gently touches the scar on her wrist that she got before the war. On the eighth day, the woman confesses that she is a nurse whom the fiancée convinced to take her place while she went to meet another man. The blind vet admits he had known the whole time since the nurse's fake scar was on the wrong wrist. This sad tale captures Gray's situation symbolically. Gray, too, has been fooled and deluded by an alluring, seductive presence, the dream of a higher class position. Faulkner, himself, had been jilted by a woman and seemed to have no real prospects for professional and financial success at the time he wrote "Victory." Like the fiancée in the story, reality is a cruel mistress, and yet both men are willingly deluded to a large extent, finding their blindness more comforting than facing the harsh light of truth.

Pylon

Faulkner wrote *Pylon* while feeling stuck with *Absalom, Absalom!*; a return to the pilots and barnstorming shows he knew and loved might get his gears turning again, and he saw *Pylon* as a somewhat salacious novel akin to *Sanctuary* (Rollyson, Vol. 2, 2–3). It is also a novel about class conflict, with the perpetually broke pilots pitted against those who own and control the airport and the airshows in which they compete against one another for meager prizes. The unnamed reporter who is the book's protagonist is obsessed with a particular group of pilots and crew due to their raw, visceral experience of life during their death-defying shows and also due to their shockingly unconventional lifestyle. Laverne Shumann is partner to two men, Roger and Jack (married to Roger only because he won a dice throw), and none of them know which one is the father of her son. The reporter latches onto this group, including their hard-drinking mechanic Jiggs, and is in awe of both their aerial exploits and their rejection of traditional social norms. The distance between the conventionally minded reporter and the intrepid aviators he follows around is encapsulated in their clothing.

The daring pilots whom the reporter idolizes all seem cut from the same cloth, "in blue serge cut apparently not only from the same bolt but folded at the same crease on the same shelf" (51). Both the blue serge worn in the hotel lobby and the matching dungarees worn in the airport hangar denote equality within the group but also demarcate their class position in wider society, distinctly below those who wear tweed "Madison Avenue jackets" (51). Faulkner similarly uses the reporter's physical appearance as a method of characterization, emphasizing his gangly body that looks like a skeleton "in the snatched garments of an etherized patient," alluding to Eliot's "The Lovesong of J. Alfred Prufrock" and "The Wasteland":

> [A] creature which, erect, would be better than six feet tall and which would weigh about ninetyfive pounds, in a suit of no age nor color, as though made of air and doped like an aeroplane wing with the incrusted excretion of all articulate life's contact with the passing earth, which ballooned light and impedimentless about a skeleton frame as though suit and wearer both hung from a flapping clothesline.
>
> (15)

His skinny body is enveloped in a "ballooning" suit (22) that gives him "the illusion of being held together by only the clothes wore" (190), while Jiggs wears clothing that accentuates, as opposed to hides, his "short thick musclebound body" (4), including pants so tight that you can see the outlines of individual coins in his pocket (6). Jiggs's tight pants are reminiscent of the young dandy Faulkner's own sartorial choices, and the novel opens with Jiggs staring longingly at a pair of fashionable boots on display in a store window.

Those boots, in fact, are important as things throughout the novel, motivating Jiggs's behavior as they assume iconic status for him as a consumer: "Slantshimmered by the intervening plate they sat upon their wooden pedestal in unblemished and inviolate implication of horse and spur, of the posed countrylife photographs in the magazine advertisements" (4). The boots seem to represent a better life to Jiggs, the kind of life of comfort and ease that has always been beyond his grasp living hand-to-mouth as his group travels the airplane racing circuit. As he enters the clothing store, he is nearly overwhelmed by the sheer amount and otherworldly appearance of the sartorial choices on display:

> [T]hat museum of glass cases lighted suave and sourceless by an unearthly daycolored substance in which the hats and ties and shirts, the beltbuckles and cufflinks and handkerchiefs, the pipes shaped like golfclubs and the drinking tools shaped like boots and barnyard fowls and the minute impedimenta for wear on ties and vestchains shaped like bits and spurs, resembled biologic specimens put into the inviolate preservative before they had ever been breathed into.
>
> (4)

Jiggs is like Sarty Snopes or the young Thomas Sutpen in this scene, overwhelmed by the amount and the allure of things, and his desire to possess the boots drives him to use Jack's prize money to pay for them, even though the group struggles to find money for food. People desire to show others who they are, and in the modern world they do that increasingly through the objects they own and display, clothing being the most common and visible. The boots in this sense resemble Alec Gray's waxed moustache and walking stick or the $75 designer tie that Ratliff purchases in *The Mansion* in that the allure of such articles of display is more than their use value, monetary worth, and aesthetic appeal. People feel compelled to purchase and display these items because of what they can say about class, status, and belonging.

A flashback to an earlier incident provides a different example of clothing exerting causality on people's behavior. The first time Laverne parachutes from the wing of a flying plane, she becomes terrified after climbing out on the wing, but it is too late to back down with "the money collected and the crowd waiting" (171). She is wearing a skirt since "they had decided that her exposed legs would not only be a drawing card but that in the skirt no one would doubt that she was a woman" (171), but she does not wear underwear "from fear she might soil one of the few undergarments which she now possessed" (172). Her response to her fear of impending death is to climb in the cockpit with Roger and have sexual intercourse while he flies the plane over the heads of the waiting crowd. When she then parachutes to the ground (apparently pulled from the plane in flagrante delicto), her skirts billow up and display her naked body like boots in a shop window to the now frenzied mob of men below: "not merely naked but clothed in the very traditional symbology—the ruined dress with which she was trying wildly to cover her loins, and the parachute harness—of female bondage" (173). She is arrested and thrown in jail, then eventually smuggled out again by two deputies in order to save her from the clutches of another deputy who has been driven mad by what he saw of Laverne and seems intent on groping or even assaulting her. This incident combines several different meanings of clothes that have been discussed so far. She and Roger choose her outfit based on the existing gender stereotypes and expectations of their society. She chooses not to wear underwear (and to do the stunt in the first place) for economic reasons, and the clothing choice begets a sexual encounter, while the cumbersomeness of the skirt and harness leads to the accidental parachuting at the wrong time. The symbolism of her falling from the sky recalls Caddy in the tree: the exposed woman above men with her sexual knowledge both repulsive and attractive, driving men crazy with lust and hate. In the aftermath, she is covered with a raincoat, like Temple, when they smuggle her out of the jail to get her away from the obsessed deputy. After Roger's death, Laverne sits with her trench coat open, now vulnerable and exposed, while her unconventional sexuality seems to be represented in another allusion to Caddy, "a long smear of oil or mud across the upper part of her white dress" (221).

Although the reporter is drawn to the pilots' seeming lack of interest in money, the demands of a capitalist society often impede on their lives, compelling them to borrow and hustle for money constantly while proclaiming its unimportance (129, 140, 155). In many ways, this is the central tension of the novel, the desire to live life free of the petty tyranny of money yet existing in a society that makes this impossible, not unlike Charlotte and Harry in "The Wild Palms." The reporter fixates on the freedom from money and conventions that he sees when the planes are soaring through the air, and he is blinded by his sexual obsession with Laverne. Faulkner shows how this freedom is, if not illusory, then only temporary. On the ground, the mundane demands of getting and spending affect these flyers as much as anyone else. The boots that captivate Jiggs in the novel's opening scene are sustained as a motif through the story while also motivating his actions as physical objects. The airplanes themselves are the objects that define the lives of the group, to the point that one critic declares, "Their entire existence—their location at a particular moment, their subsistence, their routing, their moral and spiritual values—is determined by the machines they serve ... Human relationships are subservient to relationships created by the necessity of servicing the machine" (Volpe 177). In this context, Jiggs's obsession with the fashionable new boots makes more sense; they are another object whose attraction cannot be resisted, no matter the cost.

He is overly cautious every time he wears the boots or removes them from their protective bag, always aware that he may need to return them for a refund in a financial emergency. The boots are even an actant in Roger's death since Jiggs never finishes fixing the valves on Roger's new plane before his fatal race even as he moons over his footwear. More to blame is a meeting between the race sponsors and the flight crews that Faulkner compares to the common textile mill labor disputes of his era (131) in which the organizing committee wants to reduce the prize money available in order to pay for printing new programs so that the name of a pilot who crashed and died on the first day of the events can be removed. Their callousness and the bureaucratic inefficiency of the meeting means Jiggs never finishes the valve repairs before Roger tries to fly an experimental new airplane in hopes of taking the two-thousand-dollar prize money. After Roger's death, Jiggs and the reporter collect animal bones as a home remedy for buffing a scratch out of boots so that Jiggs can sell them and buy an assortment of cheap gifts for Laverne and her son. In effect, they replace their friend with the bones and gifts, substituting things for a person. Even the reporter who nearly worships the free-spirited crew cannot help but reify rather than deify them: "they aint human ... cut him and it's cylinder oil; dissect him and it aint bones: it's little rockerarms and connecting rods" (204). Despite their apparent rejection of a system that turns their skill and bravery into commodities, they still become reduced to things with Laverne even rejecting the human connection with her own son as she leaves him to be raised by Roger's aging parents. The defeats in the capitalist arena that end *Pylon* and "Victory" are connected to the fact that the recurring theme of individual identity creation is largely missing from these stories. There is less of a connection between internal struggle and external sartorial image and more of a focus on image itself, on how clothing and objects might offer fulfillment as ends in themselves rather than, as we saw in the Clothing and Race chapter, as tools to assist identity creation and growth.

"Barn Burning"

"Barn Burning" was first published in 1939, though it seems to have been originally conceived and written as part of *The Hamlet* (Towner and Carothers 4), and the much-anthologized short story anticipates some of Faulkner's use of clothing in the later novel. The story opens with a decided emphasis on things and commodities, as Sarty sits in the store-cum-courtroom among the "ranked shelves close-packed with the solid, squat, dynamic shapes of tin cans" (3). Sarty's mother's and sisters' clothing is also described, but, significantly, they are figured almost as part of the detritus and seemingly random possessions loaded in the wagon: "His two hulking sisters in their Sunday dresses and his mother and her sister in calico and sunbonnets were already in it, sitting on and among the sorry residue of the dozen and more movings which even the boy could remember—the battered stove, the broken beds and chairs, the clock inlaid with mother-of-pearl, which would not run" (6). As they stoop to pick up de Spain's rug later in the story—a rug literally worth more than they are—Faulkner's narration again makes them less human than objects, and cheap ones at that "they presented an incredible expanse of pale cloth and a flutter of tawdry ribbons" (13). Ab's class-based complaints that he is treated no better than slave labor find resonance with the story's emphasis on people as things.

Clothing is a method of characterization early in the story, as Sarty is first described as wearing "patched and faded jeans even too small for him," while Ab is "stiff in his black Sunday coat donned not for the trial but for the moving" (4). The fact that Ab wears his Sunday coat for moving suggests he does not recognize the authority of the court or worship justice but rather makes a God of his own need for vengeance which then requires him to move constantly. Ab uses his appearance and demeanor to create an image of himself that will appear large and threatening: "the flat, wide, black hat, the formal coat of broadcloth which had once been black but which had now that friction-glazed greenish cast of the bodies of old house flies, the lifted sleeve which was too large, the lifted hand like curled claw" (11). As the story progresses, Sarty sees his father almost exclusively as the outer garments he wears and the image they project, "the depthless, harsh silhouette of the hat and coat" (14), his father's inner identity inscrutable. The solitary outfits that we see each of the Snopes family members wearing contrast with the numerous changes in apparel that de Spain undergoes, from the "linen-clad man on a fine sorrel mare" to his "collarless and even bareheaded" (15) second appearance to the "collar and cravat" (17) he wears in court. Of course, this sartorial superiority is part of de Spain's class standing, and Sarty is overwhelmed by the display of objects and possessions in the de Spain house, beginning with the "linen jacket" the Black servant wears,[5] and both the servant and Lula de Spain seem part of the opulent accumulation of stuff:

> [T]hen the boy, deluged as though by a warm wave by a suave turn of carpeted stair and a pendant glitter of chandeliers and a mute gleam of gold frames, heard the swift feet and saw her too, a lady—perhaps he had never seen her like before either—in a gray, smooth gown with lace at the throat and an apron tied at the waist and the sleeves turned back.
>
> (11–12)

Just as the Snopes women in the wagon were earlier, the person is part of the assemblage here: lady, clothes, chandelier, servant, rug, carpet, gold. All of it acts on Sarty (dazzling him like Jiggs's boots) and it is these things, not the people, that cause him to turn against his own father. He wants something different for his life, a new image or persona that will require relinquishing the old, as when the servant tries to grab Sarty at the story's end, but the boy's whole sleeve, "rotten with washing" (23), comes off like a snake shedding its skin and Sarty runs away to start his new life. Again, we do not see the work of identity formation in this story, but only its initial stage—the determination to become someone new. At this stage it is only the allure of objects and the dazzling image of Major de Spain that attracts Sarty.

The Hamlet

The Hamlet uses clothing as a method of characterization more than any of Faulkner's other novels, and clothes function similarly to money, facilitating exchange while also conveying a certain social capital on the wearer. The

---

[5] In the later story "Shall Not Perish," the Grier family dons their Sunday clothes to visit Major de Spain's house, and Res, as he shines his son's shoes, sounds just as resentful as Ab: "'De Spain is rich,' he said. 'With a monkey nigger in a white coat to hold the jar up each time he wants to spit'" (104).

Hamlet is also perhaps Faulkner's novel most concerned with exchanges, and it portrays a culture and economy that shuns actual money, preferring trading and bartering whenever possible. Fines are levied in bushels of corn; IOUs are signed over multiple times; Ratliff buys, sells, and trades all manner of goods, anything "which the owner did not want badly enough" (15), as he says; and Jody Varner tells Ab Snopes "No cash" (9) at the general store. Meanwhile, horses bought and paid for with paper money are never actually possessed by their nominal owners. Cash money has a relatively fixed value while trading offers the possibility of a good deal, a one-sided trade, a chance to better one's position. In a novel where cash is perhaps the least-used medium of exchange, the notion of clothes as currency is not a radical leap. The payment of Labove for his football heroics in the currency of shoes is the most obvious example of this function of clothing, used as a way to circumnavigate restrictions on paying collegiate athletes while also providing Labove and his family with practical goods that they lack. This literal use of clothing as currency suggests that we might also read dress similarly in metaphorical terms.[6] The farcical image of Labove's grandmother wearing football cleats while sitting in her rocking chair indicates a related aspect of clothing: clothes as a signifier to others. As mentioned in the Introduction, Barthes notes that because clothing is in contact with the body, it acts "simultaneously as its substitute and its mask" (236). Or as Elizabeth Wilson puts it in *Adorned in Dreams*, "Dress is the frontier between the self and the not-self" (3). Clothing is the nexus between an individual's self-construction and their public persona, presenting a certain version of the person to the world to be understood, interpreted, and consumed. Not only do we see the value of clothing in the eyes of others shift in the novel, but also the social standing of the people wearing the clothes.

Throughout the novel, clothing is used as a principal method of characterization. The only trace of federal revenuers who go into Frenchman's Bend are articles of their clothing worn by locals (5); Ab Snopes is described as wearing a "preacher's hat and coat" (18); Hoake McCarron has "the first riding boots the countryside had ever seen" (151); Ratliff's blue shirts "accurately assert his chosen social and sartorial territory between the overalls of workers and the broadcloth of the bourgeoisie" (Cook 9); Ike Snopes (*The Hamlet* 69–71) and Eula Varner (144, 147) are both defined by the fact that their clothes do not

---

[6] There is a similar instance in "The Wild Palms," when the striking miners are compensated with a can of beans and a wool shirt apiece (158).

fit them properly (albeit in quite different ways); Eula's suitors are unnamed, identified only by their peacock-like clothes, "the half dozen or so bright Sunday shirts with pink or lavender sleeve-garters" (145); Houston's wife, also unnamed, brings to the marriage only "a small trunk of neat, plain, dove-colored clothes and the hand-stitched sheets and towels and table-linen which she had made herself" (227), and after her death, the only remembrance Houston keeps is one gingham dress "which resembled the one in which he had first seen her that day at the school" (240); and the Armstids, before they are ever named, are defined by their "battered and paintless" old wagon which matches their clothing: "It contained a woman in a shapeless grey garment and a faded sunbonnet, and a man in faded and patched though clean overalls" (320). Thus, clothing is very often the primary identifier for many characters, even more important than their names or occupations in demarcating their individuality and social standing.

The most significant linkage of a character and clothes in the novel is, of course, Flem Snopes. Flem in this novel begins his rise from poor sharecropper's son that will culminate with him as bank president by the end of the Snopes Trilogy, using a series of smaller exchanges to swap one identity for another. His clothing is no small factor in this journey. Critics, including Patricia Gantt, Diane Roberts, and Michael Williams, have explored "the tension between powerlessness and agency in Faulkner's fiction by focusing on the clothing of female characters who engage in gendered cross-dressing," as Cook points out (9). Flem, I would argue, engages in a type of class-based cross-dressing, utilizing the same "guerilla tactic," to use Gantt's phrase (410), which women use to assert themselves and transgress social boundaries. Flem's story is something of a reworked Horatio Alger story, in which "a change of clothing usually precedes or serves as a catalyst for, rather than following and expressing the transformation of self ... a distinct move away from Thoreau's [idea] that we change our clothes only through work, work that can change us internally" (Elahi 26–7). Elahi's study asserts the growing importance of fashion in late nineteenth- and early twentieth-century literature: "As social mobility posed both promises and threats about the shape of national identity and culture, American literary realists looked to and depicted clothing as the screen on which hopes and anxieties could effectively be projected" (5). Cook echoes this point, noting that in multiple Faulkner texts "seemingly class-and caste-bound people successfully display their social mobility in their garments" (9), and Jon Smith notes the same transgressive, combative quality to Flem's dress when he calls his iconic bowtie "protopunk" ("Metropolitan Fashion" 86).

The brief tale of a drummer who courts Eula illustrates the connection of clothing and social status, though he fails where the more ruthless and shrewder Flem later succeeds. A successful dinner at the Varners's home apparently has this unnamed drummer close to marrying Eula and moving from the ranks of traveling salesmen into the landed gentry of Frenchman's Bend. Three days after the dinner, he returns in the fanciest buggy that can be rented in Jefferson, "and he not only wore a necktie, he had on the first white flannel trousers Frenchman's Bend ever saw" (147), indicating that his relationship to the Varners, Frenchman's Bend, and indeed, the world has shifted. Despite his Flem-like necktie, the locals do not accept the drummer's attempt to raise his class standing, and his rival suitors for Eula attack him and send him fleeing, those same impressive pants now mockingly described as "ruined ice cream pants" (147), showing that the clothes themselves have not changed yet their value has, a loss in currency commensurate with a loss in social capital.

This notion of a currency with wildly fluctuating value can also be linked to the renewed national debate about the gold standard in the 1930s. In her article analyzing Zora Neale Hurston's "The Gilded Six-Bits" in the context of the gold-standard debate, Hildegard Hoeller notes the almost-religious zeal proponents had for the idea of gold as "an essential measure of value" and argues that "the issue of democratic distribution versus plutocratic centralization of money" was at the heart of the debate:

> For gold-standard supporters, revoking the gold standard was not only an economic and political mistake but also a sacrilege, an abandonment of civilization, a kind of unanchoring of the world. For gold-standard opponents, it was a much needed democratization of American money, a way of making money circulate among all people and all parts of the United States, including the West and the South, and of overthrowing the un-American "monarchy" of gold.
>
> (766–7)

Democratizing American money, allowing the common man a shot at the wealth and capital previously reserved for the wealthy few—one could hardly describe better the phenomenon of Flem Snopes. His clothes are a new currency not tied to an essentialist arbiter of value.

Arthur A. VanderVeen has argued that in both *Go Down, Moses* and *The Hamlet*, Faulkner "investigates the period's fear that reliable standards of value were mere arbitrary constructs" (46) in relation to the prominent gold-standard debate. He goes on to suggest that "*The Hamlet* represents Frenchman's Bend as a series of exchanges that highlight the performativity of every transaction" (48), a notion that is particularly germane to my contention that clothing operates as currency. Flem's clothing allows him to exchange an old identity for a new one, a net profit, while he also exploits the traditional faith in the essential, fixed value of cash money to trick Ratliff, Armstid, and Bookwright into buying the old Frenchman Place in order to get their hands on some coins whose perceived value far outweighs their true exchange value.

In order for Flem to rise, he must first usurp Jody Varner, whose clothes Faulkner describes at some length in the novel's first description of him:

> He wore, winter and summer (save that in the warm season he dispensed with the coat) and Sundays and week days, a glazed collarless white shirt fastened at the neck with a heavy gold collar-button beneath a suit of good black broadcloth. He put on the suit the day it arrived from the Jefferson tailor and wore it everyday and in all weathers thereafter until he sold it to one of the family's negro retainers, so that on almost any Sunday night one whole or some part of one of his old suits could be met—and promptly recognized—walking the summer roads, and replaced it with the new succeeding one. In contrast to the unvarying overalls of the men he lived among he had an air not funereal exactly but ceremonial.
>
> (7-8)

Jody's role as manager of the businesses and real estate that he and has father "together had been acquiring during the last forty years" (8) is signaled as much by his fashionable difference from the farmers in their overalls as anything. The fact that he wears the same outfit every day suggests a sort of uniform that demarcates his class position, a fact Faulkner highlights when he calls Jody's attire "a costume at once ceremonial and negligee" (11). The fact that he sells his old suits to Black servants and workers, however, suggests and foreshadows the possibility of the lower classes becoming the equals of their supposed betters, while simultaneously recalling feudal lords handing down their used fine clothing to their domestic servants.[7] Jody's donations also relate back to

---

[7] Elizabeth Wilson, in her seminal study of fashion *Adorned in Dreams: Fashion and Modernity*, describes how domestic help in preindustrial times were often "given the cast-off fashionable garments of their employer, still in good condition, and thus it was that they were able to parade the city streets in finery that appalled the moralists and conservatives of the day" (23).

the Clothing and Race chapter in that they allow Jody to solidify his whiteness. The hand-me-downs are only worn by Black men, and his act of charity also establishes Jody in a paternalistic role.[8] As Patricia Yaeger points out, white Southerners are compelled to define the objects their Black neighbors possess as "rubbish" in order to reaffirm racial difference (*Dirt and Desire* 209), though the similarity of these garments worn by Black and white men further insinuates the permeability of the color, as well as class, barrier.

When Flem shows up in the very next paragraph, his outfit is mentioned before his name or anything else about him as a way of defining him: "a man, smaller than common, in a wide hat and a frock coat too large for him, standing with a curious planted stiffness" (8). The clothes he wears do not fit him, as if he is trying to be something he is not, trying, like Jody, to differentiate himself from "the half dozen overalled men" on the store gallery (10). As Veblen asserts, garments that show no evidence of wearing or soiling are crucial to telegraphing the elegance of the upper class: "The pleasing effect of neat and spotless garments is chiefly, if not altogether, due to their carrying the suggestion of leisure—exemption from personal contact with industrial processes of any kind" (170). Flem is described initially as "soft in appearance like Varner himself, though a head shorter, in a soiled white shirt and cheap gray trousers" (24). This description emphasizes his relative position beneath the Varners, but a quick costume change precipitates his rapid rise in the social hierarchy. The farmers on the store porch, Jody, and Ratliff are all noted as wearing the same outfit day after day, never changing their clothes nor their position in the world. In fact, virtually no characters in *The Hamlet* other than Flem ever change clothes, despite their garments being frequently mentioned throughout the novel. It is worth recalling a quote used in the first chapter from Sandra M. Gilbert noting the traditional ties of clothing to social roles: "[U]ntil the middle or late nineteenth century most people wore what were essentially uniforms: garments denoting the one form or single shape to which each individual's life was confined by birth, by circumstance, by custom, by decree" (196). Clothing is an important aspect of hegemonic structures that make inequalities and hierarchies appear to be natural. By the same token, clothing can be used to expose the fact that these iniquities are merely social constructions that are therefore subject to change.

[8] Blotner relates that Ned Barnett, the African American man employed by the Faulkners for decades, inherited many articles of fine clothing from "the Young Colonel," Faulkner's grandfather, J. W. T. Faulkner, that he wore even while doing farm chores (Vol 1 52-3), which also resembles the descriptions of Lucas Beauchamp's clothes that Chick compares to his own grandfather's.

When Flem soon reappears in a brand-new white shirt, it is immediately noticeable, and he looks strange, almost ridiculous, to others who note the newness of the hand-made shirt, as well as its "sun-browned streaks" that look like zebra stripes (56), underscoring Flem's exotic, out-of-place appearance as a store clerk and wanna-be Varner. He wears the same shirt all week, until it is noticeably soiled, then shows up with an identical new one the next week, which then becomes soiled in the exact same pattern. Faulkner's narration suggests a connection between the shirt and its wearer's suitability for his new job: "It was as though its wearer, entering though he had into a new life and milieu already channelled [sic] to compulsions and customs fixed long before his advent, had nevertheless established in it even on that first day his own particular soiling groove" (57). He so immediately and convincingly inhabits the role of clerk that, to the amazement of the onlookers, even Will Varner pays Flem for the nickel's worth of tobacco he gets from his own store. Flem's silent approach and departure between store and galley on which Ratliff comments in this scene are attributed to his tennis shoes, and these sneakers are emblematic of his stealthy rise to prominence.[9] When the citizens finally realize that Flem is now living in the village itself, it is when he arrives for the first time at church on Sunday morning and their "incredulous astonishment" (64) seems due as much, if not more, to his new clothes as to his presence: "In addition to the gray cloth cap and gray trousers he wore not only a clean white shirt but a necktie—a tiny machine-made black bow" (64). Flem's tie (just the second in the whole county, after Will Varner) is compared to "an enigmatic punctuation symbol" (64), in this case a sign of his intention and ambition to overtake the other man with the tie. First, though, it is the son, Jody, whom Flem must surpass, and his tie and white shirt "gave him Jody Varner's look of ceremonial heterodoxy raised to its tenth power" (64). Faulkner tells us parenthetically in this passage that Flem would later become bank president, thereby signaling that this article of clothing is directly connected to his rise through the social and economic ranks.

Again, the clothes act as currency in the sense that Flem is able to trade off them, leveraging his unusual yet commanding appearance into a stealthy series of trades: swapping sharecropping for clerking, then a country shack eight miles

---

[9] Flem's sneaking in this scene recalls his initial appearance in the novel: "One moment the road had been empty, the next moment the man stood there beside it ... the same cloth cap" (24). Chick Mallison, in *Intruder in the Dust*, is also glad to wear sneakers, "thinking how he had never really appreciated rubber soles before, how nothing could match them for giving you time to make up your mind what you really wanted to do" (28).

from the store for a rented room in town. Just a page later, it is *Flem* who is weighing the cotton while Jody clerks in the store, and the locals flock again to see the moment that Jody has been passed by Flem, or as Ratliff says with a nod to those sneakers, "You mean, that was when Jody begun to find it out" (66). While Jody's outfit does not seem to ever change, Faulkner's later frumpy description of his clothes befit his lowered status: "the heavy bagging broadcloth, the white collarless shirt with a yellow halfmoon of sweat at each armpit, the dusty, lint-wisped black hat" (177). Just a year later, Flem has Jody's horse, lives in the Varners's house, and rides side-by-side with Will in a new buggy "with bright red wheels and a fringed parasol top" (99), an ostentatious sartorial choice for the buggy that announces new money has arrived (reminiscent of Jay Gatsby's yellow "circus wagon"). As the chapter ends, Flem is sitting in Will's bespoke chair at the Old Frenchman Place, suggesting a further rise is imminent. He even has Will's mannerisms, jerking his head at the porch sitters in the same fashion, further suggesting an almost Gatsby-like performance. Numerous critics have read James Gatz as "passing" in ways connected to both race and class, and Flem's cross-dressing might be read similarly, particularly in light of Duvall's arguments that Ab Snopes dresses in Black face in "Barn Burning" and that Ab and Sarty are both figuratively Black in the story (*White Identity* 14–15), as well as Godden's contention that Flem is figured as Black at least three times in *The Hamlet* (14).[10] Faulkner suggests something similar in his description of Flem sitting at the knee of Varner as the two settle up tenants' accounts: "Varner and Snopes resembled the white trader and his native parrot-taught headman in an African outpost" (67). Flem must differentiate himself sartorially from the overalls of the peasant class, and imitating Varner in other ways is an example of what Veblen describes as a trickle-down theory of fashion, manners, and lifestyle: "The leisure class stands at the head of the social structure in point of reputability; and its manner of life and its standards of worth therefore afford the norm of reputability for the community. The observance of these standards, in some degree of approximation, becomes incumbent upon all classes lower in the scale" (84).

The Spotted Horses section of the novel also relates to these issues of currency, value, and the gold standard in a variety of ways. As Flem returns

---

[10] Michael Wainwright points out that since the strange Black man who warns Harris does not limp, it could not be Ab in disguise. Wainwright argues Flem (though unnamed in "Barn Burning") would therefore be "the sole candidate for the unknown African American" (91–2) according to Duvall's argument, which would add another layer to the notion of Flem passing.

to Yoknapatawpha in the opening of "Book Four: The Peasants," it is again his clothes that are most prominent: "He might have departed only this morning. He wore the same cloth cap, the minute bow tie against the white shirt, the same gray trousers" (300). Buck Hipps, the strange Texan who accompanies Flem, "wore a heavy densely black moustache, a wide pale hat … [and] tight jeans pants" (300), as well as a vest that is soon ripped by one of the horses "from collar to hem down the back exactly as the trick swordsman severs a floating veil with one stroke" (302). This lifting of the veil, as it were, nearly scuttles the entire auction by exposing the reality that the horses are untameable and therefore worthless as investments. It is an emperor-has-no-clothes moment, but the crowd is too eager to see what they want to see and so do not grasp that they, too, are about to be ripped off. Buck leaps into the pen of stampeding horses with his "flapping vest" (303) in an effort to regain control as the crowd's perception of events threatens to change and expose his scheme: "It had seemed like a big lot until now, but now the very idea that all that fury and motion should be transpiring inside any one fence was something to be repudiated with contempt, like a mirror trick" (304). This image of a mirror, along with that of lifting of the veil, suggests nakedness, an uncovering of what should be covered, what is meant to remain hidden. This is how clothing functions as well, not only projecting a certain image to the world which may or may not jibe with our actual selves, but also covering up and hiding our nakedness, that irreducible sign of our own weak flesh and mortality.

Thus, it is fitting that the next sentence details the stranger emerging "carrying the wire-cutters and his vest now completely gone" (304). A few sentences later he rips off and throws aside his torn shirt sleeve, as the horses slowly shear away his clothing, threatening to expose both his ruse and his human weakness. At this moment Eck's son appears, looking for his father: "The boy went on to the end of the veranda, in diminutive overalls—a miniature replica of the men themselves" (304). Grammatically this sentence can be read not only with the boy as the referent of "miniature replica," but also the overalls themselves as the replica of the men. Indeed, their veneer of pride and envy covers over all and leads them into falling for the wild horses scam, despite Ratliff's warnings and the evidence staring them in the face in the form of "mirage-like clumps" (305) of manic animals. Caroline Miles's article referenced in the Clothing and Race chapter that argues for Caddy's fluctuating monetary value also cites these Texas ponies as a prime example of "value with no basis in reality" (58), relating the auction to debates of the era about government tools to fix fluctuating values.

The next morning, Buck emerges for the auction with a new shirt and vest (309), and the crowd of men is all too obliging in having the wool pulled over their eyes by the Texan's smooth talk. Here, Barthes's focus on the discourse around clothing is more relevant. Barthes explains that an abundant discourse of clothing is necessary so that there is a disparity of consciousness between seller and buyer: "In order to blunt the buyer's calculating consciousness, a veil must be drawn around the object—a veil of images, of reasons, of meanings; … in short, a simulacrum of the real object must be created" (*The Fashion System* xi-xii). This idea is even more readily observed earlier in the novel when Pat Stamper trades Ab Snopes his own horse back to him by clothing the horse, modifying its appearance with decorative paint and air pumped under its skin with a bicycle pump (47-9). Dressing up the horse and employing strategic discourse around the object actually changes the animal's value. This returns us to the gold-standard debate and the "fear that reliable standards of value were mere arbitrary constructs" (VanderVeen 46). Allowing common people access to money and wealth comes with the destabilizing counter proposition of unmooring value from a stable referent: things that seem valuable may only be dressed up as something they are not, even cash money as Ratliff and Bookwright find out with the coins they unearth. Moreover, the spotted horses that the locals must forever chase but never truly possess, never truly harness for their value, could represent any material goods, such as mass-produced fashionable clothing, introduced from outside the community that disrupt the local culture of home manufacture.

The democratization of American money is complete as Flem's wheeling and dealing quickly enables him to begin making loans to townspeople at what we can only assume to be advantageous interest rates (67-8). As in the gold-standard debate, Flem's fashion allows him access to what had been previously the preserve of the patrician class. The fact that his "patented necktie" (173) is "made for him by the gross" (64) suggests machine-made, modern clothing as well, as opposed to the hand-made, home-spun goods of the past, which most of his fellow Frenchman's Bend residents still use. He is emblematic of the machine-made, mass-produced, profit-driven future. However, there is still a nagging question of how Flem pulls off this rapid rise. Flem outsmarts practically everyone he deals with, yet the Snopes clan as a whole is not renowned for their intelligence. The similarities of all the Snopeses to one another are commented upon numerous times in the novel, yet it is a *lack* of intelligence that more often than not is a defining feature. So what might account for Flem apparently being smarter than not only the rest of his extended family, but everyone in Frenchman's Bend? Godden also notes the curiosity of Flem's success, and he suggests that luck explains Flem's successful rise, but what if the clothes themselves as actants are responsible for making Flem smarter?

Fashion historian and critic Anne Hollander notes that when clothes stop being produced by hand and at home, they ironically become more personal: "Ever since industrialized fashion began to offer everybody a vast array of constantly varying mass-produced garments and adornments to play with, it has in fact been possible for many of the suggestions and satisfactions of clothing to be aimed mainly at the self, not the viewer" (107). Flem and his clothing are figured as modern in the novel, and we therefore might see him dressing for himself as much as for his audience. Bill Brown's thing theory, as discussed in the Introduction, investigates "how inanimate objects constitute human subjects, how they move them, how they threaten them, how they facilitate or threaten their relation to other subjects" ("Thing Theory" 7), and Flem's clothing behaves as an actant on not only his audience but himself. The relatively new concept of enclothed cognition offers a specific, scientific explanation of how objects can shape, influence, and constitute human subjects.

Hajo Adam and Adam D. Galinsky, researchers at Northwestern University, coined the term enclothed cognition in the publication of their experimental results in the *Journal of Experimental Social Psychology*. The authors point out that there has been significant research about the effects of clothes on *viewers* and how the wearer is perceived, but very little on the effects of clothes on the wearers themselves: "Indeed, research on the effects of clothing on people's own perceptions and behavior is relatively scattered and disintegrated" (918). Their article offers "a potentially unifying framework to integrate past findings and capture the diverse impact that clothes can have on the wearer by proposing that enclothed cognition involves the co-occurrence of two independent factors—the symbolic meaning of the clothes and the physical experience of wearing them" (918). Their experiment showed significant gains in attention-related tasks when participants wore a doctor's white lab coat. The results were also greater when participants *wore* the lab coat as opposed to only being shown it and exposed to it, which leads Hajo and Galinsky to conclude that wearing clothes has a more significant effect than the already accepted phenomenon of "material priming," a term that refers to "the phenomenon that simply being exposed to a physical item ... can increase behaviors consistent with the symbolic meaning of that item" (919).

Moreover, they found that similar gains on the same activities were not found when the participants wore the same coat but were told that it was a painter's coat rather than a doctor's coat. The researchers conclude that two components are important for enclothed cognition to occur, the physical act of wearing the clothes and the symbolic meaning attached to the clothes:

> We argue, however, that actually wearing a piece of clothing and having the accompanying physical experiences (e.g., seeing it on one's body, feeling it on one's skin, etc.) will make it significantly more likely for the piece of clothing to influence the wearer's psychological processes, above and beyond basic material priming effects. That is, embodying the clothing's symbolic meaning is a critical element in our enclothed cognition perspective.
>
> (919)

Therefore, Flem may actually become smarter, more aware, and more perceptive when he dons his white shirt and tie. The clothing affects him as well as the impressions of him that others have. Whether his outfit is *actually* one that a store clerk, loan shark, horse dealer, or bank president would wear would not alter the effects of enclothed cognition, so long as Flem believes that it is. That is, the symbolic meaning of the clothes to him could engender the effects of enclothed cognition, regardless of what they might signify to others. Thus, Flem's much commented upon clothing may not only be a symbol of his change in socio-economic position, but, in fact, the cause of it, allowing him to fashion a new, prosperous, and modern self. Noting the possibility that clothing affects Flem directly suggests that perhaps other characters experience similar, if less dramatic, effects. Alec Gray almost succeeds in pulling off a similar rise, but never has Flem's luck. Temple's change of clothing at Miss Reba's might help explain her altered mental state, though of course the trauma she endures is much more significant. Joe Christmas and Rosa Coldfield are perhaps negative examples in that they never try to alter their dress and their lives stagnate. Charles Etienne Bon's enforced change into "the harsh and shapeless denim ... of the sons of Ham" (160) certainly seem to impact his mental state, and he tries to recapture his former self by wearing his old clothes (162). Lucas Beauchamp's pride and dignity are conceivably more created by his regal clothing than reflective of it, though to recognize that in no way diminishes his own role as author of his own life: the mutually constitutive nature of clothing and self is what Faulkner reveals.

The Town and *The Mansion*

As the Snopes Trilogy continues, so does Flem's rise in Jefferson. *The Town* opens with Flem taking over the restaurant co-owned by Ratliff, and while he and Eula both have to wear a "greasy apron" (4, 10), that garment soon passes to I. O. Snopes (40) while Jefferson's new power couple continues their climb. The Cotillion Ball turns out to be Flem's coming-out party. While Gowan and Gavin Stevens wear white bow ties and suits and the women wear diamond earrings and white gloves, Flem shows up in "a rented dress suit" (76)—no mention of whether he wears his trademark black bow tie on this occasion. Chick as narrator of this section summarizes the town's reaction to Flem's outfit, first calling it "the second footprint" he has made on the town (the water tank being the first [4]), but he then immediately revises this characterization: "it wasn't anymore just a footprint than that water tank was a monument: it was a red flag. No: it was that sign at the railroad crossing that says Look Out For The Locomotive" (76).

Compared to his metamorphosis in *The Hamlet*, Flem does not undergo as dramatic of a sartorial change in the second Snopes novel. The bow tie continues as a trademark, but he makes a significant alteration to his wardrobe when he jettisons his checked cap in favor of a hat "of the broad black felt kind which country preachers and politicians wore" (146), a hat that, according to *The Mansion*, "somebody told him was the kind of hat bankers wore" (72). If Flem has designs on climbing the ladder—first to superintendent of the power plant, then vice president of the bank—he needs to look the part, and the garb of a politician or preacher is more befitting the echelon of society to which he aspires than that of restaurateur of a back-alley greasy spoon. Not only that, but the effect of enclothed cognition depends on the wearer believing the clothing to be associated with a profession: if Flem thinks he's wearing a banker's hat, he may actually think more like a banker. Things and objects are important for Flem to play his new role convincingly, and even his family are mere props to him: "a vice president's wife and child along with the rest of the vice president's furniture in the vice president's house" (234). The family rifts between Flem and both his wife and daughter that we see play out over the course of *The Town* and *The Mansion* have their roots in his inability to treat people as anything other than more material goods that either aid or hinder his rise.

Overalls are the uniform of the poor, common farmer that Flem has left behind, and Gavin Stevens narrates an encounter between just such a farmer and

Clothing and Class 149

the now-powerful vice president that accentuates the importance of clothing to not only Flem, but also to the unnamed tenant farmer:

> [O]ne still in the overalls and the tieless shirt and still thrall, attached irrevocably ... to the worn-out tenant farm which—the farm and the tie-less shirt and the overalls—he had not wrenched free of yet as Snopes himself had, nor ever would probably and who for that very reason had watched the rise of one exactly like himself, from the overalls and the grinding landlord to a white shirt and a tie and the vice presidency of a bank; watched this not with admiration but simply with envy and respect (ay, hatred too), stopping Snopes on the street one day, calling him mister, servile and cringing because of the white shirt and the tie but hating them also because they were not his.
> (281)

This passage recalls Faulkner's more famous expression of socio-economic forces tying agricultural laborers to the land in *Go Down, Moses*: "two threads frail as truth and impalpable as equators yet cable-strong to bind for life them who made the cotton to the land their sweat fell on" (279). The cotton in the clothing and the clothing likely bought on credit or made at home with precious resources keep these farmers tied to the worn-out land of an anachronistic tenant farming system. Flem has seen this reality, as does his cousin Ab in "Barn Burning," and he has escaped what must have seemed his fate. The shirt and tie are now not just symbols of Flem's new status but more like the crown and scepter of the king, tools that are part of what help him attain and maintain that status, tools that make others cringe before him. The servile farmer waits for change to happen that will allow him to own fine clothes, but Flem has figured out how to make objects work for him.

A funny thing happens in the latter half of the Snopes Trilogy, though: Flem stagnates. He is described as being seen about town "placid, inscrutable, unchanged in the broad black planter's hat and the minute bow tie seen somewhere about the Square at least once during the day as regular as the courthouse clock itself" (304). The tie that once seemed so novel is commonplace, "the tiny bow tie which he had worn for eighteen years now" (323–4), and just as boring as his (now not-so) new hat: "and him sitting there in that black hat that still looked brand new and like he had borrowed it, and that little bow tie that never had and never would look anything but new" (372). The description of the hat as looking "borrowed" recalls Flem's rented suit from early in *The Town*, suggesting a lack of movement or even a reversal, since now Eula, the wife who was so important as a prop on his ascent, has killed herself to escape this stultifying life. As Jon Smith puts it, for Faulkner "the problem with the traditional South is—in *The Mansion*, at least—boredom ... Eula Varner Snopes is agreed to have committed suicide out of boredom and even Flem Snopes is hypothesized to have done so" (*Finding Purple* 92). The second installment of the Snopes Trilogy ends, in fact, with shabbily dressed Snopeses on the move, albeit leaving Jefferson, in the form of Byron's children being shipped back to El Paso like so much cargo: "the girl and the two boys in overalls and Ratliff's least un in its ankle-length single garment like a man's discarded shirt made out of flour- or meal-sacking or perhaps the remnant of an old tent. We never did know which it was" (390). The town, "all of us; we represented Jefferson," may have been unable to prevent Flem's clothing-based rise, but they make sure to strip these Snopses down to literal rags and affix shipping tags to their garments, as if to confirm that these children do not belong in Jefferson and barely count as human (390).

In *The Mansion*, Flem's torpor continues, and the rhetorical emphasis is on consistency and uniformity rather than change. Multiple times, descriptions of "the one Snopes of them all who had risen, broken free" (39) highlight not his rise, movement, or change, but the lack of those things. Montgomery Ward Snopes disdainfully refers to "that white shirt and that damn little ten-cent snap-on bow tie; they said the same one he had worn in from Frenchman's Bend sixteen years ago" (72). Ratliff refers to Flem as the man the town "had done got accustomed to for twenty years now: the same little snap-on bow tie he had got outen the Frenchman's Bend mule wagon in and only the hat was new and different" (172). When Mink finally comes face to face with his successful cousin toward the end of the novel, his reaction is again centered on continuity in clothing and character:

> [A] little changed of course: the black planter's hat he had heard about in Parchman but the little bow tie might have been the same one he had been wearing forty years ago behind the counter in Varner's store, the shirt a white city shirt and the pants were dark city pants too and the shoes were polished city shoes instead of farmer's brogans. But no different, really.
>
> (453)

The new hat is a minor alteration, and we even learn that he sold his former cloth cap to a young Black boy, a return or even regression to Jody Varner's behavior at the beginning of *The Hamlet*. Flem's biggest move in the latter half of the Snopes Trilogy is from bank vice president to president, accompanied by a physical move to De Spain's former house. The house may be the final prop needed for his veneer of respectability to be "completely complete," but the rut into which he has fallen has the rest of the town realize that "it was jest the house that was altered and transmogrified and symbolised: not him" (172). That is, when Flem first began his ascent, he was able to use his exterior appearance to disguise, and even alter, his interior makeup. After so many years, however, the town sees through his purchase of the De Spain house for the superficial gesture it is, with no concomitant change in internal identity.

Significantly, Flem makes no changes to the house's interior, "all them big rooms furnished like De Spain left them," and never allows anyone to see what's inside (173). The novel suggests that his sole devotion to money has prevented Flem from evolving, describing him as "belonging simply to Money" (461) and saying that he "died in his prime (financially anyway)" (460). Ratliff speculates that Flem was "bored" (472) like Eula prior to her suicide and that he therefore let himself be killed. His inner stagnation is reflected in and caused by his lack of exterior change, especially clothing, while his resistance to changing his appearance also forestalls any further development. In terms of fashion, Flem's shift from a renegade outsider to part of the establishment is unsurprising. Bernard explains how the "new" in fashion is always co-opted as when, for instance, punk and hip-hop fashions that at first challenged and destabilized fashion paradigms become co-opted into safe and marketable commodities (45–6, 129). Flem's "proto-punk" bowtie eventually becomes a marker of his insider, establishment status as he becomes absorbed by the mainstream. Ultimately, Flem is perhaps most like Judge Howard Allison in "Beyond," a story set in the afterlife. Upon his death, the Judge forsakes the opportunity to meet his own son who died years before at the age of ten. Instead, he returns home to climb in his coffin, first changing out of the uncomfortable outfit of pajamas and overcoat into a comfortable familiarity: "they were his own, and he fitted himself to the olden and familiar embrace ... this is best after all. An old man is never at home save in his own garments: his own old thinking and beliefs; old hands and feet, elbow, knee, shoulder which he knows will fit" (797). In a letter to a *Harper's* editor (where the story originally appeared), Faulkner explains that the Judge "naturally and humanly prefers the sorrow with which he has lived so long that it not only does not hurt anymore, but is perhaps even a pleasure, to the uncertainty of change, even when it means that he may gain his son again" (*Selected Letters* 71–2). Flem similarly rejects his child and chooses stasis signified by a familiar set of clothes, in effect choosing the comfort of death over the unknown disquiet of change.

Ratliff makes his own trademark blue shirts himself while also selling sewing machines to help women create clothing for their families at home. Thus, he is aligned with older, traditional models of consumer consumption, even as he sells the latest technology on his traveling route. His distrust of and distaste for Flem's ascent and the subsequent waves of Snopes in Yoknapatawpha likewise establishes a role of gatekeeper for proper Jefferson society wary of outsiders who do not or should not belong. Ratliff's encounter with a designer necktie in New York City illustrates the cyclical nature of consumer fashion. Ratliff is shocked that one tie could be displayed in a shop window alone and could cost $75 (185–8). Its value comes from the fact that it is a one-of-a-kind Allanovna creation, the designer's name justifying the price. Hoke McCarron immediately recognizes the tie as "an Allanovna" (190), but Ratliff tries to reject Myra Allanovna's attempt to give him two of her creations.[11] This is perhaps the culmination of the saga of Flem's tie: whereas his machine-made tie signaled modernity and a new identity available to the common man in *The Hamlet*, now the handcrafted, artisan piece is more valuable, meaningful, and status-laden than the mass-produced item, a throwback to home manufacture but with the modern twist of the artist's name attached to the item conferring value. Ratliff's sexual attraction to Allanovna signals his desire for the luxury goods she represents, but the $75 ties are a threat to Ratliff's conception of himself as a humble traveling salesman: "I sells sewing machines in Missippi. I cant have it knowed back there that I paid seventy-five dollars a piece for neckties" (196). Ratliff does accept the ties but apparently never wears them after returning from New York (352). He instead indulges their symbolic meaning as well as their importance as things, keeping one on display "under a glass bell" (256) in a room he describes as a shrine to Eula, the confirmed bachelor's desire for her hermetically sealed in glass as well.[12]

Ratliff's tie is not, then, an example of Veblen's conspicuous consumption, where this chapter began. He is not interested in the communication aspect of

---

[11] According to the editors of Digital Yoknapatawpha, "Faulkner almost certainly bases this character on Lucilla Mara de Vescovi, an Italian immigrant who opened Countess Mara, a men's neckwear company, in New York in the early 1930s; Countess Mara ties are still sold today" ("Faulkner's *The Mansion*").

[12] Gordon argues that Ratliff is hiding (sometimes openly) his homosexuality throughout the Trilogy (229–55). If one follows this reading, then Ratliff's true desires are, perhaps, what is safely sealed away rather than released. On the other hand, if one takes Allanovna's directive to Ratliff at the end of their encounter—"Then kiss me" (197)—to be evidence of heterosexual desire, then the preserved tie in Eula's shrine might indicate that she was his true object of desire with Allanovna a poor replacement. Of course, there is no need to read his sexuality as either/or, which could further complicate possible readings.

fashion here, not wearing the tie to impress, and even worries about the damage to his reputation if word gets out how much he paid for a necktie. It is not significant as a marker of status or tool to advance class striving but because it was designed by Myra Allanovna personally or perhaps purely for its aesthetic properties as an object of design. It is important as a thing, that is, not for what it might communicate to others, to Ratliff at least, though it does hold different meanings for others when he wears it to a party. Smith writes about this incident and reminds us both of "Faulkner's lifelong and obvious love of well-designed objects" and that the 1950s are a time when Americans placed great promise in the transformative power of things (93). Ratliff purchases the designer tie because Stevens will not allow him to wear the ugly pink and green tie he bought in Jefferson. Smith notes that Ratliff's new tie is recognized at a New York party as an Allanovna and he is mistaken for either an Oklahoma oilman or Texas cattleman (*The Mansion* 192) and describes the encounter as "a comic case of mistaken identity, of unexpected social mobility" (Smith 97). Although it may seem that Faulkner is mocking Ratliff as well as consumerism-run amok in the form of $75 neckties, Smith argues that it is "an important step for Faulkner, whose characters up to this point have generally, in their progress from peasantry to respectability, amassed design objects solely as markers of their status" (102). Here, there is appreciation of the object as art and Ratliff displays the tie next to Barton Kohl's sculpture in his home, and Smith's reading of the necktie helpfully draws attention to the object itself, as well as its connection to Ratliff's sense of personal identity: "It is a celebration of beauty, an assertion of personal dignity, and, most of all, an affirmation of selfhood" (105).

In texts written from the beginning to the end of his career, Faulkner consistently links clothing and class in similar ways. Clothing can demarcate class boundaries, and clothing can be a part of overcoming those boundaries. Dress may reflect the reality the wearer wishes to enact, but it also can act itself and help bring that desired change into reality. The costuming of Faulkner's youth is a component of his fiction throughout his life, but he also increasingly becomes aware of the value of clothing as thing, as object, as art, something with both private and public meaning that endures and leaves a mark on the world. Faulkner's mocking of crass, bourgeois materialism in *Flags in the Dust* changes to a more complex understanding of the power of objects in The Snopes Trilogy. Across Faulkner's career, he creates characters who learn to adapt to the new and the modern, while holding on to the useful parts of the past. Characters who remain stuck in the past, like Bayard and, eventually, Flem, get left behind and die off. Clothing is often a tool for those seeking to move forward to change their station in life. The fact that these attempts are sometimes unsuccessful shows a healthy dose of skepticism on Faulkner's part about the ability of the modern world to deliver its alluring promises, as the ultra-modern pilots of *Pylon* crashing to earth attests. The themes of escaping or transcending boundaries that run through the chapters on gender and race continue in relation to class. The pilots of *Pylon* try to escape but are ultimately bound by an inflexible class system, echoing Alec Gray's post-First World War experience. In relation to class, the theme of identity creation is related to the use of objects. That is, people attempt to use objects, especially clothing, to improve their status and standing but this can lead to prioritizing the image over one's interior identity in the process. Characters like Thomas Sutpen, Flem Snopes, and Alec Gray lose a sense of self as they treat others like objects after some initial success using things to further their goals.

It is not the case that using objects necessarily entails treating people as objects—that is perhaps just the case for these white men. Patricia Yaeger, in *Dirt and Desire*, quotes from Harriet Jacobs's slave narrative that "a slave, *being* property, can *hold* no property" as part of a discussion about the importance of things in Southern literature. Yaeger discusses the importance of objects as property in African American literature because in a world where "self-definition" is defined through property, the lack of it creates "identity trauma" and racial animus (196). She uses Charles Chesnutt's "Po' Sandy" to illustrate the power of objects, as even when Sandy is transformed from subject to object (turned into a tree then cut down for lumber), he still exerts some degree of agency in the story (198), a version of the idea of objects as actants. Yaeger explains the importance of objects in her analysis by saying that "things acquire such an aura in southern literature because they are shadowed by a world where people have been defined as things" (206). This point underpins my analysis in the preceding chapters, and it emphasizes how clothing is perhaps especially important for women and African Americans, those groups most often defined as things in Faulkner's South. If the power of things can be harnessed by people in these marginalized groups, then they can perhaps disrupt or undermine or challenge the hegemony of the dominant group who has been defined historically by their ownership of property. Harnessing the power of clothing to self-fashion (to return to Greenblatt's term) a new identity is empowering to the individual and challenging to the status quo, in both cases because the power of the actant object is utilized by, even transferred to, the subject. This empowerment is recognized by the dominant white male culture, resulting in what Yaeger calls "white object panic" to describe "the terror that blacks might use the moving objects that have become the calling cards of capitalist and late capitalist society as a route to self-possession" (216).

Of course, this same logic applies to male fears of female self-possession, even if this threat is ultimately neutralized in the vast majority of Faulkner's fictions. That is, the women characters who manage to fashion a new, modern identity either die, like Charlotte Rittenmeyer and Eula Varner, flee altogether, like Miss Quentin and Laverne Shuman, or are shamed and "put in their place," like Caddy Compson, Temple Drake, and Drusilla Sartoris. Perhaps only Linda Snopes Kohl fashions herself a modern identity successfully with the aid of and reflected by her clothing. It is important to note that in his characterization of her in *The Mansion*, Faulkner no longer defines the masculine garments she wears in the same transgressive terms as those worn by Drusilla and Charlotte. Faulkner himself and perhaps the era have shifted considerably from the 1920s, perhaps in part due to women like those listed above, and the resistance to what once would have been shocking challenges to notions of feminine propriety elicit comparatively little concern in the 1950s. Faulkner's later novels also show the most evidence of Black characters becoming fully modern subjects through their dress and attendant behavior. Roth Edmond's unnamed mistress in *Go Down, Moses*, the great, great-granddaughter of Tomey's Turl, although a minor character, is another woman who dons masculine clothing and defines herself on her own terms. The intersectionality of gender and race complicates her situation further, and she verbally and morally bests the white male Ike McCaslin in her only scene. Her great-uncle Lucas Beauchamp also fashions a strong and defiant identity in the face of white racism, and his clothing is a substantial part of that self-fashioning in both *Go Down, Moses* and *Intruder in the Dust*. Their common ancestor, Tomey's Turl, utilizes the power of clothing even at a time when he is legally defined as an object of property himself, succeeding at self-fashioning where characters like Joe Christmas and Charles Etienne Bon fail. Their failure at self-definition is very much related to what Watson describes as characters who fail at becoming white "[who] are not so much subjects without properties as subjects without *property*, the most valuable property of all: Lockean self-ownership" ("Introduction" xiii). Thus, identity creation is bound in complex ways with the function of clothes as objects. The symbolic power of clothing conveys layers of meanings to viewers, the ability to own and wield clothing as a possession can provide agency and identity, while the concept of enclothed cognition suggests a powerful effect of clothing on the mental state of the wearer.

After *Go Down, Moses* and *Intruder in the Dust*, Faulkner shifts his attention away from race toward issues of economics and class. As this final chapter has shown, however, the seeds for these topics are present in numerous early works as well, presaging the concerns of the Snopes Trilogy. Even without the added burden of racial difference, Faulkner's characters are often failures at climbing the social ladder, though they at times use clothing in ways that bring them closer to success. Seduced by the allure of objects, multiple characters come to believe that if they can just possess the right amount and type of things, the power of the things might improve their class standing and then allow them to own even more material goods. Flem Snopes and Thomas Sutpen find some success, while Alec Gray, the pilots of *Pylon*, and Bayard Sartoris fail to become modern middle-class subjects in the way that Ratliff achieves by the end of *The Mansion*. Even in the numerous instances of characters who unsuccessfully refashion their identities, Faulkner reveals the power of clothing. Indeed, it is often the clothing that provokes reactions that doom the characters to failure, defeat, or death. Clothing is the outer manifestation of inner change, a signal or warning to others of internal contravention, and a catalyst for change itself through its status as actant. Faulkner's personal love of fine clothing and interest in fashion suggests why he is so attuned to the power of clothing in his fiction and the transformative effect that dress can have on both the wearer and the audience. To emphasize the importance of seeing clothing as not just a semiotic text but as an object is really to argue for understanding humans as nodes in a network as opposed to solitary autonomous beings. This viewpoint decenters humans and recognizes the mutual influences and complicated causal relationships among animals (in Faulkner, Old Ben, Lion, Jewel's horse, and many mules), systems (tenant farming or the judicial/penal systems, for instance), objects (the way Cash's tools are an integral part of his identity, for example), and people. Even people who have died continue to exert influence, as is the case with Hightower's parents, Johnny Sartoris and his powerful coat, and even Old Carothers McCaslin hanging like a specter over Ike's life. This study of clothing argues for the value of paying attention to nonhuman things and the ways they help fashion our reality, our lives, our selves.

Works Cited

Adam, H. and A. D. Galinsky "Enclothed Cognition." *Journal of Experimental Social Psychology*, Vol. 48, No. 4 (2012), pp. 918–25.
Anderson, Mark M. *Kafka's Clothes: Ornament and Aestheticism in the Habsburg Fin de Siècle*. Clarendon, 1995.
Appadurai, Arjun, ed. *The Social Life of Things: Commodities in Cultural Perspective*. Cambridge UP, 1986.
Baker, Patricia. *Fashions of a Decade: The 1940s*. Facts on File, 1992.
Baldwin, James. "No Name in the Street." *The Price of the Ticket: Collected Nonfiction, 1948-1985*. St. Martin's/Marek, 1985, pp. 449–552.
Barnard, Malcolm. *Fashion as Communication*. 2nd Edition. Routledge, 2002.
Barthes, Roland. *The Fashion System*. Translated by Matthew Ward and Richard Howard. Hill and Wang, 1983.
Barthes, Roland. *The Pleasure of the Text*. Translated by Richard Miller. Hill and Wang, 1975.
Beckert, Sven. *Empire of Cotton: A Global History*. Vintage, 2014.
Bennett, Jane. "Systems and Things: On Vital Materialism and Object-Oriented Philosophy." *The Nonhuman Turn*, edited by Richard Grusin, U of Minnesota P, 2015, pp. 223–39.
Bennett, Jane. *Vibrant Matter: A Political Ecology of Things*. Duke UP, 2010.
Blotner, Joseph. *Faulkner: A Biography*. 2 Vols. Random House, 1974.
Blotner, Joseph. *Faulkner: A Biography*. One-Volume Edition. Random House, 1984.
Blotner, Joseph. The Joseph Blotner Papers. Louis Daniel Brodsky Collection of William Faulkner Materials. Southeast Missouri State University.
Blotner, Joseph, ed. *Selected Letters of William Faulkner*. Random House, 1977.
Blotner, Joseph and Frederick L. Gwynn, eds. *Faulkner in the University*. U of Virginia P, 1959.
Brevda, William. "'Without Even His Hat Took Off': Falkner's *Sanctuary*." *Mississippi Quarterly*, Vol. 74, No. 4 (2021), pp. 393–422.
Brodsky, L. D. *William Faulkner, Life Glimpses*. U of Texas P, 1990.
Brooks, Cleanth. *Toward Yoknapatawpha and Beyond*. Yale UP, 1978.
Brown, Bill. *A Sense of Things: The Object Matter of American Literature*. U of Chicago P, 2003.
Brown, Bill. "Thing Theory." *Critical Inquiry*, Vol. 28, No. 1, Things (Autumn, 2001), pp. 1–22.

Brydon, Anne and Sandra Niessen. *Consuming Fashion: Adorning the Transnational Body*. Berg, 1998.

Burgers, Johannes H., John Corrigan, and Ben Robbins. "Faulkner's *The Mansion*." Added to the project: 2018. Digital Yoknapatawpha, U of Virginia, http://faulkner.iath.virginia.edu

Cavallaro, Dani and Alexandra Warwick. *Fashioning the Frame: Boundaries, Dress and Body*. Berg, 1998.

Cofield, J. R. "Many Faces, Many Moods." *William Faulkner of Oxford*, edited by James W. Webb and A. Wigfall Green. Louisiana State UP, 1965, pp. 107–13.

Commins, Dorothy. *What Is an Editor? Saxe Commins at Work*. U of Chicago P, 1978.

Constantino, Maria. *Fashions of a Decade: The 1930s*. Facts on File, 1992.

Cook, Sylvia Jenkins. "Reading Clothes: Literary Dress in William Faulkner and Erskine Caldwell." *The Southern Literary Journal*, Vol. XLVI, No. 1 (Fall 2013), pp. 1–18.

Cowdrey, Albert E. *This Land, This South: An Environmental History*. UP of Kentucky, 1983.

Dattel, Gene. *Cotton and Race in the Making of America: The Human Costs of Economic Power*. Ivan R. Dee, 2009.

Davis, David. *World War I and Southern Modernism*. UP of Mississippi, 2019.

Davis, Fred. *Fashion, Culture, and Identity*. U of Chicago P, 1992.

Davis, Thadious M. "From Jazz Syncopation to Blues Elegy: Faulkner's Development of Black Characterization." *Faulkner and Race*. UP of Mississippi, 1987, pp. 70–92.

Davis, Thadious M. *Games of Property: Law, Race, Gender and Faulkner's Go Down Moses*. Duke UP, 2003.

Denton, Ren. "Telling the White Man: Decoding the Gendered Blues and Domestic Violence in Hurston's 'Sweat' and Faulkner's 'That Evening Sun.'" *Faulkner and Hurston*, edited by Christopher Rieger and Andrew B. Leiter. Southeast Missouri State UP, 2017, pp. 91–110.

Doyle, Don H. *Faulkner's County: The Historical Roots of Yoknapatawpha*. U of North Carolina P, 2001.

Duvall, John. "Faulkner's Crying Game: Male Homosexual Panic." *Faulkner and Gender*, edited by Donald M. Kartiganer and Ann J. Abadie. UP of Mississippi, 1996, pp. 48–72.

Duvall, John. *Race and White Identity in Southern Fiction: From Faulkner to Morrison*. Palgrave Macmillan, 2008.

Eig, Jonathan. *Get Capone: The Secret Plot That Captured America's Most Wanted Gangster*. Simon & Schuster, 2010.

Elahi, Babak. *The Fabric of American Literary Realism: Readymade Clothing, Social Mobility, and Assimilation*. McFarland, 2009.

Evans, Medford. "Oxford, Mississippi." *Southwest Review*, Vol. xv, No. 1 (Autumn 1929), pp. 46–63.

Faulkner, John. *My Brother Bill: An Affectionate Reminiscence*. Trident, 1963.

Faulkner, William. *Absalom, Absalom!* 1936. Vintage International, 1990.

Faulkner, William. "Appendix: Compson 1699–1945." *The Sound and the Fury*, 3rd Norton Critical Edition, edited by Michael Gorra. W.W. Norton and Company, 2016, pp. 258–71.

Faulkner, William. *As I Lay Dying*. 1930. Vintage International, 1990.

Faulkner, William. *Collected Stories of William Faulkner*. Vintage International, 1995.

Faulkner, William. *Essays, Speeches, and Public Letters*. Edited by James B. Meriwether. Random House, 1966.

Faulkner, William. *Flags in the Dust*. Vintage International, 2012.

Faulkner, William. *Go Down, Moses*. 1942. Vintage International, 2011.

Faulkner, William. *The Hamlet*. 1940. Vintage International, 1991.

Faulkner, William. *Intruder in the Dust*. 1948. Vintage International, 2011.

Faulkner, William. *Knight's Gambit*. 1949. Vintage International, 2011.

Faulkner, William. *Light in August*. 1932. Vintage International, 1990.

Faulkner, William. *The Mansion*. 1959. Vintage International, 2011.

Faulkner, William. *Mosquitoes*. 1927. Liveright, 1997.

Faulkner, William. *Pylon*. 1935. Vintage International, 2011.

Faulkner, William. *The Reivers*. 1962. Vintage International, 2011.

Faulkner, William. *Sanctuary*. 1931. Vintage International, 1993.

Faulkner, William. *Soldiers' Pay*. 1926. Liveright, 1997.

Faulkner, William. *The Sound and the Fury*. 1929. Vintage International, 1990.

Faulkner, William. *The Town*. 1957. Vintage International, 2011.

Faulkner, William. *The Unvanquished*. 1938. Vintage International, 1991.

Faulkner, William. *The Wild Palms [If I Forget Thee, Jerusalem]*. 1939. Vintage International, 1995.

Fischer, Gayle V. *Pantaloons and Power: A Nineteenth-Century Dress Reform in the United States*. Kent State UP, 2001.

Gammon, Katherine. "Groundbreaking Study Finds 13.3 Quadrillion Plastic Fibers in California's Environment." *The Guardian*, 16 Oct. 2020, www.theguardian.com/us-news/2020/oct/16/plastic-waste-microfibers-california-study. Accessed November 11, 2020.

Gantt, Patricia. "'This Guerilla Warfare of Everyday Life': The Politics of Clothing in Faulkner's Fiction." *Mississippi Quarterly*, Vol. 49, No. 3 (Summer 1996), pp. 409–23.

Gatrell, Simon. *Thomas Hardy Writing Dress*. Peter Lang, 2011.

Gilbert, Sandra M. "Costumes of the Mind: Transvestism as Metaphor in Modern Literature." *Writing and Sexual Difference*, edited by Elizabeth Abel. U of Chicago P, 1982, pp. 193–219.

Godden, Richard. *Fictions of Labor: William Faulkner and the South's Long Revolution*. Cambridge UP, 1997.

Godden, Richard. *William Faulkner: An Economy of Complex Words*. Princeton UP, 2007.

Gordon, Phillip. *Gay Faulkner: Uncovering a Homosexual Presence in Yoknapatawpha and Beyond*. UP of Mississippi, 2020.

Greenblatt, Stephen. *Renaissance Self-Fashioning: From More to Shakespeare*. U of Chicago P, 1980.

Grusin, Richard, ed. *The Nonhuman Turn*. U of Minnesota P, 2015.

Gurung, Regan A. R., Rosalyn Stoa, Nicholas Livingston, and Hannah Mather. "Can Success Deflect Racism? Clothing and Perceptions of African American Men." *The Journal of Social Psychology*, Published online 29 June 2020, https://doi.org/10.1080/00224545.2020.1787938. Accessed December 16, 2020.

Gwin, Minrose. "Did Ernest Like Gordon?: Faulkner's *Mosquitoes* and the Bite of Gender Trouble." *Faulkner and Gender*, edited by Donald M. Kartiganer and Ann J. Abadie. UP of Mississippi, 1996, pp. 120–44.

Gwin, Minrose. *The Feminine and Faulkner: Reading (Beyond) Sexual Difference*. U of Tennessee P, 1990.

Hamblin, Robert. "Beyond the Edge of the Map: Faulkner, Turner, and the Frontier Line." *Faulkner in the Twenty-First Century*, edited by Robert W. Hamblin and Ann J. Abadie. UP of Mississippi, 2003, pp. 154–71.

Haynes, Gavin. "The White Polo Shirt: How the Alt-Right Co-Opted a Modern Classic." *The Guardian*, August 30, 2017, www.theguardian.com/fashion/2017/aug/30/the-white-polo-shirt-how-the-alt-right-co-opted-a-modern-classic. Accessed October 20, 2020.

Hempstead, Susanna. "Once a Bitch, Always a Bitch: Rereading Caddy in *The Sound and the Fury*." *The Faulkner Journal*, Vol. 31, No. 1 (Spring 2017), pp. 23–42.

Herald, Jacqueline. *Fashions of a Decade: The 1920s*. Facts on File, 1991.

Hoeller, Hildegard. "Racial Currency: Zora Neale Hurston's 'The Gilded Six-Bits' and the Gold-Standard Debate." *American Literature*, Vol. 77, No. 4 (December 2005), pp. 761–85.

Hollander, Anne. *Feeding the Eye*. Farrar, Straus and Giroux, 1999.

Hollander, Anne. *Seeing through Clothes*. The Viking Press, 1978.

Hughes, Clair. *Dressed in Fiction*. Berg, 2005.

Ibrahim, Habiba. *Black Age: Oceanic Lifespans and the Time of Black Life*. New York UP, 2021.

Kartiganer, Donald. "'So I, Who had Never had a War …': William Faulkner, War, and the Modern Imagination." *Modern Fiction Studies*, Vol. 44, No. 3 (1998), pp. 619–45.

Kern, Stephen. *The Modernist Novel*. Cambridge UP, 2011.

Kuhn, Cynthia. *Self-Fashioning in Margaret Atwood's Fiction*. Peter Lang, 2005.

Latour, Bruno. *Reassembling the Social: An Introduction to Actor-Network-Theory*. Oxford UP, 2005.

Leach, William R., "Transformation in a Culture of Consumption: Women and Department Stores, 1890–1925." *Journal of American History* 71 (September 1984), pp. 319–42.

López, Alfred J. "Queering Whiteness, Queering Faulkner: Hightower's 'Wild Bulges.'" *Faulkner and Whiteness*, edited by Jay Watson. UP of Mississippi, 2011, pp. 56–74.

Marx, Karl. *The Poverty of Philosophy*. International Publishers, 1963.

Matei, Adrienne. "Your Polyester Sweater Is Destroying the Environment. Here's Why." *The Guardian*, October 23, 2020, www.theguardian.com/commentisfree/2020/oct/23/your-polyester-sweater-is-destroying-the-environment-heres-why. Accessed November 11, 2020.

Matterson, Stephen. *Melville: Fashioning in Modernity*. Bloomsbury, 2014.

Matthews, John T. *William Faulkner: Seeing through the South*. Wiley-Blackwell, 2009.

McHaney, Thomas L. "Faulkner and Autobiography in Fiction." *Constructing the Self: Essays on Southern Life-Writing*, edited by Carmen Rueda-Ramos and Susana Jimémez Placer. Universitat de València, 2018.

McNeil, Peter, Vicki Karaminas, and Catherine Cole, eds. *Fashion in Fiction: Text and Clothing in Literature, Film and Television*. Berg, 2009.

Miles, Caroline. "Yankee Dollars: The Challenge to Southern Values in 'Two Dollar Wife' and *The Sound and the Fury*." *Philological Review*, Vol. 42, Nos. 1 and 2 (Spring/Fall 2016), pp. 47–63.

Miller-Idriss, Cynthia. "Why Does the Far Right Love Fred Perry? Mainstream Fashion Is Its New Camouflage." *The Guardian*, August 29, 2019, www.theguardian.com/commentisfree/2019/aug/29/far-right-fred-perry-mainstream-fashion-camouflage-brands. Accessed October 20, 2020.

Morton, Timothy. *Hyperobjects: Philosophy and Ecology after the End of the World*. U of Minnesota P, 2013.

Morton, Timothy. "They Are Here." *The Nonhuman Turn*, edited by Richard Grusin. U of Minnesota P, 2015, pp. 167–92.

Munns, Jessica and Penny Richards. "Introduction: 'The Clothes That Wear Us.'" *The Clothes That Wear Us: Essays on Dressing and Transgressing in Eighteenth-Century Culture*. U of Delaware P, 1999, pp. 9–32.

Nisetich, Rebecca. "When Difference Becomes Dangerous: Intersectional Identity Formation and the Protective Cover of Whiteness in Faulkner's *Light in August*." *The Faulkner Journal*, Vol. 31, No. 1 (Spring 2017), pp. 43–66.

Pitcher, Laura. "New Study Links Major Fashion Brands to Amazon Deforestation." *The Guardian*, November 29, 2021, https://www.theguardian.com/us-news/2021/nov/29/fashion-industry-amazon-rainforest-deforestation. Accessed December 1, 2021.

Rieger, Christopher. *Clear-Cutting Eden: Ecology and the Pastoral in Southern Literature*. U of Alabama P, 2009.

Rieger, Christopher. "'The Front Door and the Back Door of the World': Flowers, Sex, and Death in Faulkner and García Márquez." *Faulkner and García Márquez*, edited by Christopher Rieger and Andrew B. Leiter. Southeast Missouri State UP, 2020, pp. 108–24.

Roberts, Diane. *Faulkner and Southern Womanhood*. U of Georgia P, 1994.

Rollyson, Carl. *The Life of William Faulkner, Volume 1: The Past Is Never Dead, 1897–1934*. U of Virginia P, 2020.

Rollyson, Carl. *The Life of William Faulkner, Volume 2: This Alarming Paradox, 1935–1962*. U of Virginia P, 2020.

Sensibar, Judith L. *Faulkner and Love: The Women Who Shaped His Art*. Yale UP, 2009.

Sensibar, Judith L. *The Origins of Faulkner's Art*. U of Texas P, 1984.

Sheldon, Rebekah. "Form/Matter/Chora: Object-Oriented Ontology and Feminist New Materialism." *The Nonhuman Turn*, edited by Richard Grusin, U of Minnesota P, 2015, pp. 193–222.

Skrbina, David. *Panpsychism in the West*. Revised edition. MIT Press, 2017.

Smith, Jon. "Faulkner, Metropolitan Fashion, and 'The South.'" *Faulkner's Inheritance*, edited by Joseph R. Urgo and Ann J. Abadie. UP of Mississippi, 2007, pp. 82–100.

Smith, Jon. *Finding Purple America: The South and the Future of American Cultural Studies*. U of Georgia P, 2013.

Snead, James A. "*Light in August* and the Rhetorics of Racial Division." *Faulkner and Race*. UP of Mississippi, 1987, pp. 152–69.

Stallybrass, Peter. "Worn Worlds: Clothing, Mourning, and the Life of Things," *The Yale Review*, Vol. 81, No. 2 (April 1993), pp. 35–50.

Towner, Theresa M., and James B. Carothers, eds. *Reading Faulkner: Collected Stories*. UP of Mississippi, 2006.

Valentini, Chris, director. *Al Capone: Icon*. PBS, 2014.

VanderVeen, Arthur A. "Faulkner, the Interwar Gold Standard, and Discourses of Value in the 1930s" *The Faulkner Journal*, Vol. 12, No. 1 (1996), pp. 43–62.

Veblen, Thorstein. *The Theory of the Leisure Class*. 1899. The Modern Library, 1934.

Volpe, Edmond. *A Reader's Guide to William Faulkner*. Farrar, Strauss, and Giroux, 1964.

Volpe, Edmond. *A Reader's Guide to William Faulkner: The Short Stories*. Syracuse UP, 2004.

Wainwright, Michael. "Authorial Irresponsibility: Hemingway's 'The Battler' and Faulkner's 'Barn Burning.'" *Faulkner and Hemingway*, edited by Christopher Rieger and Andrew B. Leiter. Southeast Missouri State UP, 2018, pp. 80–102.

Wales-Freedman, Eden. "'Something Is Happening to Me': Witnessing Trauma in Faulkner's *Sanctuary*." *Faulkner and Morrison*, edited by Robert W. Hamblin and Christopher Rieger. Southeast Missouri State UP, 2013, pp. 231–48.

Walford, Jonathan. *Forties Fashion: From Siren Suits to the New Look*. Thames & Hudson, 2008.

Wardrop, Daneen. *Emily Dickinson and the Labor of Clothing*. U of New Hampshire P, 2009.

Watson, James G., ed. *Thinking of Home: William Faulkner's Letters to His Mother and Father, 1918–1925*. W.W. Norton and company, 1992.

Watson, James G. *William Faulkner: Self-Presentation and Performance*. U of Texas P, 2000.

Watson, Jay. "Introduction." *Faulkner and Whiteness*, edited by Jay Watson. UP of Mississippi, 2011, pp. vii–xxix.

Watson, Jay. *William Faulkner and the Faces of Modernity*. Oxford UP, 2019.

Webb, James A. and A. Wigfall Green, eds. *William Faulkner of Oxford*. Louisiana State UP, 1965.

Werner, Craig. "Minstrel Nightmares: Black Dreams of Faulkner's Dreams of Blacks." *Faulkner and Race*. UP of Mississippi, 1987, pp. 35–57.

White, Shane, and Graham White. *Stylin': African American Expressive Culture from Its Beginnings to the Zoot Suit*. Cornell UP, 1998.

Williams, Michael. "Cross-Dressing in Yoknapatawpha County." *Mississippi Quarterly*, Vol. 47, No. 3 (1994), pp. 369–90.

Williams, Patricia J. *The Alchemy of Race and Rights: Diary of a Law Professor*. Harvard UP, 1991.

Wilson, Elizabeth. *Adorned in Dreams: Fashion and Modernity*. Revised and updated Edition. Rutgers UP, 2003.

X, Malcolm with the assistance of Alex Haley. *The Autobiography of Malcolm X*. Ballantine, 1964.

Yaeger, Patricia. *Dirt and Desire: Reconstructing Southern Women's Writing, 1930–1990*. U of Chicago P, 2000.

Yaeger, Patricia. "Faulkner's 'Greek Amphora Priestess': Verbena and Violence in *The Unvanquished*." *Faulkner and Gender*, edited by Donald M. Kartiganer and Ann J. Abadie. UP of Mississippi, 1996, pp. 197–227.

Zeitlin, Michael. *Faulkner, Aviation, and Modern War*. Bloomsbury, 2022.

Zeitlin, Michael. "Faulkner, Marcuse, and Erotic Power." *Faulkner's Sexualities*, edited by Annette Trefzer and Ann J. Abadie. UP of Mississippi, 2010, pp. 54–72.

Zeitlin, Michael. "The Passion of Margaret Powers: A Psychoanalytic Reading of *Soldiers' Pay*." *Mississippi Quarterly*, Vol. 46, No. 3 (Summer 1993), pp. 351–72.

Index

Absalom, Absalom! (Faulkner) 12, 36 n.1, 92–103, 126–7, 131
   Charles Bon 98–102
   Charles Etienne St. Valery Bon 99, 107, 147, 155
   Clytie 99–100, 102
   Ellen 96–8
   Goodhue Coldfield 97
   Henry 101–2
   Judith 98–9, 101–2
   Milly Jones 96–7
   Quentin 97
   Rosa 97–8, 102
   Thomas Sutpen 92, 94–8, 101–3, 127
   Wash Jones 96–7
   young Thomas Sutpen 93
Actor-Network Theory (ANT) 6–12, 31
Adam, Hajo 146
"Ad Astra" (Faulkner) 124–5
African Americans fashion 77–80, 78 n.1, 82, 116, 119, 154
Allanovna, Myra 152–3, 152 n.12
"All the Dead Pilots" (Faulkner) 125, 129
American material culture studies 5
American money, democratization 139, 145
androgynous clothing 32, 74
antiestablishment sentiments 66
Appadurai, Arjun, social life of things 3
Art Deco style 17
As I Lay Dying (Faulkner) 28, 30
   Dewey Dell 29–30
   MacGowan 29
   Vardaman 29–30
   Vernon Tull 29
Ataturk, Mustafa Kemal 16
Atwood, Margaret 2, 33

Baldwin, James 79
Barnard, Malcolm 13, 33, 58, 62–3, 68, 100
   Fashion as Communication 13, 33

"Barn Burning" (Faulkner) 11, 135–6, 143, 149
   Major de Spain 95, 135–6
   Sarty Snopes 96, 135–6
Barnett, Ned 24, 141 n.8
Barr, Caroline 85
Barthes, Roland 72, 137, 145
   erotic in dress 72
   The Fashion System 13–14
Beckert, Sven, *Empire of Cotton: A Global History* 15
Bennett, Jane 5, 9 n.5, 13, 37, 52
   environmentalism to vital materialism 9 n.5, 10–11
   Vibrant Matter: A Political Ecology of Things 8–9
Bergson, Henri, *L'évolution créatice* 10
Bernard, Malcolm 151
Berry, Wendell 8
"Beyond" (Faulkner) 151
Bezzerides, Albert "Buzz" 25
Birch, Reginald 99 n.4
Blotner, Joseph 19, 21, 24, 27, 61, 61 n.11, 75, 79, 141 n.8
brand of modernism 3
Brazilian leather (Pitcher) 10
Brevda, William 54, 57, 84, 113
bricolage 79
Brodsky, Louis Daniel 25
   William Faulkner, Life Glimpses 23–4
Brown, Bill 146
   A Sense of Things 5–6
Burnett, Frances Hodgson, *Little Lord Fauntleroy* 99 n.4
Butler, Judith 61

Cab Calloway zoot suit 79, 111
Cajun clothing 70
Caldwell, Erskine 2
Capone, Al 53–4
Carlyle, Thomas, *Sartor Resartus* 1

Carpenter, Meta 67–8
Cavallaro, Dani 30, 39, 56–7, 120
Center for 21st Century Studies 4
Chanel, Coco 17, 17 n.9
Chesnutt, Charles, "Po' Sandy" 154
Chicago Defender 79
children's clothing 99 n.4
city clothes 87, 128
civilian-military act 90
Civil War 62, 102, 121
class 2, 9, 14, 31–3, 38, 46, 62, 76, 82–3, 92–3, 100, 118, 119, 125
  consciousness and mobility 118
  leisure class 93, 117–18, 141, 143
clothes/clothing 1, 3, 7, 9, 19–20, 30, 34, 40–1, 43–4, 47, 56, 62 n.12, 63, 65–6, 70, 76, 96, 104–5, 115, 117, 119, 121, 135, 141, 153–4
  as actants 11, 30, 32–3, 40, 44, 52, 61, 63, 65, 71, 76, 80, 84–5, 88, 92, 100, 104, 107, 113, 146
  ads 18
  body and 73, 76
  change 66, 100, 104, 138, 147
  as currency 137, 139–40, 142
  and fashion 18, 32–3, 80, 82
  and identity/identity construction 2–3, 28–32, 69, 76–7, 80, 89, 92, 95, 98, 100, 154–6
  as objects 14, 32, 35, 61, 76, 85, 96, 109, 112, 122–3, 135, 153–6
  racial identity and 77, 90, 95, 105, 112
  social function of 76
  and social mobility 2, 138, 153
  as things 11–14, 54, 76, 123, 148
  touching and smelling 92, 121–2
  unreliability of 89
Cofield, J. R. 19, 26
Cole, Catherine, *Fashion in Fiction* 2
Commins, Dorothy 25–6, 99 n.4
  What Is an Editor? Saxe Commins at Work 99 n.4
Commins, Saxe 25–6, 99 n.4
Confederacy in the Civil War 92
consumers of clothing 83
containment 32–4, 43, 45, 64, 73, 76, 115
Cook, Sylvia Jenkins 2, 138
Cosmopolitan magazine 53

cosmopolitan persona 23
cotton 83
cotton clothing 9, 14–15, 70, 83, 108–10, 149
Cowley, Malcolm 22
"Crevasse" (Faulkner) 126–7
cross-dressing 61, 69, 74–5, 138, 143

dandy 20–1, 25, 53, 132
dandyism with homosexuality 20
Dattel, Gene, *Cotton and Race in the Making of America* 14, 108
Davis, David, *World War I and Southern Modernism* 130
Davis, Fred, *Fashion, Culture, and Identity* 66
Davis, Thadious M. 79, 82, 101, 103–5, 111–13, 115–16
  Games of Property 80, 87, 116
Defoe, Daniel 2
demystification 8
Denton, Ren 84
Dickinson, Emily 2
Digital Yoknapatawpha 8 n.3, 78 n.1, 152 n.11
Dior, Christian, the New Look 17
"Divorce in Naples" (Faulkner) 75–6
  Carl 75
  George 75
Duvall, John 122, 125–6, 143, 143 n.10

Elahi, Babak, *The Fabric of American Literary Realism* 2–3, 5, 14, 138
Eliot
  "The Lovesong of J. Alfred Prufrock" 131
  "The Wasteland" 131
Esquire magazine 26
Evans, Medford 126 n.3

fashion 2–3, 13, 33, 58, 68, 78–9, 85, 115, 118, 120, 138, 151, 155
  in Faulkner's time 15–18 (*see also* Faulkner's fashion)
  and natural world 9
  rebellion 68
Faulkner and Race 79
Faulkner, Estelle 20, 22, 24, 61, 67
Faulkner, Jack 22

Faulkner, Jill 24
Faulkner, John 22
Faulkner, J. W. T. 141 n.8
Faulkner's fashion 18–28
    Delta State College 27
    fictional 28–32
Faulkner, William 1–2, 7, 9–10, 14–15, 18, 20–2, 25–6, 28, 36, 45, 52 n.4, 55, 55 n.9, 67, 69, 75–80, 78 n.1, 81, 83, 85, 87, 89–90, 92, 99 n.4, 100, 111, 115–16, 118, 121, 123, 128 n.4, 131, 142, 147, 153. *See also specific works of Faulkner*
female sexuality 32–3, 38, 43–6, 49, 68, 76, 86, 97
femininity 33, 55, 58, 61, 63
    blackness and 101
First World War 10, 18, 22–3, 53 n.7, 78, 81, 90, 127, 129–30
First World War stories 119, 122–30, 123 n.2
    "Ad Astra" 124–5
    "All the Dead Pilots" 125, 129
    "Crevasse" 126–7
    "Turnabout" 124–5
    "Victory" 126–7, 129–30, 134
Fischer, Gayle V., *Pantaloons and Power* 15–16, 61–2
Flags in the Dust (Faulkner) 101, 118–23, 127, 153
    Caspey Strother 81–2, 119
    Harry Mitchell 121
    Horace Benbow 53 n.5, 119, 123
    Isom 81, 119, 123
    Joby Strother 109
    Johnny Sartoris 119, 121–2, 125
    Miss Jenny 81, 119
    Narcissa 120
    Young Bayard Sartoris 118–19, 121, 123
Ford, Henry 16
Foucault 120
Franklin, Cornell 24

Galinsky, Adam D. 146
Gantt, Patricia 66, 69, 138
Gatrell, Simon, *Thomas Hardy Writing Dress* 2

Gatz, James 143
gender, clothing and 2, 9, 14, 31–3, 38, 62, 77, 80, 82, 92–3, 101, 117–18, 125, 155
    identity 33, 62–4, 68, 101, 104
    nonconformity 82
    and sexuality 126, 129
    switching 69
Gibson, TP 109
Gilbert, Sandra M. 38, 141
Gilded Age United States 5
Godden, Richard 69, 118, 143, 146
Go Down, Moses (Faulkner) 12, 15, 59, 80, 103–11, 139, 149, 156
    Boon 105
    Butch Beauchamp 104, 109–11, 115
    Fonsiba 108
    hunting scenes 104–5
    Ike McCaslin 59, 83, 105–9, 112, 155
    Isaac McCaslin 87
    Lucas Beauchamp 105–6, 109–10, 112, 115, 155
    Major de Spain 104–5
    McCaslin-Edmonds plantation 108–9
    "Pantaloon in Black" 107–8
    Rider 107–8
    Roth Edmond 108–9, 111, 155
    Sophonsiba Beauchamp 103, 106
    Tomey's Turl 103–6, 108–9, 111, 155
    Uncle Buck 103–4, 106
    "Was" 103–4
    wilderness 104–5
Good Housekeeping magazine 5
Gordon, Phillip 42–3, 75, 152 n.12
    Gay Faulkner 20
Greenblatt, Stephen, *Renaissance Self-Fashioning* 3, 31
Grove, Lena 29 n.12
Grusin, Richard, *The Nonhuman Turn* 4–5
The Guardian newspaper 91
Gwin, Minrose, "Did Ernest Like Gordon?: Faulkner's *Mosquitoes* and the Bite of Gender Trouble" 42

"half concealed" outfit 100
Hamblin, Robert 27, 28 n.11

Index

The Hamlet (Faulkner) 70–2, 135–47
    Ab Snopes 137, 143, 145
    Armstid 138, 140
    "Book Four: The Peasants" 144
    Bookwright 140, 145
    Buck Hipps 144–5
    Eula Varner 32, 70–3, 72 n.14, 76, 137–9
    Flem Snopes 70–2, 74–5, 96, 120, 138–9, 141–3, 142 n.9, 145–8, 150, 152
    Frenchman's Bend 71–2, 129, 137, 139–40, 145, 150
    Hoake McCarron 137, 152
    Ike Snopes 86, 137
    Jody Varner 71, 137, 140–3, 150
    Labove 71–2, 137
    Mink 74–5
    Pat Stamper 145
    Ratliff 137, 140–5, 152–3, 152 n.12
    The Spotted Horses 143
    Will Varner 71, 142–3
Harlem Renaissance 16
Harmon, J. W. "Bill" 25
Harper magazine 151
Haynes, Gavin 91 n.3
Head, Herbert 97
Hempstead, Susanna 45
Hoeller, Hildegard 139
Hollander, Anne 146
    angularity 14
    Seeing Through Clothes 12–13
The House Beautiful magazine 5
Hughes, Clair, *Dressed in Fiction* 2
humanities and social sciences 4, 78, 116
Hurston, Zora Neale
    "The Gilded Six-Bits" 139
    "Sweat" 86
hyperobjects 11, 14, 109

Ibrahim, Habiba, *Black Age: Oceanic Lifespans and the Time of Black Life* 82
If I Forget Thee, Jerusalem (Faulkner) 65–70, 76
    Charlotte Rittenmeyer 46, 64–70, 74
    Flint 65
    Harry Wilbourne 65–70
    "Old Man" 65, 69
    "The Wild Palms" 65, 76, 133
Intruder in the Dust (Faulkner) 62 n.12, 112–16, 142 n.9, 155–6
    Aleck Sander 114–15, 114 n.7, 125
    Chick Mallison 112–14, 112 n.6, 114 n.7, 142 n.9
    Crawford Gowrie 114
    Gavin Stevens 114
    Lucas 112–16, 155
Ivy League fashions 53

James, Henry 2, 5
jazz clubs of New York 16
jeans 66, 66 n.13
Jewett, Sarah Orne 5
Jim Crow era, clothes 78
Journal of Experimental Social Psychology 146
Journal of Social Psychology 115

Kafka, Franz 2, 8
Karaminas, Vicki, *Fashion in Fiction* 2
Kartiganer, Donald 22–3
Kern, Stephen 45
King Cotton 9, 14–15, 110
Kingsolver, Barbara 8
Klopfer, Donald 26
"Knight's Gambit" (Faulkner) 23
Kristeva, Julia 40
Kuhn, Cynthia 33
Ku Klux Klan 16

Lacan's objet a 30, 95
The Ladies Home Journal magazine 5
Latuour, Bruno 6, 8 n.4, 10, 40, 52
    Reassembling the Social: An Introduction to Actor-Network-Theory 6–8
laundry 55, 83–6, 86 n.2, 116
Leach, William 78
leisure class 93, 117–18, 141, 143
Lerner, Laurence 122
A Life on Paper 25
Light in August (Faulkner) 12, 29 n.12, 55 n.8, 86–92
    Bobbie 88–9
    Byron Bunch 87, 92

Doc Hines 87
Gail Hightower 87, 91–2, 100–1
Joanna Burden 86, 88–9
Joe Christmas 55 n.8, 86–90, 100–1
Lena 92
Lucas Burch 87
McEachern 87–8
patriotism and white supremacy 91
Percy Grimm 90–1, 100
literary clothing 2–3, 5, 31, 33, 120
López, Alfred J. 122
Lopez, Barry 8
Lost Generation 34, 118, 123

male homosexuality and homoeroticism 42, 125
The Mansion (Faulkner) 73–6, 95, 132, 148–56
masculinity 33–6, 46–7, 49, 58, 68, 74, 104, 125–6
masking and costuming 42, 79–81
mass manufacture of goods 16
materialist localism 6
material objects 1, 5–6
 and nonhuman actants 11
 regionalism and modernism 5
material priming 146–7
Matterson, Stephen, *Melville: Fashioning in Modernity* 31, 33, 48 n.3
Matthews, John T. 47, 85
McHaney, Thomas 19
McNeil, Peter, *Fashion in Fiction* 2
Melville, Herman 2
microcosm 68
Miles, Caroline 96, 144
 "Yankee Dollars: The Challenge to Southern Values in 'Two Dollar Wife' and *The Sound and the Fury*" 96–7
military uniforms 17, 21, 32–5, 90–1, 118, 125, 128
Miller-Idriss, Cynthia 91 n.3
The Mississippian newspaper 18–19
modernism/modernity 3, 5–6, 17–18, 32, 53, 59, 85, 109, 121, 130
Montreal 21

Morton, Timothy 4, 11, 109
 Hyperobjects: Philosophy and Ecology After the End of the World 11, 14, 109
Mosquitoes (Faulkner) 23, 38–9, 44, 67, 76, 82
 David 41–3
 Dawson Fairchild 41, 43
 Eva Wiseman 43
 Jenny Steinbauer 42–3
 Julius Wiseman 40, 43
 Major Ayers 41
 Mark Frost 41
 Mrs. Maurier 40–1
 Patricia Roby 41–3
Munns, Jessica, *The Clothes That Wear Us: Essays on Dressing and Transgressing in Eighteenth Century Culture* 2–3
Mussolini, Benito 16

Nabokov, Vladimir 122
Native Americans 15, 50–1
neo-Nazis 91
"New Woman" 38
New York Times newspaper 79
Nisetich, Rebecca 89–90
nonhuman(s) 20
 actants 10–11
 humans and 8–9
 and things 3–6, 8, 14, 67, 69, 112, 114, 156

object-oriented ontology (OOO) 4, 12, 31, 84, 89
 feminism and 4
 hyperobjects 11
Occupy movement 5
Oxford Eagle newspaper 18

panpsychism 11
Parisian fashion 16, 98
patriarchy 7 n.2, 29–30, 38, 60–1, 69
personae 14, 19, 22–3, 85
Phil A. Halle Department Store 19
The Portable Faulkner (Faulkner) 22
power of clothing 22, 29, 32–3, 44, 60, 65, 70, 96, 101, 106–7, 122, 154–6

Index

Pylon (Faulkner) 12, 131–5, 154, 156
   Jack 131–2
   Jiggs 131–2, 134
   Laverne Shumann 131–4
   Roger 131–4

quasi-agents 8, 32, 37, 40, 47

race 2, 9, 14, 31–2, 46, 55, 76, 82–3, 89, 92–3, 100–1, 104, 116, 118, 155–6
ready-to-wear garments 17
real Fashion 13
Rebner, Wolfgang 68
"Red Leaves" (Faulkner) 50–2
The Reivers (Faulkner) 86 n.2
restrictions and recriminations 78
Richardson, Samuel 2
Richards, Penny, *The Clothes That Wear Us: Essays on Dressing and Transgressing in Eighteenth Century Culture* 2–3
Rieger, Christopher, *Clear-Cutting Eden: Ecology and the Pastoral in Southern Literature* 9
Roberts, Diane 69, 72 n.14, 138
"A Rose for Emily" (Faulkner) 83
Roth, Philip 122

Sanctuary (Faulkner) 29, 52–9, 76, 84, 123, 128 n.4, 131
   Brevda 57, 84, 113
   Goodwin 55
   Gowan Stevens 57
   Horace Benbow 52–3, 55, 123
   Miss Reba 54–5, 58–9, 86, 147
   Nacrcissa Benbow 55
   Popeye 52–4, 57–9
   Ruby 54–6
   Temple 53–9, 59 n.10, 72, 86, 147
Sargent, John Singer 5
The Saturday Evening Post magazine 50, 123 n.2
"Scarface" 53 n.7
The Scream magazine 18
Second World War stories 123 n.2. See also First World War stories
self-fashioning 3, 31, 33, 154–5

Seneca Falls Convention (1848) 16
Sensibar, Judith 21, 23–4
"Shall Not Perish" (Faulkner) 123 n.2, 136 n.5
Sheldon, Rebekah 4
Sinners in Silk 54
slave clothing 77–9, 85, 93, 108
Smith, Jon 138, 150, 153
Snead, James A. 80
Snopes Trilogy (Faulkner) 32, 73, 76, 118, 138, 148–50, 153, 156. See also *The Hamlet* (Faulkner); *The Mansion* (Faulkner); *The Town* (Faulkner)
social standing 83, 137–8
soiled garments 85, 87–8, 106, 141–2
Soldiers' Pay (Faulkner) 23, 34–40, 49, 67, 76, 129
   Cecily Saunders 37–40
   Donald Mahon 34–40, 56
   Emmy 37–9
   George Farr 39
   Januarius Jones 36–8
   Joe Gilligan 35
   Julian Lowe 34–6, 49, 123
   Margaret Powers 35, 37–9
The Sound and the Fury (Faulkner) 11–12, 44–52, 54, 76, 80–2, 117, 126, 126 n.3
   "Appendix: Compson 1699–1845" 109
   Benjy 44–5, 50–2, 55 n.9, 60
   Caddy 12, 39, 44–52, 55, 55 n.9, 85, 87, 97
   Dalton Ames 48–9
   Deacon 14, 80–2, 90
   Dilsey 45, 55, 60, 82, 85
   Gerald Bland 48–9
   Jason 11, 44–9, 51, 55, 71, 85
   Quentin 12, 14, 39, 46–51, 55, 71, 80–1, 85, 87
South Carolina's Negro Act (1735) 77
speculative realism 4
Spencer, Hubert, *The Principles of Sociology* 5
Stallybrass, Peter 121
Stand.earth 10
Stone, Emily 25
Stroll 79, 82

Sunday clothes 28–9, 72, 77–8, 78 n.1, 82, 85, 87, 103, 135, 136 n.5, 138
Susan Reed ("Hair") 61
swagger stick 19

"That Evening Sun" (Faulkner) 83–6
   Jesus 86
   Nancy 83–4
   Quentin 83–4
"There Was a Queen" (Faulkner) 109
These Thirteen (Faulkner) 126
top hat revolution 16
The Town (Faulkner) 73–6, 81, 114 n.7, 125, 148–56
   Chick 148
   Eula 73, 148–52
   Flem 148–9, 151–2
   Gowan and Gavin Stevens 148
   Linda Snopes Kohl 73–5, 155
   Montgomery Ward Snopes 150
Tribune newspaper 53
"Turnabout" (Faulkner) 124–5
   Bogard 124–5
Twain, Mark, *Pudd'nhead Wilson* 77
"Two Dollar Wife" (Faulkner) 97
two-piece swimsuit (bikini) 17 n.10
"Two Soldiers" (Faulkner) 123 n.2

ubiquitous clothing 8 n.3
"Uncle Willy" (Faulkner) 52
uniforms 19, 21–3, 33–8, 40, 49, 69–70, 80–1, 89–91, 97, 100, 115, 118–21, 123–6, 128–9, 140–1, 148
Unite the Right rally (Charlottesville) 91 n.3
University of Wisconsin-Milwaukee, Center for 21st Century Studies 4
The Unvanquished (Faulkner) 60–4, 76
   "Ambuscade" 61
   Aunt Louisa 61–3
   Bayard 60, 63, 106, 156
   Drusilla Hawk 46, 60–4, 66
   Granny 60–1, 63
   Grumby 60
   John Sartoris 63, 70
   "An Odor of Verbena" 63
   Ringo 60, 64, 106
urbane clothing 101

VanderVeen, Arthur A. 139
Veblen, Thorstein 19, 38, 62, 93, 95, 141, 143, 152
   The Theory of the Leisure Class 117–18
   trickle-down theory 143
"Victory" (Faulkner) 125–7, 129–30, 134
   Alec Gray 126–30, 132, 147, 154, 156
Volpe, Edmond 126–7

Wainwright, Michael 143 n.10
Wales-Freedman, Eden 57, 59
Walker, Mary 62
Warner Brothers 25
war-time clothing 16–17, 62
Warwick, Alexandra 30, 39, 56–7, 103–4, 120
Wasson, Ben 20
Watson, James G. 18, 23, 53
   William Faulkner: Self-Presentation and Performance 18–19
Watson, Jay 6, 17, 53, 105, 155
   introduction (*Faulkner and Whiteness*) 105
Werner, Craig 79
Wharton, Edith 2
White, Graham, *Stylin': African American Expressive Culture from Its Beginnings to the Zoot Suit* 77
whiteness 83–6, 90, 100, 105, 112, 141
White, Shane, *Stylin': African American Expressive Culture from Its Beginnings to the Zoot Suit* 77
Wilde, Oscar 20
The Wild Palms (Faulkner) 11, 65
Wilkins, Mary Holland 61
William Scully, Ltd. 21
Williams, Michael 138
   "Cross Dressing in Yoknapatawpha County" 64
Williamson, Joel 23
Williams, Patricia J., *The Alchemy of Race and Rights* 116
Williams, William Carlos 5
Wilson, Elizabeth
   Adorned in Dreams 20, 137, 140 n.7
   zoot suits 110

women's dress/fashion 16, 42, 62–3, 62 n.12, 69, 75, 82, 115–16, 152, 154–5
   newspaper coverage 16
   reform 15
   suffrage movement 16
   two-piece swimsuit (bikini) 17 n.10
Woolf, Virginia, *Orlando* 1
Worsham, Samuel 109
written clothing/Fashion 13

X, Malcolm, "Detroit Red" persona 111

Yaeger, Patricia 36, 61, 64, 141, 154, 155
   Dirt and Desire 154
   white object panic 155
Yoknapatawpha County 18, 21, 115, 120, 129, 144

Zeitlin, Michael 31, 124
   Faulkner, Aviation, and Modern War 34–5
zoot suits 79, 110–11, 115

www.ingramcontent.com/pod-product-compliance
Lightning Source LLC
Chambersburg PA
CBHW052048300426
44117CB00012B/2026